D1592575

INTENTIONALIST
INTERPRETATION

INTENTIONALIST INTERPRETATION

A Philosophical Explanation and Defense

WILLIAM IRWIN

Contributions in Philosophy, Number 73

GREENWOOD PRESS
Westport, Connecticut • London

Library of Congress Cataloging-in-Publication Data

Irwin, William, 1970–
    Intentionalist interpretation : a philosophical explanation and
    defense / William Irwin.
        p. cm.—(Contributions in philosophy, ISSN 0084–926X ; no.
  73)
    Includes bibliographical references and index.
    ISBN 0–313–31151–X (alk. paper)
    1. Interpretation (Philosophy) 2. Intentionality (Philosophy)
  I. Title. II. Series.
  B824.17.I78   1999
  121'.68—dc21   99–31576

British Library Cataloguing in Publication Data is available.

Library of Congress Catalog Card Number: 99–31576
ISBN: 0–313–31151–X
ISSN: 0084–926X

First published in 1999

Greenwood Press, 88 Post Road West, Westport, CT 06881
An imprint of Greenwood Publishing Group, Inc.
www.greenwood.com

Printed in the United States of America

The paper used in this book complies with the
Permanent Paper Standard issued by the National
Information Standards Organization (Z39.48–1984).

10 9 8 7 6 5 4 3 2 1

Dedicated to My Parents

Contents

Acknowledgments   ix

1. Normative and Descriptive Approaches to Hermeneutics: 1
   How *Should* We Interpret? How *Do* We Interpret?

2. A Critical Survey of Author Constructs: 17
   Does It Matter Who Is Speaking?

3. A Defense of an Intentionalist Approach: 39
   Urinterpretation

4. Gadamer's Hermeneutics: 73
   Descriptive and Normative

5. Conclusions and Implications   111

Select Bibliography   127

Index   135

Acknowledgments

Many people have supported and encouraged me in the preparation of this book. Let me take this opportunity to acknowledge them.

The list of friends and colleagues from whom I have learned so much includes: Alan Clune, Gregory Bassham, Eric Bronson, Daniel Barwick, Mark Conard, William Drumin, Margaret Monahan Hogan, Henry Nardone, Andrew Schwartz, Aeon Skoble, Sarah Worth, and all members of the original Buffalo Rectangle. In addition I thank my friends, colleagues, and students, who read the entire manuscript and offered valuable criticisms and suggestions: Michael Henshaw, Terri Jennings, Megan Lloyd, and Kate Ruth Williams. I would, of course, be remiss if I did not also thank, albeit in a summary fashion, my family and friends outside of academia.

Let me conclude by thanking those who contributed most directly and most substantially to the realization of this project. I thank James Lawler for always offering criticism of my work, which stuck at the very heart of the matter. I thank Kah-Kyung Cho for teaching me Heidegger and for introducing me to the work of Gadamer. I thank Peter H. Hare, who has helped me in many ways and whose unlimited philosophical interest and curiosity are virtues to be emulated for a lifetime. I thank E.D. Hirsch, Jr., who generously agreed to read the entire manuscript and offered a wealth of helpful criticisms and suggestions. Professor Hirsch's own work has been an inspiration to me, and so it was quite an honor to have him involved in this project. Above all, I thank my mentor, Jorge J.E. Gracia, who provided a bounty of encouragement and support from the beginning. The extent to which he contributed to and improved this project is beyond measure.

Parts of this book were presented as papers at professional conferences, including meetings of the American Philosophical Association in Pittsburgh and Los Angeles, and at conferences at the University of Memphis and in Estes Park, Colorado. On all occasions I profited greatly from questions posed by the audience.

I gratefully acknowledge the editors *Diálogos* and *International Studies in Philosophy* for permission to reprint my "An Author Construct There Must Be," originally printed in *Diálogos* 74 (1999): 169-177, which constitutes part of chapter 2, and "A Critique of Hermeneutic Truth as Disclosure," *International Studies in Philosophy*, forthcoming, which constitutes part of chapter 4. In addition I gratefully acknowledge the permission granted to me to quote from the following volumes: Hans-Georg Gadamer, *Truth and Method*, translated by Joel Weinsheimer and Donald G. Marshall, published by Sheed and Ward and The Continuum Publishing Company; Martin Heidegger, *Being and Time*, translated by John Macquarrie and Edward Robinson, published by Blackwell Publishers and HarperCollins; E.E. Cummings, "r-p-o-h-e-s-s-a-g-r," in *Complete Poems: 1904–1962*, edited by George J. Firmage, published by Liveright Publishing Corporation.

1

Normative and Descriptive Approaches to Hermeneutics: How *Should* We Interpret? How *Do* We Interpret?

HERMENEUTIC CONFLICT

Hermeneutics is the discipline that deals with the interpretation of texts; it is the discipline that seeks an understanding of the meaning of texts and all that this involves. Contemporary hermeneutics is marked by scholarly conflict, disagreement, and differing points of emphasis. To some, the conflict has seemed unfortunate and unnecessary. If the disputants would truly listen to one another they would realize that they are pursuing independent projects, that there is in fact no need for the quarreling.[1] Such a simple and straightforward solution is highly desirable in all conflicts, but in this case such a resolution does not appear to be forthcoming. There are indeed genuine areas of disagreement to be settled.

To begin, there are seemingly innumerable conflicts among hermeneutic theorists, and to document them all would be to verge on the trivial. Instead we shall be concerned in this study with what is arguably the primary and most interesting conflict, that between those dedicated to normative pursuits and those dedicated to descriptive pursuits. The terms "normative" and "descriptive" have been employed in hermeneutics by such disparate theorists as E.D. Hirsch, Jr.[2] and Jean Grondin. Hirsch sees the mixing of normative and descriptive approaches as at the root of much trouble and confusion. "I propose that interpretive theories should not lump together the descriptive and normative aspects of interpretation; that theorists should disengage the descriptive dimension of hermeneutics, which concerns the nature of interpretation, from the normative dimension which concerns its goals."[3] Grondin sees normative hermeneutics as a thing of the past and descriptive hermeneutics as the only genuine concern of the present and future:

Classical hermeneutics tried to be essentially technical and *normative*. Its purpose was to show the rules or the method to follow when one seeks to interpret writings scientifically with a view to eliminating arbitrariness and subjectivism in the realm of interpretation. Contemporary hermeneutics renounces this *normative* and technical project to place itself on a more elementary level. It will no longer teach how one must interpret (envisaged *normatively*) but how, in effect, one interprets; not what we *should* do, but "what happens to us over and above our wanting and *doing*" when we interpret. What we have here is an approach that is resolutely phenomenological or *descriptive*.[4]

The conflict between the normative and descriptive is most clear in the quarrels and debates between Hirsch and his followers on the normative side and Hans-Georg Gadamer and his followers (such as Grondin) on the descriptive side. As we shall understand these terms, a normative approach to hermeneutics is one concerned with the aims and goals of interpretation while a descriptive approach is one concerned with the very nature of interpretive understanding.[5] A normative approach is one concerned with establishing the criteria or guidelines interpreters *should* follow in seeking the meaning of a text. A descriptive approach, by contrast, is one concerned with depicting the kind of understanding which *does* take place in interpretation. This phenomenon of interpretive understanding is frequently depicted as beyond our complete control.

Having made this distinction, it at first appears as if there is no room for conflict between the normative and descriptive theorists. Surely the project of defining the goals of interpretation is separate from the project of describing the nature of interpretive understanding. In practice such is decidedly not the case, however. Genuine conflicts do indeed arise, largely because while each side emphasizes one approach it still engages in the other. For example, as we shall see, there is some element of the normative in Gadamer's descriptive approach and some element of the descriptive in Hirsch's normative approach. Still, I submit that a harmonious resolution between the descriptive and normative is possible. While in the act of interpretation descriptive and normative elements necessarily intertwine, in hermeneutic theory the descriptive and the normative can (to a great extent) and should be distinguished. That is, when we are actually interpreting a text we experience both the process of interpretive understanding and the search for meaning in accord with established (or sometimes presumed and tacitly understood) criteria. It is in theory, however, that we can reflect on the act of interpretation and separately consider the process of understanding and the criteria for meaning. We shall detail this claim in a subsequent section of this chapter.

Let us take an example often discussed in the literature, William Blake's "London,"[6] to clarify the distinction between normative and descriptive approaches.

London

I wander thro' each charter'd street,
Near where the charter'd Thames does flow,
And mark in every face I meet
Marks of weakness, marks of woe.

In every cry of every man,
In every Infant's cry of fear,
In every voice, in every ban,
The mind-forg'd manacles I hear.

How the Chimney-sweeper's cry
Every blackning Church appalls;
And the hapless Soldier's sigh
Runs in blood down Palace walls.

But most thro' midnight streets I hear
How the youthful Harlot's curse
Blasts the new-born Infant's tear,
And blights with plagues the Marriage hearse.[7]

A normative approach to Blake's "London" asks: How are we to understand the meaning of the poem? What method shall we employ? One normative method would be to seek the poet's intention in composing his work, taking that intention to be the key to the poem's meaning. Is the poet, for example, calling for social reform, the abolition of the "mind-forg'd manacles," or just despairing in *Experience*? What we do not ask is how such understanding of meaning occurs or is even possible. (This is the concern of a descriptive approach.) We seek the meaning through an established method, but we do not explore the ontology of the phenomenon of understanding. How interpretive understanding occurs, and what its ontological basis is, are the concerns of a descriptive approach. How is it that "London" can speak to me? How do the "mind-forg'd manacles" have meaning for me? How can this line from the past speak into my present? What is the nature of this interpretive understanding?

As I have suggested, then, the primary conflict in contemporary hermeneutics occurs between those who *emphasize* a normative approach and those who *emphasize* a descriptive approach. The conflict has persisted because despite the differing emphases, each side does engage in the other's basic approach. The discipline of hermeneutics encompasses a vast array of issues, and no one to my knowledge has truly addressed them all. Despite the variety of issues and the great difference between normative and descriptive, theorists tend to have the egocentric belief that they are addressing the true issues of hermeneutics and that others are simply naive. A universal hermeneutics must be free of this egocentric tendency, and must examine both normative and descriptive issues. Still, we should attempt to keep these issues separate, as far as possible, in articulating theory.

We must make a number of choices in establishing the normative criteria for interpretation. In the end, as we shall argue in chapter 3, these choices prove to be ethical ones. On the other hand, the descriptive task is a phenomenology of understanding. Gadamer's descriptive hermeneutics is the most comprehensive philosophical account to date, and so it is to his account that we shall direct our descriptive focus in chapter 4.

After taking a more detailed look at normative and descriptive approaches, we shall turn to the possibility of separating the issues in articulating theory, and then proceed to a preliminary examination of different types of interpretation.

NORMATIVE APPROACHES

A normative approach in its pure form would be concerned primarily with epistemological and ethical issues. Ethical analysis, as we shall see in chapter 3, serves as an arbiter when questions arise that epistemological analysis alone cannot settle. In this chapter, however, we shall be concerned with the epistemological basis of a normative approach. The most important epistemological question a normative approach will address is: What method should we employ in securing knowledge of the meaning of a text? As we shall see, the two great rival answers to this question are: (1) discovering the author's intention and (2) letting the text stand on its own.[8] Beyond this, we must also decide how to implement our epistemological method and how to adjudicate among competing interpretations. Having said this much, let us turn to an examination of Hirsch's normativism.

E.D. Hirsch, Jr. is the preeminent contemporary advocate of the normative approach known as intentionalism.[9] In his influential work *Validity in Interpretation,* Hirsch takes up the epistemological question: How does one gain knowledge of the meaning of a text? His answer, in short, is that one gains knowledge of the meaning of a text by discovering authorial intention, because it is the author's intended communication that is the meaning of a text. For Hirsch, utterer's meaning is utterance meaning, as long as the utterance can support the utterer's meaning.[10] As he says, "Verbal meaning is whatever someone has willed to convey by a particular sequence of linguistic signs and which can be conveyed by those linguistic signs."[11] This meaning, moreover, is determinate despite any attendant ambiguity or vagueness,[12] and includes the author's unconscious (nonconscious, and not fully conscious) intentions. For Hirsch the meaning of a text is the author's intended communication, as long as that communication can be supported reasonably by the text chosen to express it. We shall take up Hirsch's account of meaning and intention in detail in chapter 3.

Hirsch grounds his argument for the determinateness of verbal meaning in Husserlian intentionality. Briefly put, the argument concludes that the meaning of a text is an unchanging intentional object. We should note that here Hirsch is not using the word "intentional" in the ordinary sense, but in the sense in which Husserl uses it in his phenomenology. That is, an intentional object is an object of awareness. As Husserl and Hirsch explicate the intentional object, it does, however, have intimate ties to both meaning and "intention" in the ordinary sense of the word.[13] The meaning of a text may appear different from different "angles," but it is in actuality always the same. It is, then, our task as interpreters to achieve a comprehensive view of the communication the author intended. Achieving this view includes learning to the best of our ability the unconscious intentions of the author. This too, Hirsch believes, is consistent with Husserlian intentionality. As he says, "The unseen sides of a box belong to my 'intention' in precisely the same way that the unconscious implications of an utterance belong to the author's intention."[14] Hirsch, as I understand him, does not necessarily mean logical implications, but rather what the author intends to imply (logically, conversationally, or otherwise) by the text but of which she is not aware. Chapter 3 shall take up the potential conflict between conscious and unconscious intentions.

For Hirsch, an adjudication must take place when we have two or more possible meanings for a text based on possible authorial intentions, that is, when we have not secured knowledge of the meaning of the text. The practice of validation, for Hirsch, is the process that shows that in a particular case knowledge has probably been achieved.[15] This is as opposed to verification, in which we achieve certainty of truth. In validation we strengthen our justification in light of what appears to be a true belief. In verification our justification becomes so strong that we are certain we have a true belief. Verification is common in everyday experience. Being uncertain as to whether I have forgotten my wallet, I simply check my pocket and discover it is there. In this way I achieve certainty that the proposition, "I have my wallet," is true. Hirsch holds that verification is not possible for interpretive knowledge; our evidence in this area is always partial and so our belief is always subject to being false. Rather, interpretive knowledge is the product of a process of validation that never fully comes to rest. I may believe that I know the meaning of "London," but that belief does not achieve the level of certainty that "I have my wallet" does. My evidence and justification may be strong, but I am open to the possibility that my belief is false in a way that I am not regarding my wallet.

As Hirsch explains the validation process, "The interpreter's primary task is to reproduce in himself the author's 'logic,' his attitudes, his cultural givens, in short—his world."[16] Having performed the epistemological task of recreating in himself the author's mindset, at least as far as is necessary to understand his communication, the interpreter must then decide among competing interpretations.

The question may arise, however, that even if we are to grant Hirsch that the meaning of a text is determinate in accord with Husserlian intentionality, why is it that authorial intention is responsible for the determinacy?[17] Why not the text itself? Why not the original audience, or any of the other innumerable criteria that could be proposed? Hirsch finds this question to be a matter for ethical analysis. To disregard an author's intention, he argues, is to disregard the very soul of speech (spoken or written); the soul of speech is, of course, communication. Along Kantian lines, Hirsch argues that to treat a person's words as grist for one's own mill is ethically analogous to treating a person as a means only.[18] It appears, then, that the author's intention must be the cause of the determinacy of textual meaning. This is certainly a bold and important claim, but it is beyond the scope of the mainly expository aims of this chapter to examine it. Chapter 3 shall take this issue up in detail.

Before leaving Hirsch for the moment we should note how it is that he fails to remain purely normative. For the most part, Hirsch leaves aside the description of the phenomenon of interpretive understanding. Still, he does engage in descriptive hermeneutics to some extent. His analysis of the hermeneutic circle, along with his reconception of validation as not only a tool of a normative approach but an explanation of understanding itself, are prime examples.[19] We shall discuss Hirsch's reconception of validation in detail in chapter 3.

The other major normative approach to consider is that represented by Monroe C. Beardsley, who holds that the text itself determines its own meaning. (What a text is, of course, is an intricate question. We shall take it up in chapter 2.) Beardsley, in collaboration with W.K. Wimsatt, actively opposes the method that Hirsch later adopted, calling it, "The Intentional Fallacy."[20] As he says, "[T]he design or intention of the author is neither available nor desirable as a standard of judging the success of a literary work of art."[21] According to Beardsley, the meaning of a text is not determined by its author's intention; it could not be, because meaning changes and is simply inconsistent with authorial awareness. The meaning of a text can change after an author dies, and a dead author certainly cannot change her mind or the meaning. Also, a text can have meanings of which an author is not aware, and therefore have meanings its author did not intend.[22] An essential part of the conflict between Hirsch and Beardsley is a disagreement concerning the connection between authorial awareness and authorial intention. According to Hirsch, we can have unconscious intentions, that is, intentions we are not aware of (or, sometimes, just not fully aware of).

Beardsley gives his own epistemological criterion for the interpretation of texts in what he calls the principle of autonomy: literary works are self-sufficient entities whose properties are decisive in checking interpretations and judgments.[23] In other words, once the author has written the text it flies off on wings of its own; its correct interpretation is not tied to its author but to its own constitution. Texts acquire determinate meaning through the interaction of their words without the intervention of an authorial intention.[24]

The process of validation is less clear for Beardsley than for Hirsch. Presumably we must still adjudicate among competing interpretations as we must in Hirsch's theory. Malcolm Bradbury explains this process in the New Criticism, of which Beardsley is a proponent, as follows: "[I]t was the text that was postulated as an empirical experience independent of the persons experiencing—an ideal text to which all critics, provided they purge themselves of quirks of personality, misfortune of upbringing, environmental, social, and political preferences, might share in as a common find."[25] In adjudicating among competing interpretations, then, interpreters must ask themselves how successfully they have rid themselves of their own interpretive prejudices.[26] A certain amount of determinacy is dictated by the text's structure and possibly its sounds,[27] but beyond that an acceptable interpretation seems to be one that produces an aesthetic experience. For Beardsley, in fact, this seems more important than being free of interpretive prejudices. As he says, "the primary purpose of literary interpretation . . . is to help readers approach literary works from the aesthetic point of view."[28] Using Jorge J.E. Gracia's term, we might speak of the cultural function[29] of literary texts as that of producing aesthetic experience. This is the way, Beardsley believes, that our interpretive community approaches and should approach literary texts. The case may be different for other kinds of texts, as he makes clear with the example of interpreting a will.[30]

Beardsley does not have the kind of rigorous process of validation that Hirsch does. Having established the epistemological criterion that the text is the determiner of its own meaning, we simply look for interpretations that meet that criterion and produce an aesthetic experience. Perhaps the better the aesthetic experience the better is the interpretation for Beardsley.[31]

Beardsley's normative approach, even more clearly than Hirsch's, involves a descriptive element. That literary interpretation involves an aesthetic experience is certainly a matter of description, and, as we shall note later, this is somewhat akin to Gadamer's aesthetic grounding of his descriptive account. Beardsley, in fact, is caught somewhere between the normative and descriptive, between saying what *should* happen and what *does* happen in interpretation. His primary concern is an epistemological one, the methodological acquisition of textual meaning. He is very concerned with refuting the intentionalist approach, and with establishing his own approach. Still, he does engage in descriptive hermeneutics with his account of literary interpretation as aesthetic.

As we have seen, the place of the author's intention is the primary area of disagreement within normative hermeneutics. For Hirsch authorial intention is of the utmost importance, whereas for Beardsley the text itself governs its own interpretation. The author's intention is unimportant to him, except inasmuch as it is clearly expressed in the text itself. In preparation for settling the normative debate in chapter 3, in chapter 2 we will have to provide an answer to the question: What is an author? Neither Hirsch nor Beardsley has addressed this question, and yet answering it will prove vital to settling the conflict between them. For now, however, we turn to an exposition of descriptive hermeneutics.

DESCRIPTIVE HERMENEUTICS

Although descriptive elements have long been incorporated into hermeneutic theories, it is only in this century that we have seen the development of a descriptively based hermeneutics. This descriptive project has its roots in Heidegger's hermeneutic of *Dasein*, as explicated in *Being and Time*, but was developed most fully by Gadamer in his *Truth and Method*. As Gadamer has said, "In both rhetoric and hermeneutics . . . theory is subsequent to that out of which it is abstracted; that is, to praxis."[32] In descriptive hermeneutics we are concerned, then, with a phenomenology of praxis, with describing what occurs in interpretive understanding. We ask ourselves: What is the nature of interpretive understanding? What is its ontological structure?

As Gadamer makes clear, Heidegger gave an answer to these questions in *Being and Time*, where he said that understanding is the way in which the historicity of *Dasein* is itself carried out. Understanding is one of the *existenziale* structures (essential existential characteristics) of *Dasein*'s being-in-the-world.[33] "[T]he real question is not in what way being can be understood but in what way understanding *is* being."[34] Understanding is a substantial part of our being-in-the-world, and, taken in this way, it is the subject to be described by hermeneutics. Gadamer is insistent upon this, giving no place to a method[35] of interpretation à la Hirsch. Hirsch understands Gadamer's position clearly, and notes the irony of the title *Truth and Method*. This book, he says, is actually a polemic against the nineteenth-century preoccupation with objective truth and correct method.[36] In defending his *magnum opus* against the intentionalist criticisms of Emilio Betti, Gadamer claims that he is simply engaged in describing what *is* in every act of understanding; he is doing ontology not methodology.[37]

Gadamer's descriptive project is (ostensibly) unconcerned with epistemological method, but also differs from the normative accounts we have seen in its conception of truth. Hirsch (and perhaps Beardsley) employs a coherence theory of truth, or perhaps a coherence theory of validation, inasmuch as Hirsch is concerned with validation rather than verification. For the normativists, an interpretation that coheres with the information we have is an acceptable one. Gadamer, on the other hand, rejects traditional epistemology in favor of Heideggerian epistemology with truth as disclosure (*aletheia*, *Erschlossenheit*). As Richard E. Palmer explains this conception of truth, "[T]he being of something is disclosed not to the contemplative analytical gaze but in the moment in which it suddenly emerges from hiddenness in the full functional content of the world."[38] Truth is not some banal coherence, or even correspondence to fact, but an event or happening.

Gadamer grounds much of his hermeneutics and his exposition of truth in aesthetics. The work of art seizes us with an immediate truth claim; it, in a sense, takes possession of us as it discloses the truth of its being. Gadamer speaks in similar terms of textual interpretation: "Hermeneutics . . . is not 'knowledge as domination' . . . rather, it consists in subordinating ourselves to the text's claim to dominate our minds."[39] This is not the appropriate place for a critical assessment of this epistemology, its conception of truth, and its employment; we shall take up that task in chapter 4. Instead we turn to a brief exposition of the major elements of Gadamer's descriptive hermeneutics.

Gadamer describes textual understanding as a "fusion of horizons" (*Horizontverschmelzung*). His driving question is: How *do* we in the present understand a text from the past? Gadamer is asking: How is this understanding possible? He is not asking: By what method do we achieve a correct understanding? Gadamer's answer is that reproduction of the text's past understanding is both impossible and undesirable; yet we do confront the historicality of the text in some way. As he says, "Part of real understanding, however, is that we regain the concepts of a historical past in such a way that they also include our own comprehension of them. Above I called this the 'fusion of horizons.'"[40] In the fusion of horizons the foreign element in the text is overcome and, we might say, melts away such that the tension between the horizons disappears. In fact, there really are not two distinct horizons; since time moves ever onward understanding is ever changing. As Gadamer says, it is enough to say we understand in a different way if we understand at all.[41] We are to understand texts in terms of the ever-changing questions we pose to them. It follows that textual meaning is indeterminate, always growing and changing.

For Gadamer the meaning of a text is its effective history (*Wirkungsgeschichte*), its history of effects on *Dasein*. A text's meaning is comprised of all its actual and potential interpretations, and the discovery of this meaning is an infinite process. That a text can never be fully understood is implied by Gadamer's dictum, *"Being that can be understood is language."*[42] Gadamer's linguisticality (*Sprachlichkeit*) here is in accord with his Heideggerian epistemology; the being of the text offers itself to be understood through language. (We shall discuss this further in chapter 4.)

Gadamer does not stay in the realm of the descriptive, as Hirsch and Beardsley do not stay in the realm of the normative. (Of course, one may question whether it is even possible to remain purely descriptive or purely normative in hermeneutics. We shall take up this issue in the next section of this chapter. For now, let us simply note where Gadamer crosses the line into the normative.) The general thrust of *Truth and Method* is so anti-normative that in just that way it becomes normative. Gadamer is quite concerned with showing the impossibility of objective truth and the inappropriateness of "scientific" method in the discipline of interpretation. In his anti-normativism Gadamer does not simply ignore the normative but rather actively opposes it.

It is, however, the doctrine of effective history that ultimately draws him over to the normative side. To be clear, it is not the doctrine itself that crosses the normative line, but the qualifications Gadamer makes and imposes on it. In saying that the meaning of a text is the history of its effects, of all its possible interpretations, Gadamer approaches relativism. It seems as though a text can be interpreted in any way whatsoever, and that such an interpretation would be partly constitutive of the text's meaning through effective history. Gadamer does not go this far, however, but rather offers criteria for acceptable interpretation. What the criteria are is not always clear, however. In fact, they are a matter of some debate among Gadamer's followers. We shall join this debate in chapter 4. At this point let us simply note two candidates (and then a third) for the criteria.

The first criterion is that the text is the measure. An interpretation cannot be inconsistent with the elements of the text, and in fact must account for them all. (What exactly a text is for Gadamer is a question we shall have to address.) "The harmony of all the details with the whole is the criterion of understanding. The failure to achieve this harmony means that understanding has failed."[43] Entailed by the first criterion is that an interpretation must not be self-contradictory.[44] Assuming that the text under consideration is not self-contradictory, an interpretation that accounts for all of its parts will not (and should not) be self-contradictory either. Interestingly, Gadamer does not hold that one or both of two mutually exclusive interpretations must be unacceptable.

The second criterion is tradition (*Überlieferung*). The interpreter who follows the path of tradition arrives at a correct interpretation, and the interpreter who does not follow this path arrives at a wrong interpretation. Tradition is a rather complicated concept for Gadamer, and we shall explore it and its relevance to interpretation in detail in chapter 4.

Lawrence K. Schmidt has argued that neither of these two is Gadamer's criterion, though each has its role to play in correct understanding. Schmidt argues that, for Gadamer, a correct understanding is reached when one legitimizes one's pre-judgments (prejudices, *Vorurteile*) by basing them on the things themselves (*die Sachen selbst*), the subject matter under discussion, and not on mere opinion.[45]

SEPARATING THE NORMATIVE AND DESCRIPTIVE

Separating the normative and descriptive approaches to hermeneutics may seem unnatural and impossible. How one describes interpretive understanding may well influence the normative standards one develops, and the normative standards one develops may well influence how one describes interpretive understanding. There seems to be an inevitable relationship between the two approaches.

Even given this argument and evidence there is no logical reason why normative and descriptive concerns cannot be distinguished on the theoretical level. In the past, normative and descriptive elements blended in theories largely because theorists were not mindful of the distinction. One of the goals of the current project is to highlight this distinction and encourage independent study of the normative and descriptive. While in practice a normative method is inseparable from the moment of understanding to be described, in theoretical study the normative and descriptive are quite separable. It is true, however, that given a certain normative view one is more likely to accept a certain descriptive view and vice versa. Still, this does not mean that in considering one aspect we must necessarily move into the other.

Recall our example of interpreting Blake's "London." In taking a normative approach to interpreting this poem, one would choose a normative criterion. One may decide, for example, that the criterion to use in interpreting poetry is the author's intention. In accord with this criterion, it is *prima facie* clear that the poem does not speak well of marriage. "Blasts the new-born Infant's tear, / And blights with plagues the Marriage hearse." Marriage is clearly intended as one of the "mind-forg'd manacles."[46] On the other hand, one may choose the criterion of the text itself. The text itself allows a great deal of latitude, in that words may be taken in any number of ways. W.K. Wimsatt, Beardsley's ally and sometime collaborator, adopts this criterion and finds "London" to be a poem which actually favors marriage.[47] No matter what criterion one selects, the selection can be done independently of a descriptive account of interpretive understanding. Of course, in practice, the application of the normative criterion is inseparable from the moment of understanding itself. That is, the phenomenon of understanding, of which the descriptive approach seeks to provide an account, is simultaneously intertwined with the application of our normative principle. They are not separate moments, but only separate considerations.

Similarly, one can give a descriptive account of interpretive understanding, for example calling it a fusion of horizons, before in practice interpreting "London." Further, this descriptive account need not be based on a normative criterion, though in the practice of interpreting "London" one may (though not necessarily) employ a strict normative criterion in concert with the descriptive approach. It is my contention that the interaction of normative and descriptive approaches in practice has obscured the fact that they can be distinguished in theory. As I shall make clear through the course of this study, it is quite beneficial to examine the normative and descriptive elements separately on the theoretical level. To do so greatly facilitates clarity and precision, allowing us to focus on one set of concerns at a time.

TYPES OF INTERPRETATION

We have thus far looked at the two major approaches to interpretation, the normative and the descriptive. The questions we must now consider are: What types of interpretation are there? And what types of interpretation, and on what grounds, do we find acceptable? Although there is a rich variety of minor interpretive types, one may be inclined to classify only two major types.[48] Where one draws the line between them is a matter of some debate, however. Gracia, for example, in a recent study has drawn the line between what he calls textual and nontextual interpretations.[49] I will draw the line in a different place in accord with the normative position I defend in chapter 3.

As I have suggested, where one draws the line between the two major types of interpretation is a function of the normative standards one employs. Let us first, then, see what Gracia takes to be the aim of interpretation.[50] "The aim of an interpreter is to create a text that produces in the audience acts of understanding that are intensionally the same as those produced by the historical text in the historical author and the historical audience of the historical text."[51]

Gracia's view is clearly in opposition to Gadamer's fusion of horizons in that it claims that different causes can produce the same effect. For Gracia, understanding is not understanding differently; the same understanding can be reproduced despite contextual and historical differences. In light of this aim of the interpreter, Gracia distinguishes between two primary types of interpretation—textual and nontextual. Textual interpretations are those whose main or only purpose is to produce understandings of the meanings of texts and of the implications of those meanings. Nontextual interpretations are those whose primary aim is other than to produce such understandings, even where such understandings are necessary for the fulfillment of the primary aim of interpretation.[52] For example, a textual interpretation of "London" would attempt to reproduce acts of understanding intensionally the same as those of Blake and his contemporary audience. A Marxist interpretation of "London" would be nontextual in that its aim would be other than to produce understandings intensionally the same as those of Blake and his audience.

While Gracia's taxonomy makes a neat and logical division that serves his interpretive theory well, I do not find it satisfactory for my purposes. Gracia divides interpretive types by examining what kind of understandings are produced in the present audience as compared to those produced in the author and her historical audience. My concern, on the other hand, is not with understanding but with intention, and not with past audiences but with authors only. I am concerned with authors and intentions because these are the key elements of the normative theory urinterpretation, which I will briefly outline below and defend in detail in chapter 3.

I propose, then, to divide interpretation into two types, urinterpretation and non-urinterpretation. An urinterpretation is one that seeks to capture the intention of the author, though not necessarily his understanding. This aim is suggested by the German prefix "ur" which connotes origins (as in the city of Ur in the cradle of civilization), and which is found in the German word "*Urheber*," author.[53] An urinterpretation is not necessarily the original interpretation of the text, but rather the interpretation made in accord with the original meaning of the author, as he intended to communicate it. An author may not fully understand his text, and neither may his contemporaries, and so recapturing his or their understandings is not always worthwhile. Inasmuch as the author's text is an intentional effort to communicate, however, his intention is indeed worth recapturing. (More on this in chapter 3.)

A non-urinterpretation is one that does not seek to capture the intention of the author, but rather points to, what we will call with Hirsch, some significance of the text. Non-urinterpretations are not concerned with recapturing the past but with speaking to the present. Non-urinterpretations, though often of real value, are not our first concern and are, as we shall see, potentially unethical. In chapter 5 we shall argue that urinterpretation has a certain primacy over non-urinterpretation. A non-urinterpretation that is not acknowledged as such is unethical; it misrepresents the author of the text and it deceives the audience. We shall return to this issue, but for now let us consider, very briefly, what value non-urinterpretations may have. Non-urinterpretations relate some significance of the text to the reader. Such interpretations can actually bring a text to life in a new way, sowing the seeds of progress and inspiration. A world of only urinterpretations would be a dull and stagnant world indeed. In chapter 5 we shall explore the place and value of non-urinterpretation through a survey of its practice alongside urinterpretation in the interpretation of philosophical, literary, and legal texts.

CONCLUSION

This chapter has set the table for much of what is to come. We have examined and defined the normative and descriptive approaches to hermeneutics, and addressed the question of their separability. Also, we looked at the classification of two major types of interpretation, first in Gracia's view and then in mine.

We shall begin this study in earnest by addressing the normative approach to hermeneutics. Determining the place of the author in interpretation is essential to settling the major conflict within the normative camp, and essential to settling this conflict is an answer to the question: What is an author? It is to this question that we turn in chapter 2.

NOTES

1. See for example Christopher E. Arthur, "Gadamer and Hirsch: The Canonical Work and the Interpreter's Intention," *Cultural Hermeneutics* 4 (1977), p. 190.

2. E.D. Hirsch, Jr., "Three Dimensions of Hermeneutics," *New Literary History* 3 (1972), pp. 245–261; and also *The Aims of Interpretation* (Chicago: University of Chicago Press, 1976), pp. 74–91 (hereafter *Aims*). Hirsch's third dimension is the metaphysical, which we shall include in our understanding of the descriptive. In this way our use of the terms 'normative' and 'descriptive' shall differ from Hirsch's.

3. *Aims*, p. 75.

4. Jean Grondin, "Hermeneutics and Relativism," in Kathleen Wright ed., *Festivals of Interpretation: Essays on Hans-Georg Gadamer's Work* (Albany: SUNY Press, 1990), p. 44 (emphasis added).

5. "Three Dimensions of Hermeneutics," p. 246; *Aims, p.* 75. Hirsch is responsible for the distinction between normative and descriptive hermeneutics, which in part resulted from his reflection on how he had originally conceived his conflict with Gadamer. I take him to be recognizing his own work as primarily normative and Gadamer's as primarily descriptive. This distinction is important, but has not been adequately developed. I believe it sheds a great deal of light on the genuine and false areas of conflict between Hirsch and Gadamer that others, such as Arthur (above), have noted but with which they have not properly dealt.

6. E.D. Hirsch, Jr., "Counterfactuals in Interpretation," in Sanford Levinson and Steven Mailoux eds., *Interpreting Law and Literature: A Hermeneutic Reader* (Evanston, IL: Northwestern University Press, 1988), pp. 58–62. See also Hirsch, *Innocence and Experience: An Introduction to Blake* (New Haven: Yale University Press, 1964). W.K. Wimsatt, *Day of the Leopards: Essays in Defense of Poems* (New Haven: Yale University Press, 1976), pp. 30–33; W.K. Wimsatt, "Genesis: A Fallacy Revisited," in David Newton-de Molina ed., *On Literary Intention* (Edinburgh: Edinburgh University Press, 1976), pp. 132–134; P.D. Juhl, *Interpretation: An Essay in the Philosophy of Literary Criticism* (Princeton, NJ: Princeton University Press, 1980), pp. 51, 118–121.

7. William Blake, "London," in *The Norton Anthology of Poetry* 3rd edition (New York: W.W. Norton & Company, 1983), pp. 506–507.

8. Other criteria may be proposed as well, for example the understanding of the original audience or society. The possible criteria are unlimited. I shall deal with these two because they have drawn the most attention and are the most viable. To deal with every other possible criterion would take us too far afield.

9. Other advocates of intentionalism include F.D.E. Schleiermacher, *Hermeneutics and Criticism* ed. and trans. Andrew Bowie (Cambridge: Cambridge University Press, 1998); Emilio Betti, "Hermeneutics as the General Science of the *Geisteswissenschaften*," in Josef Bleicher ed., *Contemporary Hermeneutics: Hermeneutics as Method, Philosophy, and Critique* (London: Routledge & Kegan Paul, 1980), pp. 51–94; Steven Knapp and Walter Benn Michaels, "Against Theory," in *Against Theory: Literary Studies and the New Pragmatism* (Chicago: University of Chicago Press, 1985), pp. 11–36, and "Against Theory 2: Hermeneutics and Deconstruction," *Critical Inquiry* 14 (1987), pp. 49–68; P.D. Juhl *Interpretation: An Essay in the Philosophy of Literary Criticism* (Princeton, NJ: Princeton University Press, 1980); Gary Iseminger, "An Intentional Demonstration?" in Gary Iseminger ed., *Intention and Interpretation* (Philadelphia: Temple University Press, 1992), pp. 76–96; Noël Carroll, "Art, Intention, and Conversation," in Gary Iseminger ed., *Intention and Interpretation* (Philadelphia: Temple University Press, 1992), pp. 97–131; and Robert Stecker, "The Role of Intention and Convention in Interpreting Artworks," *The Southern Journal of Philosophy* 31(1993), pp. 471–481.

10. See William E. Tolhurst, "On What a Text Is and How It Means," *British Journal of Aesthetics* 19 (1979), p. 11. This is my understanding of Hirsch. I here make use of the distinction between utterer's meaning and utterance meaning, as does Tolhurst, which is essentially the difference between what the producer of a text meant and what the text as it stands seems to say.

11. E.D. Hirsch, Jr., *Validity in Interpretation* (New Haven: Yale University Press, 1967), p. 31 (hereafter *VI).*

12. *VI*, p. 230.

14   *Intentionalist Interpretation*

13. We shall see this in chapter 3.

14. *VI*, p. 221.

15. *VI*, p. 163.

16. *VI*, p. 242.

17. See Jack W. Meiland, "Interpretation as a Cognitive Discipline," *Philosophy and Literature* 2 (1978), pp. 23–45.

18. *Aims*, pp. 90–91.

19. *VI*, p. 76ff. and *Aims*, p. 33.

20. W.K. Wimsatt and Monroe C. Beardsley, "The Intentional Fallacy," in *The Verbal Icon: Studies in the Meaning of Poetry* (Lexington, KY: University of Kentucky Press, 1954), pp. 3–18. In "Genesis: A Fallacy Revisited," Wimsatt affirms that this formulation is to be taken to apply to the meaning and not just the value of the literary work, pp. 117 and 136.

21. "The Intentional Fallacy," p. 3.

22. Monroe C. Beardsley, "The Authority of the Text," in *The Possibility of Criticism* (Detroit: Wayne State University Press, 1970), pp. 19–20.

23. Ibid., p. 16.

24. Ibid., p. 30.

25. Malcolm Bradbury, "Introduction: The State of Criticism Today," in Malcolm Bradbury and David Palmer eds., *Contemporary Criticism* (London: Edwin Arnold, 1970), p. 23.

26. I am not certain that Beardsley would fully accept this criterion, though Bradbury puts it forth as the standard practice of the New Criticism. Gadamer, as we shall see, certainly would not accept anything like this. For him, prejudices are actually a condition for the possibility of understanding a text.

27. As in poetry read aloud. Cf. "The Authority of the Text," p. 37.

28. Ibid., p. 34.

29. See Jorge J.E. Gracia, *A Theory of Textuality: The Logic and Epistemology* (Albany: SUNY Press, 1995), pp. 89–96 (hereafter *ATT*).

30. Cf. "The Authority of the Text," pp. 32, 35–36. As we shall see in chapter 5, even interpreting a will is sometimes not without its problems.

31. For some discussion of what an aesthetic experience is and what constitutes a "better" one see Monroe C. Beardsley, "Aesthetic Experience Regained," *Journal of Aesthetics and Art Criticism* 28 (1969), pp. 3–11.

32. Hans-Georg Gadamer, "On the Scope and Function of Hermeneutical Reflection," in ed. and trans. David Linge, *Philosophical Hermeneutics* (Berkeley: University of California Press, 1976), p. 21.

33. Cf. Lawrence K. Schmidt, *The Epistemology of Hans-Georg Gadamer: An Analysis of the Legitimization of Vorurteile* (Frankfurt: Peter D. Lang, 1985), p. 25.

34. Hans-Georg Gadamer, "On the Problem of Self-Understanding," in *Philosophical Hermeneutics*, p. 49; Gadamer, "Zur Problematik des Selbstverständnisses," *Kleine Schriften* v. I *Philosophie Hermeneutik* (Tübingen: J.C.B. Mohr, 1967), p. 74.

35. For a discussion of Gadamer on method and its limits see Joel C. Weinsheimer, *Gadamer's Hermeneutics: A Reading of Truth and Method* (New Haven: Yale University Press, 1985), pp. 1–59.

36. *VI*, p. 245.

37. Hans-Georg Gadamer, *Truth and Method* trans. Joel Weinsheimer and Donald G. Marshall (New York: Continuum, 1989), supplement "Hermeneutics and Historicism," p. 512 (hereafter *TM*); Gadamer, "Hermeneutik und Historismus," *Wahrheit und Methode* (Tübingen: J.C.B. Mohr, 1972), p. 483 (hereafter *WM*).

38. Richard E. Palmer, *Hermeneutics: Interpretation Theory in Schleiermacher, Dilthey, Heidegger, and Gadamer* (Evanston, IL: Northwestern University Press, 1969), p. 133.

39. *TM*, p. 311; *WM*, p. 295.

40. *TM*, p. 374; *WM*, p. 356.

41. *TM*, p. 297; *WM*, p. 280.

42. *TM*, p. 474; *WM*, p. 450. Gadamer explains this dictum in this way in his "Text and Interpretation," in Brice R. Wachterhauser, ed., *Hermeneutics and Modern Philosophy* (Albany: SUNY Press, 1986), p. 382.

43. *TM*, p. 291; *WM*, p. 275.

44. Brice R. Wachterhauser, "Interpreting Texts: Objectivity or Participation?" *Man and World* 19 (1986), p. 450. I find no explicit mention of this in Gadamer, but Wachterhauser draws it out from the harmony of part and whole.

45. Schmidt, *The Epistemology of Hans-Georg Gadamer*, p. 191.

46. There is also outside evidence to justify the claim that the authorial intention was against marriage. See Hirsch, "Counterfactuals in Interpretation," pp. 59–60.

47. W.K. Wimsatt, "Genesis, An Argument Resumed," in *Day of the Leopards: Essays in Defense of Poems* (New Haven: Yale University Press, 1976), pp. 30–35. In concert with taking the "text itself" as criterion, Wimsatt employs the criterion of making the poem the best it can be—both in terms of relevance and aesthetic experience.

48. There is no necessity to this, of course. We shall see several examples, though, throughout this study: Interpretation based on meaning versus interpretation based on significance, textual versus nontextual interpretation, urinterpretation versus non-urinterpretation, and the classic distinction of interpretation versus criticism.

49. *ATT*, pp. 168–176.

50. Gracia, we should note, introduces the term "intension" into our discussion. Intension, of course, is the totality of attributes shared by all and only those objects in a term's extension. A term's extension, of course, is all the objects to which the term may be applied correctly.

51. *ATT*, p. 157.

52. *ATT*, p. 164.

53. German also, of course, has a more commonly used word for author, the cognate *Autor*.

2

A Critical Survey of Author Constructs: Does It Matter Who Is Speaking?

INTRODUCTION

What is an author?[1] This question at first appears quite strange, strange in that its answer seems so obvious as to make the question unnecessary. An author is simply the producer of a text. This understanding served interpretive theorists well for some time, but with the rejection of author-based interpretation by the New Critics and later by the structuralists and post-structuralists this understanding would no longer do.[2] The term "author construct" refers to a theorist's conception of the author, particularly as this conception applies to interpretation. We shall trace the recent historical development of author constructs and see how, although they were at first instrumental in diminishing the role of the author in interpretation, with sustained attention to them, some theorists have moved back in the direction of authorial intent.[3] No intentionalist, however, has provided us with an author construct suitable to his position. Having surveyed the development of author constructs, then, we shall offer an account of an intentionalist author construct, the urauthor.

We shall begin with an examination of the move away from author-based interpretation as found in Wimsatt and Beardsley's "The Intentional Fallacy."[4] We shall then turn to an examination of Michel Foucault and Roland Barthes, and subsequently to an appropriation of some of the developments made by Alexander Nehamas and Jorge Gracia. We shall pause to consider the dilemma that author-based interpretation poses for feminists, and finally arrive at our intentionalist author construct.

THE INTENTIONAL FALLACY

In their seminal article "The Intentional Fallacy" Wimsatt and Beardsley make a case for the move away from author-based interpretation.[5] In particular, they attempt to show that interpreting a text in strict accord with an author's intentions is a matter of confusing a text with its origins. Simply because an author produces a text does not mean that all or any of his intentions are embodied in it; some may be, but even these need not be considered. As they say, "There is a gross body of life, of sensory and mental experience, which lies behind and in some sense causes every poem, but can never be and need not be known in the verbal and hence intellectual composition which is the poem."[6]

The meaning and correct interpretation of a text are to be known in another way, through an analysis of the text itself.

The text itself, not the author's intention,[7] is the best indication of what it means. As Wimsatt and Beardsley say, one judges a poem like one judges a machine by asking the question: Does it work? If it works that is fine, but if it does not work there is nothing to know about the manufacturer of the machine or the writer of the poem that will make their creations work.[8] Still, Wimsatt and Beardsley do not rule out biographical information altogether. "The use of biographical information need not involve intentionalism because while it may be evidence of what the author intended, it may also be evidence of the meaning of his words and the dramatic character of his utterance."[9] Wimsatt and Beardsley distinguish among three types of evidence: internal, external, and intermediate. The text itself constitutes internal evidence; it is public. Information about the author's intentions is external evidence; it is private and/or idiosyncratic. Intermediate evidence "is about the character of the author or about private or semiprivate meanings attached to words or topics by an author or by a coterie of which he is a member."[10] There is no clear line between external and intermediate evidence, "they shade together," and so Wimsatt and Beardsley are of the mind that we need always be on guard against a lapse into intentionalism.[11]

What is most noteworthy about "The Intentional Fallacy" for our purposes is its tone with regard to the author. Wimsatt and Beardsley do not offer a formal author construct, but they do have a definite stance on the place of the author in interpretation. They do not depict the author as a benevolent supplier of meaning, but as something quite the opposite. Wimsatt's and Beardsley's moves may be the first steps along a road that leads to seeing the author as repressive. They appear to have seen intentionalism (or, more accurately, biographicalism) as having been carried to burdensome extremes, for example in Lowes's *The Road to Xanadu*, in which Lowes tried to get inside the mind of Coleridge and find the source of his images by reading everything the poet is likely to have read.[12] Certainly if we had to read everything an author had read in order to understand her work, we would have little time for anything else. This indeed would be repressive, limiting freedom by placing such exhausting demands on the interpreter. Of course intentionalism need not be practiced in such a fashion, but it was against the backdrop of such biographical excess that Wimsatt and Beardsley formed their critique in "The Intentional Fallacy." The author, as they saw it, had become a detrimental intrusion on interpretation. It was time to let the text speak for itself.

Wimsatt and Beardsley work within the understanding that the author is simply the producer of the text. They do not (themselves) pose the question: What is an author? Rather, they are narrowly concerned with the normative issue of how best to interpret a text. It took a much more radical approach to broach this concern underlying the normative issue, an approach popularized by Foucault and Barthes. In their wake "The Intentional Fallacy" seems a tame and conservative criticism of the author, and has become, as Cheryl Walker calls it, an "old chestnut."[13] Still, it is a chestnut on which we must continue to chew.

FOUCAULT AND BARTHES:
BEYOND THE INTENTIONAL FALLACY

"What matter who's speaking, someone said, what matter who's speaking."[14] This often quoted line from Beckett suggests the positions of Michel Foucault[15] and Roland Barthes[16] on the author. The idea that it is not the author but the text that matters in interpretation was to be found earlier in "The Intentional Fallacy," among other places, but Foucault and Barthes push the issue further, asking what an author is and why we should put so much stock in him and his intentions.[17] They conclude that the author is a repressive figure, and it matters not at all who is speaking. Ironically, Foucault cites Beckett as the source of this line.[18] Does it after all matter that Beckett gave us this refrain?

Let us begin our discussion of Foucault and Barthes by examining the common themes of "What Is an Author?" and "The Death of the Author." Peter Lamarque has insightfully captured these themes in four theses: the historicist thesis, the death thesis, the author function thesis, and the *écriture* thesis.[19] Given that structuralism and post-structuralism engage in a critique of history, it is not surprising to find that both Foucault and Barthes criticize the author as a mere historical construct. Barthes's words capture the historicist thesis for both theorists, "The author is a modern figure, a product of our society."[20] Both see the author as a product of the Enlightenment and the rise of individualism. According to Foucault, authors came to be seen as owners of their words at the end of the eighteenth and beginning of the nineteenth centuries, when a system of ownership and strict copyright rules were established.[21] For Barthes, the author is a product of the Enlightenment with secular society's attempt to replace the divine with the human.[22]

In either case, the point is that the concept of the author we have did not always exist in the past and so it need not always exist in the future. Actual human beings have always written texts, but we have not always made authors of these human beings the way we do today. The question we must ask of the historicist thesis is: Is it true? Is it true that our conception of the author is a peculiarly modern one? Foucault does little to substantiate this claim[23] and Barthes does even less. Let us look at what evidence Foucault does offer, however. In the Middle Ages, he claims, literature did not need an author but only the sanction of antiquity.[24] Certainly this is not true. The medievals had their canons of revered authors just as we do today; the reverence for Homer in the Middle Ages, for example, far exceeded that in our own time. Foucault claims that in the Middle Ages scientific works, on the other hand, did require the authority of their authors in a way they do not today.[25] The only point this illustrates, however, is that the amount of weight vested in the author of a particular type of text is subject to change. Scientific texts still have authors today;[26] well-known and respected scientific authors have some impact on how their texts are read, although of course they are not read as gospel in the way they may have been in earlier times.[27]

Barthes makes no attempt to actually show that things were different in earlier times. He simply claims without support that:

The author is a modern figure, a product of our society insofar as, emerging from the Middle Ages with English empiricism, French rationalism and the personal faith of the Reformation, it discovered the prestige of the individual, or, as it is more nobly put, the "human person." It is thus logical that in literature it should be this positivism, the epitome and culmination of capitalist ideology, which has attached the greatest importance to the "person" of the author.[28]

The historicist thesis is at the core of the views of both Foucault and Barthes, and for that reason it is unfortunate to see it so poorly supported. Foucault offers more of an argument than does Barthes, but even he is only able to establish that the weight vested in authors of various textual types has varied somewhat through time. Still, it could be that the author of a given textual type could fade (even if she could not disappear) over time. Let us grant them this much then, and proceed to examine the other theses.

As Lamarque explains, the death thesis can be stated flatly: The author is dead.[29] This thesis is explicit in Barthes's very title, "The Death of the Author," and throughout that essay. The thesis is also an essential feature of Foucault's "What Is an Author?" We must first ask of the death thesis: What does it mean? And then, Is it true? Unfortunately both Foucault and Barthes are quite vague as to what exactly the death of the author means. Is the author dead? Is he dying? Should we kill him? That is, is the death of the author a present matter of fact or a future goal? Has the funeral already been held? Or is the author still lying on his deathbed?

The death thesis is inextricably bound to the historicist thesis. The reasoning of the death thesis is that if the author as we know him did not always exist, he need not exist—we can kill him. Barthes, more so than Foucault, presumes that the author is already dead. As he says, "The removal of the Author . . . is not merely an historical fact or an act of writing; it utterly transforms the modern text.[30] "The Author is reputed the father and the owner of his work. . . . As for the text, it reads without the inscription of the father."[31] Barthes's words imply that the author is already dead; it is a present matter of fact. Still, Barthes was not oblivious to the fact that many critics still value the author, and indeed, he admits, "the sway of the Author remains powerful."[32] Further, he closes his essay by saying, "it is necessary to overthrow the myth: the birth of the reader must be at the cost of the death of the author."[33] Surely this suggests that the author is but moribund. It makes sense then to read Barthes charitably, as understanding that the author is not yet dead, though some of his words suggest that the author is already entombed.

Foucault is much clearer about the present situation; he would certainly accept that literary criticism works within a conception of the authored-text. Foucault most often claims that the author is to be eliminated in the future. As he says, "I think that as our society changes, at the very moment when it is in the process of changing, the author function will disappear."[34]

Is the death thesis true? If we understand it to mean that the author is dead, then certainly it is not true. The author still plays a prominent role in much criticism and interpretation. If we understand the death thesis, more charitably, to mean that the author is dying and should be killed, our answer is not as clear.

In some way it is true that the author is or was dying. The interpretive pendulum has indeed, at least at some point, swung away from its earlier author-based tendencies. Much criticism and interpretation both inside and outside the postmodern camp is done without regard for the author. The more important question is: Should we pull the plug on the author, or should we revive her? Foucault and Barthes would certainly favor author-euthanasia. In sharp contrast, in chapter 3 I shall suggest reviving the author through the intentionalist author construct I offer at the end of this chapter.

The author function thesis is the most valuable French contribution to the theory of authorship. It is with it that we see the birth of the author construct.[35] The thesis is most prominent in Foucault but is also operative in Barthes. To be clear, neither Foucault nor Barthes denies that men and women write texts; it is only that these theorists oppose a certain approach to the author-as-person. They may be understood as opposing attempts at elaborate historical reconstruction of the author-as-person on the grounds that such a figure is repressive: It limits the freedom of the reader. As Lamarque explains, the core of the author function thesis can be stated: "the author function is a property of a discourse (or text) and amounts to something more than its just being written or produced by a person."[36] We construct a figure in our minds, an author function, rather than refer to the historical being who produced the text, the author-as-person. As Foucault explains it,

[T]he author is not an indefinite source of significations which fill a work; the author does not precede the works; he is a certain functional principle by which in our culture one limits, excludes, and chooses; in short, by which one impedes the free circulation, the free manipulation, the free composition, the free decomposition, and recomposition of fiction.[37]

Clearly for Foucault the author is a repressive figure, and yet he does grant the author function some permanency. As he says, "It would be pure romanticism, however, to imagine a culture in which the fictive would operate in an absolutely free state, in which fiction would be put at the disposal of everyone and would develop without passing through something like a necessary constraining figure."[38]

For Foucault the author is a repressive force or function. It "prevents us from thinking of criticism as an extension and elaboration of literature, as an activity essentially continuous with its object, aiming to produce new meanings not to describe old ones."[39] The problem is that Foucault does not keep clear his own distinction between the author function and the historical person who produces the text. It is not in fact the author function itself that is repressive but (for Foucault) the author function constructed in strict accord with the historical author-as-person. It is not the mere existence of the mental construct, known as the author function, that is repressive. Rather, what Foucault intends to depict as repressive, in the demands it makes on the interpreter and the limitations it places on his free creativity, is the feeling of obligation to form the author function on the model of the historical producer. Nehamas suggests that this essential confusion between the author function itself and the author function formed in strict accord with the historical producer is the weak point of Foucault's theory.[40] Foucault's confusion is evidenced by two of the passages quoted above, in that on the same page he speaks of both the coming disappearance of the author function and of the necessity of such a constraining figure.[41] What he likely means (if he himself was not unclear but only his words), but does not actually say, is that the author function formed in strict accord with the author-as-person may disappear. As we shall see, however, a historically based construction of the author function need not be repressive.[42]

Barthes's version of the author function is the scriptor, which differs from Foucault's author function in being essentially unrelated to the text. The scriptor is not a filter through which interpretation must pass, but rather is both created and destroyed in the act of writing. The scriptor, unlike Foucault's author function, is not considered at all in the process of interpretation. The scriptor is recognized as the point of the text's genesis, but somehow this agent is destroyed in the process of giving birth. Writing, Barthes holds, is the cause of this destruction.

This brings us to what Lamarque calls the *écriture* thesis, "writing is the destruction of every voice, of every point of origin."[43] Here there is an intimate link with the death thesis; writing itself is the death of the author. As Foucault explains, "[T]his relationship between writing and death is also manifested in the effacement of the writing subject's individual characteristics. Using the contrivances of what he sets up between himself and what he writes, the writing subject cancels out the signs of his particular individuality."[44]

The *écriture* thesis is certainly counterintuitive, and unfortunately Foucault and Barthes offer no argument to support it;[45] it stands on its own, appearing contrived and programmatic, meant to take the text from the author and put it in the hands of the reader. Consider how often writing relies on its author as a source of authority, and how difficult it is for the author to hide even when she wants. As Lamarque says, "Far from being the destruction of a 'voice of origin' the successful performative relies crucially on the disposition and authority of the speaker."[46] It is, I submit, not only the performative utterance that is so heavily reliant on its author's authority. Indeed, we quite naturally search for an author even when she attempts to hide. Consider the efforts to find the real Kierkegaard behind the various pseudonyms of *Either/Or*.[47] I am inclined to agree with Wayne C. Booth, who says, "the author can choose his guise but never choose to disappear."[48]

As mentioned above, Barthes makes clear that his motivation in killing the author is the liberation of the reader. "[A] text's unity lies not in its origin but in its destination. . . . [T]he reader . . . is that *someone* who holds together in a single field all the traces by which the written text is constituted."[49] Barthes and Foucault call for a proliferation of meaning. The *écriture* thesis is not a logical basis on which to make this call, however. Foucault and Barthes move from an *is* to an *ought*, from the premise that what *is* sometimes the case (that texts are interpreted without regard to authors) to the conclusion that this *ought* to be the case. Further, even if the *écriture* thesis were such a logical basis, it would still need a hermeneutic theory on which to proceed. Neither Foucault nor Barthes offers any hermeneutic guidelines along which the liberated reader is to proceed.[50]

One issue Foucault and Barthes leave largely untouched is the range of texts with which they are concerned. Are they speaking only of literary texts? It would appear not, particularly in the case of Foucault, who makes references to scientific texts and also at one point says, "we do not construct a philosophical author as we do a poet."[51] What about the authors of criticism and interpretation? It is a curious phenomenon that those who make a practice of disregarding authors' intentions are often quite upset when their own intentions are disregarded by others. I will briefly address the question of authors of different textual genres in a later section of this chapter and in greater detail in chapters 3 and 5. We turn now to an examination of Nehamas, who has usefully appropriated the author function thesis, showing that the author is not necessarily repressive.

NEHAMAS: WRITER AND AUTHOR

Nehamas has understood and made sense of Foucault in an important and interesting way. In "What Is an Author?" Foucault had some difficulty in keeping the author function distinct from the author-as-person. For Nehamas the author is not necessarily an intruder, but can be an aid. In forming his author construct he distinguishes between the "writer" and the "author" of a text. The writer is a historical person firmly situated within a specific context, the efficient cause of a text's production,[52] while the author is whoever can be understood to have produced the text as we have construed it.[53] The author, as Nehamas conceives it, allows for a great deal more freedom than Foucault realized was implicit in his own author function.

To Nehamas the author is not necessarily a repressive or constraining figure. This makes sense, but it is doubtful that Foucault would accept it. As Pappas has explained, Nehamas "argues in ontological terms—concentrating on what the author is, instead of what our attachment to the author is like—and as a result fails to avoid Foucault's critique of authorship."[54] That is, Nehamas attempts to solve the problem by clarifying the ontological distinction between the author function and the historical producer, whereas Foucault is most truly concerned with the relationship between the interpreter and the author function.[55] Indeed, Foucault had himself distinguished between the historical agent and our conception of the historical agent. It is just never completely clear in Foucault which of the two or what combination of the two is repressive. Nehamas suggests that only the historical agent—the writer—could be repressive, but then urges us to construct the author on the model of the historical agent. As he says, "The author is to be constructed as a plausible historical variant of the writer, as a character the writer could have been."[56] This, of course, is exactly what Foucault seems to want to avoid.

We can, then, both criticize Nehamas for not advancing Foucault and praise him for surpassing Foucault. Nehamas does not offer a theory of authorship that Foucault (or anyone else who considers the author figure repressive) would find congenial. Inasmuch as the historical agent (the writer) influences our conception of the author, the supposed repression is still fully operative. The question is just how repressive such an author really is. Nehamas's sympathy for Foucault is apparent, but their views are actually quite different on the central question. Nehamas does not find the author even when modeled after the writer to be repressive, and in fact it would be more accurate to say that these figures are enabling in Nehamas's view. They are an integral part of, and a facilitating tool in, interpretation.

Nehamas approaches, but stops short of, a theory of authorship that an intentionalist such as Hirsch would find appealing. Nehamas does indeed pull up quite short of an intentionalist position, but for no clear reason. It is almost as if out of sympathy for and allegiance to Foucault, he cannot allow himself to go this far. Let us examine some of what Nehamas says. "Meaning depends on an author's intentions even if a writer is not aware of it. Since the author's intentions depend on what the writer could have meant, a text's meaning is to that extent a thing of the past, though its understanding itself is a thing of the future."[57] This is a view I suspect most intentionalists would find quite acceptable, though perhaps incomplete. Nehamas also says, "A methodological constraint on this view is that the postulated author be historically plausible: the principle is that a text does not mean what its writer could not historically have meant by it."[58]

In the above passage Nehamas is concerned with ruling out anachronistic interpretations; we must understand a text to mean only what its writer could have meant in his time and given his biography. This position puts Nehamas in league with the intentionalists, and puts him squarely in opposition to the kind of anachronistic interpretation practiced by Foucault, Derrida, and others. Still, Nehamas is not comfortable in intentionalist shoes and clings to Foucault's belief that there is something repressive about author-based interpretation. Nehamas's solution is that the writer can be repressive, but the author is not a real person and so cannot be repressive. As he says, "The charge of repression is appropriate to the use of the historical writer as a (supposedly) independent principle by which to judge interpretation."[59] The author is only a function; he is not who is speaking, but who can be speaking. Withdrawing further from his intentionalism, Nehamas says, "Now in one sense there is something arbitrary about constructing a historically plausible figure as a text's author. In principle we could always constitute a different context and a different author to give an unhistorical reading."[60]

There is much of value in Nehamas's theory of authorship. His pointed distinction between the historical agent who produces the text and the figure we construct in interpreting the text is an invaluable contribution. Of course this distinction was already implicit in Foucault, but it is Nehamas who clarifies it and makes it attractive. Still, there are some problems with Nehamas's terminology that we should address. The term "author," though quite natural, is ambiguous and misleading. It is too easily confused with the historical producer. Foucault had been more direct in speaking of the author function. Also, "author" as Nehamas uses it applies only to literature, "to say a text has an author is to say it is subject to literary interpretation."[61] Surely we would want to say that nonliterary texts have authors as well. The *Prior Analytics* has an author, as does *The Origin of Species*, although neither of these texts is subject to literary interpretation.

The term "writer" is also less than ideal, because one can be the writer of many things of which one is not the author.[62] If I were to copy the text of *Hamlet*, I would be its writer but certainly not its author.[63] Nehamas can respond, of course, that not every writer is an author. Still, this terminology leads too easily to confusion.

We turn next to an examination of Gracia's theory of authorship, one that has profited from and advanced beyond both Foucault and Nehamas.

GRACIA: HISTORICAL AUTHOR
AND PSEUDO-HISTORICAL AUTHOR

Gracia further clarifies the distinction between the historical agent who produces the text and the figure we create of the historical agent in interpreting the text. He also has much of interest to say on the issue of authorial repression and supplies what I take to be a refutation of the *écriture* thesis.

Gracia rejects Nehamas's terminology of "author" and "writer" in favor of a more careful distinction, speaking instead of the "historical author" and the "pseudo-historical" author. The historical author is the actual agent who produced the text. A text, as Gracia defines it, is a group of entities used as signs selected, arranged, and intended by an author in a certain context to convey a specific meaning to an audience.[64] Our knowledge of the historical author is necessarily limited, at least from a practical standpoint. We will never know all there is to know about the historical author, perhaps not even everything it would be important to know. Further, even the historical author may not know everything of importance or relevance about herself.

The pseudo-historical author is a construct, not a real person; it is a composite of what we know or think we know about the historical author.[65] Because our knowledge of the historical author is always limited and approximate, our pseudo-historical author will always be an imperfect match for the historical author. Still, it is important to note that for Gracia the author construct is no arbitrary figure, but is based as far as possible on historical fact. As he says,

The pseudo-historical author is always posited as the historical author of the text and thus as a historical person who actually produced the historical text. This implies that the figure of the pseudo-historical author must be historically credible. The author of *Don Quixote*, for example, cannot be a pharaoh of ancient Egypt.[66]

This certainly has implications for the theory of interpretation, moving Gracia in the direction of intentionalism. He recoils from and resists this position, however. "[T]he author of a text need not be regarded as creator of the meaning of a text or even the relation between that meaning and the entities that constitute the text."[67] For Gracia it is not the author's intentions that dictate the meaning of a text but rather the cultural function of the text; it is up to the community of interpreters to decide how much weight, if any, to give the author's intention in interpreting texts of a particular genre.[68]

Still, Gracia does leave the door open to the use of authorial intention in interpretation; such use is not, according to his theory, always repressive. The use of an author function, in Gracia's terms a pseudo-historical author, limits the range of understanding, denying unbridled creativity on the part of the reader or audience. This does not necessarily mean that Gracia's author construct is repressive, however; it can actually be enabling, leading (in his view) to correct understanding. We must ask ourselves whether creativity on the part of the audience is always necessarily a good thing. Certainly creativity in general is to be valued, but it has a restricted place. As Gracia suggests, it is good for a surgeon to be creative if her creativity will lead to a successful operation, but if her creativity is not called for, or may actually impede an operation, then certainly it should not intrude.[69] The point by analogy is, of course, that creativity has its limited place in the interpretation of texts as well.

Gracia would defer to the text's cultural function, as determined by the community of interpreters, in deciding what role creativity is to play. I would suggest a quite different approach, which I shall detail in chapter 3. Gracia holds, as does Nehamas, that the repressive power of the author is real but has been exaggerated. "There is, therefore, a good deal of sense in the notion that authorship is repressive, but the current balance of opinion has swung too far in that direction."[70]

Gracia also offers the basis of a refutation of the *écriture* thesis. We shall not develop this argument in detail; to do so would take us too far afield. Rather, let us simply sketch the moves in the argument. Gracia has shown convincingly that we cannot have texts without historical authors.[71] His argument, it should be noted, is contingent upon acceptance of his definition of "text." The kind of question that prompts the argument is, for example: Are entities such as pebbles on a beach blown into the configuration of words, or a literary masterpiece randomly typed by a monkey, texts? At first it appears difficult to deny that these are texts, for they can be used as such. The problem is that they are not produced by historical agents and hence have no historical context. The signs that compose these entities were not selected, arranged, and intended by an agent in a certain context to convey a specific meaning to an audience. They therefore do not meet the definition of a text, although they may potentially be used as texts.[72]

The *écriture* thesis in its most radical form denies that texts have contexts. Foucault's version of the *écriture* thesis is not quite this extreme, but Barthes's perhaps is. He calls for an explosion or dissemination of meaning in which the author and presumably all context is killed in the very process of writing. To treat a text as if its author and context have been annihilated is, in its effects, not altogether different from treating a monkey's *Hamlet* as a text. If the author and context are truly killed in the process of writing, textuality is killed as well. We no longer have texts but entities resembling texts that we use as texts, and certainly this is an undesirable conclusion. Of course most proponents of the *écriture* thesis are unlikely to accept Gracia's definition of "text," but for those of us who do accept that definition, the *écriture* thesis is shown to be untenable.

Gracia argues that although all texts must have historical authors, not all texts must have pseudo-historical authors. That is, we do not necessarily form a conception of the historical producer of every text we encounter; many simple and common texts such as "No Smoking" do not ordinarily produce pseudo-historical authors.[73] It is, of course, logically possible that such texts could have pseudo-historical authors, but in practice they rarely do. Nehamas takes an even stronger position on this issue, claiming that there are entire classes of texts that we do not interpret and therefore do not have authors.[74] In a subsequent section of this chapter I shall argue that all texts, recognized as such, result in the production of an author construct. For now, we take a brief detour to examine feminist reactions to the author.

THE FEMINIST DILEMMA

The role of the author construct in interpretation poses an interesting dilemma for feminist critics. Should they take the side of the French in fighting repression (repression caused by author constructs, in this case), or should they preserve a place for the author-as-person and so further the cause of promoting lesser known women writers?[75] This question presents some difficulty, but upon reflection an answer is clear. The place of the woman author, and with it the place of the author in general, must be preserved.[76]

To read texts as if they were authorless and anonymous is to deny part of a feminist agenda. Lesser-known women writers and poets are frequently pushed outside the canon and habitually excluded from anthologies, and it is only in making women's voices heard that this problem can be corrected. Part of a feminist agenda is to promote the work of women and other marginalized groups; in particular there has been much effort to promote the work of the most disenfranchised groups among women—lesbians and women of the third world.[77]

The solution of some feminist critics has been to ignore the attack on the author,[78] while others have adhered to a revised concept of authorship.[79] Paula Bennett's book, *My Life a Loaded Gun*, draws heavily on the biographies of Emily Dickinson, Sylvia Plath, and Adrienne Rich in interpreting their work. Bennett's constant theme is that understanding female rage is critical to understanding the work of these artists.

Camille Paglia is actively hostile toward French theorists in her *Sexual Personae*.

Most pernicious of French imports is the notion that there is no person behind a text. Is there anything *more* affected, aggressive, and relentlessly concrete than a Parisian intellectual behind his/her turgid text? The Parisian is a provincial when he pretends to speak for the universe. Behind every book is a certain person with a certain history. I can never know too much about that person and that history. Personality is western reality. It is a visible condensation of sex and psyche outside the realm of word. We know it by Apollonian vision, the pagan cinema of western perception. Let us not steal from the eye to give to the ear.[80]

Paglia draws heavily on biography in her interpretations of literary works and figures from antiquity to the present. Perhaps her most interesting interpretive study is that of Emily Dickinson, whom she calls, "Amherst's Madame de Sade," making explicit the rage and sexuality within Dickinson's often obscure verse.[81]

These feminist critics are justified in their rejection of the French. The author construct is not a repressive figure but an enabling one, whether one pursues a feminist agenda or not. We turn now to the articulation of an intentionalist author construct.

AN INTENTIONALIST AUTHOR CONSTRUCT: URAUTHOR

From our survey of theories of authorship at least one point has become clear: There is an actual historical agent who produces a text and there is a figure we construct in interpreting that text. Foucault and Barthes consider the author in an effort to move interpretation away from this "repressive" figure. Further considerations of the author by Nehamas and Gracia have led to views somewhat congenial to the normative position known as intentionalism, but no intentionalist per se has articulated an author construct. Though there are differences among intentionalists, one thing they share in common is a conspicuous lack of an author construct. What I propose then, is to articulate an author construct suitable for intentionalism.[82] To simplify matters we shall restrict our focus to the intentionalist theories of E.D. Hirsch, Jr. and P.D. Juhl.

Though Hirsch himself does not develop an author construct, he does, at times, point to one as being implied by his theory.

> On the surface it would seem impossible to invoke the author's probable outlook when the author remains unknown, but in this limiting case the interpreter makes his *psychological reconstruction* on the basis of fewer data. Even with anonymous texts it is crucial to posit not simply some author or other, but a particular subjective stance in reference to which the construed text is rendered probable. That is why it is important to date anonymous texts. . . . In this sense all texts including anonymous texts are attributed.[83]

> The speaking subject is not, however, identical with the subjectivity of the *author as an actual historical person*; it corresponds, rather, to a very limited and special aspect of the author's total subjectivity; it is, so to speak, that "part" of the author which specifies or determines verbal meaning.[84]

A reconstruction of the historical producer, then, is implied by Hirsch's position, although except in scarce few instances he does not make it explicit and never actually develops the details of an author construct. In an article published over three decades after he first took up the subject of interpretation,[85] Hirsch finally declares, "an author function there must be."[86] Even in this later article, however, he does not develop his own account of the author construct. Another indication that Hirsch means to deal with a construct, rather than a historical person, is his assertion that we must concern ourselves with what the author intended and not everything that may have been "going on in his mind" at the time of composition.

Why should anyone with common sense wish to equate an author's textual meaning with all the meanings he happened to entertain when he wrote? Some of these he had no intention of conveying with his words.[87]

If that is the principle (*everything present to the mind of the author*), all hope for objective interpretation must be abandoned, since in most cases it is impossible (even for the author himself) to determine precisely what he was thinking of at the time or times he composed his text.[88]

The author with whom Hirsch is concerned in interpretation is not the historical person with his innumerable idiosyncratic thoughts, but a limited reconstruction of the author—one that is composed only of what the historical person likely intended. Unfortunately, Hirsch himself is not clear about this distinction, and so refers to both the historical person and the construct implied in interpretation as "author." Hirsch is clear in his essential point, however. We need only be concerned with what the author intended to convey by his text.[89] Hirsch seems to have resisted the need for an author construct, at least prior to his declaration of, "an author function there must be," because such constructs had been used so readily by anti-intentionalists and because he could not yet see the value of and need for an author construct as a supplement to his intentionalism. "Those who keep abreast of literary theory know that the communicative model of textual interpretation has come under disdainful attack by Derrida and other influential French writers (Foucault and Barthes), who have made the quasi-metaphysical objection that the author of a text, being absent, does not really exist for interpretation. The author is just a construct."[90]

Juhl similarly resists developing an author construct, identifying such a figure too closely with the anti-intentionalist position he opposed. In arguing against Wayne Booth's implied author, Juhl throws the proverbial baby out with the bath water. He gets rid of Booth's implied author and fails to replace it with an intentionalist author construct, leaving us with only the real historical author. "But what could be the point of giving a name ('implied author' or 'author personality') to those aspects of the author which are relevant to our understanding of his work and another (the 'real author') to those aspects of the author which are not and saying that it is only the former we are concerned with?"[91] Juhl does not adequately recognize that an intentionalist needs an author construct because we can never even hope to "have" the real historical author. All we ever have is a more or less accurate version of him as related to his text, an author construct. Juhl admits, as does Hirsch, that we do not need to know everything about the historical author. "Few would be inclined to say it matters what the author believed to be the causes of hair loss or tooth decay."[92] In one instance Juhl hints at some realization of the difference in ontological status between what we consider in interpretation and the real historical author. "I have been arguing that it is our *picture* of the real, historical author which determines how we construe a literary work."[93]

I propose that we call the historical agent the author. To call him the writer (as Nehamas does) involves some confusion, and to call him the historical author (as Gracia does) in some way diminishes his importance by making him just another type of author.[94] I propose that we call the intentionalist author construct *urauthor*. This designation suggests that we should go back to the origin in forming this figure. We should not form our author construct arbitrarily, but rather seek as far as possible to create it in the likeness of the original, the author himself. Of course there are practical limitations as to how accurately we reproduce the original, and in some cases the restrictions will be greater than others. We need also to restrict ourselves in forming the urauthor by taking into account only what is relevant for interpretation. It is impossible to say in advance and in precise terms what is relevant in a particular case, but generally speaking we need to take into account all that contributes to the intended communication. We shall discuss this shortly.

There is also a notable difference in ontological status. The author is, or was, an actual person, whereas the urauthor is a mental construct, and consequently the urauthor can never be exactly the same as the author. Disregarding the obvious difference in ontological status, however, we can have greater and lesser matches between the two entities.

The urauthor is constituted by several elements. In constructing our author figure on the model of the original we need to take into account whatever information is at our disposal, and all of this is to be subsumed under the author construct, urauthor. Relevant biographical information will be very important.[95] Who was the author and how did she think? What likely were her intentions in composing the text?[96] How is language used in the text itself?[97] What was her historical context, and who was her audience?[98] Some of what is written only between the lines, that which is elliptical, is revealed by an analysis of the author's context and audience. What attitudes and knowledge did the author presuppose of her readers? What other texts of the author do we have at our disposal?[99] We may, in fact, construct the urauthor of a text, in part, through interpreting other texts by the same author.

The construct of the urauthor, then, will be composed of relevant available biographical information, likely intentions, use of language in the text itself, information concerning the author's context and audience, and other texts of the author inasmuch as they inform the other elements of the urauthor. Which elements are most important will vary, depending on the text to be interpreted, but always of greatest importance will be likely intentions inasmuch as all other elements of the urauthor are simply clues to those intentions.[100] How much effort we put into constructing the urauthor is a function of how much evidence we have, how clear the text as indicator of authorial intent seems to be, and how concerned we are that our interpretation be faithful to authorial intent.

The urauthor is just the sort of figure that elicits cries of repression from some theorists. I would argue, however, that the urauthor is not repressive but enabling. Interpretation must first involve historical understanding and only later creativity. (I argue for the primacy of such historical understanding in detail in chapter 5.) As Gracia has so aptly explained it, the author figure is repressive only if creativity in interpretation is a priority, and it is not clear that such creativity is a priority in all interpretation. Whether or not the urauthor is a repressive or enabling figure will have to be decided in light of the normative theory I articulate in chapter 3 and the primacy of historical understanding I argue for in chapter 5.

All texts have authors, historical agents who produced them. An entity without such a historical producer is not a text although it may resemble one. Do all texts have author constructs, however? The immediate and obvious answer would be no. Gracia holds that it is logically possible for any text to have a pseudo-historical author, but in point of fact many texts do not. We do not ordinarily form any conception of the author of the text "No Smoking," for example.[101] Nehamas is even more restrictive in the range of texts that he believes have "authors." "[S]ome texts are essentially incapable of having authors, and therefore of being interpreted. . . . [W]e can read texts, learn from them, and perhaps even like or dislike them without necessarily interpreting them."[102] Nehamas has a very strict conception of what constitutes interpretation and thus generates an author, in fact suggesting that much popular fiction may be "authorless."[103]

My position is that we do generate an author construct, an urauthor in my terms, for every text we confront.[104] The detail in which we form the construct varies greatly. At the very least, however, we assume that the author wrote[105] in the language in which we are reading or was read by someone who translated her work into that language. This is not much, but it is something. It can be the first weave in the tapestry which is to become the author construct. My point is simply that we do begin to form the author construct immediately, even if only in simple and pre-reflective terms.

This psychological argument may arouse some doubt and suspicion, but we can confirm it on logical grounds. If we accept Gracia's definition of a text as a group of entities, used as signs, which are selected, arranged, and intended by an author in a certain context to convey some specific meaning, then by definition all texts have authors (historical authors in Gracia's terms). Does the presence of an author, then, logically imply the presence of an author construct? Indeed it does, whenever we recognize something as a text. To recognize an entity as a text is, in part, to recognize it as having an author (a historical producer) and to recognize an author is, as we shall see, to recognize an author construct.

To recognize a text as having an author is to recognize it as having an author construct because any thought of the author (whether reflective or pre-reflective) gives rise to the creation of an author construct. It is only the author construct and not the author who, ontologically speaking, can be contained in our thoughts. The author is a real person not a thought content. The author construct, on the other hand, is not a real person but is precisely a thought content. In sum, to recognize an entity as a text implies recognizing it as having an author, recognizing a text as having an author is in some way to give thought to the author, and to give thought to the author is to form an author construct. All texts recognized as such, therefore, have author constructs.[106]

We tend to form the author construct through our pre-reflective assumptions about the text we confront. As mentioned above, one way in which we do this is in making assumptions about the language in which the text is written. Another important way is in assuming that the producer of the text was a rational human being using the language in a conventional way.[107] For this reason, the power of the text to determine its own meaning is often overestimated. It is routinely taken for granted that the author was rational and that her word choice and sentence structures were conventional. Such assumptions are of course defeasible, and it is in cases in which they are shown to be false that we come to realize how reliant upon the author we actually are.[108]

The drive or instinct to form the author construct is natural and pervasive. We must fight it when circumstances call for authorial anonymity. Consider the instructions for preparing a manuscript for blind review. In most cases not only is the author's name to be omitted, but all self-references as well. It is not enough that the author leave her name off the manuscript; if she even leaves a clue as to who she is, the reviewer may be tempted to follow-up the clue and identify the author. Such is the interpreter's instinct. Given an anonymous text he wants to identify the author. Something inside urges him to do so. Consider the grading of essay exams or term papers. Despite the ideal of impartiality, we teachers are influenced by the authors of these texts. We may give the benefit of the doubt to a student we consider bright or hard-working, or refuse the benefit of the doubt to a student we consider mediocre or lazy. Any teacher who grades without any consideration of the author has gained this ability only through considerable effort. It is not natural.[109]

The interpretation of any type of text logically implies the construction of an author construct. The degree of effort we put into and are satisfied with in this construction will vary a great deal, however. One cause of the variability will be the interpreter's degree of concern with being faithful to authorial intent. This is indirectly connected to another cause of the variability, the type of text being interpreted. We will ordinarily be satisfied with little or no effort in the case of simple anonymous texts such as "Please Wait in Line." Here we presume a rational author and conventional word use, and go no further in forming our construct. For more complex texts we will generally be satisfied with only more complex constructs. Still, how complex the construct must be depends on our own interpretive aims. For example, I may be highly concerned or relatively unconcerned with the formation of the author construct of a newspaper article. I may make little effort at the formation of the construct of a general information piece, while I may make substantial effort at the formation of the construct of a controversial editorial. I ask myself who was the person who wrote the editorial, and why would she say such things? Of course I could ask myself the same things about the author of the general information piece, but I am less likely to be moved to do so. I am more likely simply to presume a rational author who gives me conventional word use and sentence structure.

Some texts seem to be designed to avoid the production of an author construct, or at least a construct resembling the author. Kierkegaard, for example, was concerned that his audience not read some of his texts as his. Hence we get the pseudonyms of *Either/Or*.[110] Hume expressed much of his thought on God in dialogue form, rather than in the form of a treatise. Perhaps he did not want *everyone* to know what he, Hume, thought, and so instead put words in the mouths of dialogue characters. Even in these cases, however, the author construct is too seductive a temptress to forgo. Has not philosophical scholarship sought to form the author construct Hume, despite the author's efforts to hide? Cannot much the same be said of Kierkegaard?

CONCLUSION

Our survey of theories of authorship has led us to my account of the urauthor. In light of the ubiquitous debate of the question—What is an author?—it is impossible or at least ill-advised to leave this question unanswered. Perhaps it does matter who is speaking. N'est-ce pas?

NOTES

1. This question involves description, but it is not, strictly speaking, a concern of descriptive hermeneutics as that term was defined in chapter 1. That is, it is not an essential part of describing the process of interpretive understanding. (Although it may possibly inform that description.) Rather, the question of what an author is, is one that we must ask in order to properly articulate a normative approach. A normative approach, of course, is one concerned with the goals of interpretation, with developing a method for gaining knowledge of the meaning of a text. In this way, then, our inquiry here is in preparation for chapter 3, which deals with selecting a normative approach.

2. Of course the death of the author has an earlier history as well. Cf. Friedrich Nietzsche, *On the Genealogy of Morals* (New York: Vintage Books, 1989), pp. 100–101 (third essay, section 4); Nietzsche, *Human, All Too Human: A Book for Free Spirits* (Cambridge: Cambridge University Press, 1986) pp. 96–97 (section 208); and Nietzsche, *The Will to Power* (New York: Vintage Books, 1968), p. 327 (section 606). (It is ironic that Nietzsche is popularly credited for first pronouncing the death of God; whereas Hegel may more rightly deserve that distinction. At the same time Nietzsche is popularly overlooked in his implications for the death of the author while credit is given to Foucault and Barthes.) Gadamer also deserves some credit for the death of the author. Cf. *Truth and Method* trans. Joel Weinsheimer and Donald G. Marshall (New York: Continuum, 1989), pp. 296, 393, and 395; and Gadamer, *Wahrheit und Methode* (Tübingen: J.C.B. Mohr, 1972), pp. 280, 371, and 373. Gadamer was, in a sense, a prophet crying out in the wilderness, making way for the French merchants of authorial doom.

3. The survey we shall trace is not intended as exhaustive, nor do I mean to suggest that sustained attention to author constructs inevitably caused a move back toward intentionalism. Rather, what I offer here is one way of viewing some developments in the theory of authorship. One author construct to which we will not devote a sustained study, but rather to which we shall refer at times in discussing other author constructs, is the implied author. See Wayne C. Booth, *The Rhetoric of Fiction* (Chicago: University of Chicago Press, 1961), pp. 70–77, 86, 137–139, 151–152, 157–158, 200, and 211–221. For an excellent argument against relying on the implied author in interpretation see P.D. Juhl, *Interpretation: An Essay in the Philosophy of Literary Criticism* (Princeton, NJ: Princeton University Press, 1980), pp. 191–192, cf. pp. 163 and 194.

4. W.K. Wimsatt and Monroe C. Beardsley, "The Intentional Fallacy," in *The Verbal Icon: Studies in the Meaning of Poetry* (Lexington, KY: University of Kentucky Press, 1954), pp. 3–18.

5. Cf. W.K. Wimsatt, "Genesis: A Fallacy Revisited," in David Newton-De Molina ed., *On Literary Intention* (Edinburgh: Edinburgh University Press, 1976), p. 118. Wimsatt asserts that no revision to the earlier "Intentional Fallacy" is necessary.

6. Ibid., p.12.

7. Wimsatt and Beardsley do not rule out authorial intention altogether; authorial intention is relevant to interpretation as long as it is inferred from the text itself. Cf. W.K. Wimsatt, "Genesis: An Argument Resumed," in *Day of the Leopards: Essays in Defense of Poems* (New Haven: Yale University Press, 1976), p. 26. We should note also that one of the reasons the New Critics opposed authorial intention was that they feared it would lead to relativism—that the interpreter would impose his own intentions in place of the author's. This is ironic in that the intentionalist counterattack on the New Criticism accused it of leading to relativism. Clearly, both sides at least agree that relativism is to be avoided.

8. Ibid., p. 4.

9. Ibid., p. 11.

10. Ibid., p. 10.

11. Ibid., p. 10.

12. John Livingston Lowes, *The Road to Xanadu: A Study in the Ways of the Imagination* (Boston: Houghton Mifflin Co., 1927), Cf. "The Intentional Fallacy," p. 11.

13. Cheryl Walker, "Feminist Literary Criticism and the Author," *Critical Inquiry* 16 (1990), p. 563.

14. Samuel Beckett, *Texts for Nothing* (London: Carder and Boyars, 1974), p. 16.

15. Michel Foucault, "What Is an Author?" trans. Josué V. Harari, in Paul Rainbow ed., *The Foucault Reader* (New York: Pantheon Books, 1984), pp. 101–120 (hereafter WIA); "Qu'est-ce Qu'un Auteur?" *Bulletin de la Société Francaise de Philosophie* 63 (1969), pp. 75–95 (hereafter QA).

16. Roland Barthes, "The Death of the Author," in *Image, Music, Text* (New York: Hill and Wang, 1977), pp. 142–148 (hereafter DA); "La Mort de l'Auteur," *Manteia* 5 (1968), pp. 12–17 (hereafter MA).

17. For an excellent discussion of Foucault and Barthes see Seán Burke, *The Death and Return of the Author: Criticism and Subjectivity in Barthes, Foucault and Derrida* (Edinburgh: Edinburgh University Press, 1998) 2nd edition, pp. 20-115.

18. WIA, p. 101; QA, p. 77.

19. I am indebted for this classification of theses and much of their analysis to Peter Lamarque, "The Death of the Author: An Analytical Autopsy," *British Journal of Aesthetics* 30 (1990), pp. 319-331.

20. DA, p. 142; MA, p. 12.

21. WIA, p. 108; QA, p. 84. Cf. Mark Rose, *Authors and Owners: The Invention of Copyright* (Cambridge, MA: Harvard University Press, 1993).

22. Merold Westphal, "Kierkegaard and the Anxiety of Authorship," *International Philosophical Quarterly* 34 (1994), p. 11. Cf. DA, pp. 142-143; MA, p. 12.

23. WIA, p. 110; QA, p. 85. Here Foucault admits that he has offered only generalizations.

24. WIA, p. 109; QA, p. 84.

25. WIA, p. 109; QA, p. 84.

26. As we shall see later in this chapter, this is true even of anonymous texts and texts made anonymous for blind review.

27. Cf. Steve Woolgar, "What Is a Scientific Author?" in Maurice Biriotti and Nicola Miller eds., *What Is an Author?* (Manchester: Manchester University Press, 1993) pp. 175-190.

28. DA, pp. 142-143; MA, p. 12.

29. Lamarque, pp. 322-324.

30. DA, p. 145; MA, p. 14.

31. Roland Barthes, "From Work to Text," *Image, Music, Text* (New York: Hill and Wang, 1977), p. 161.

32. DA, p. 143; MA, p. 13.

33. DA, p. 148; MA, p. 17.

34. WIA, p. 119; QA, p. 95.

35. Of course, Foucault and Barthes were not the first theorists ever to speculate on the nature of the author. There is a long history of such speculation. Still, it is with them that such speculation and the attempt to name such a figure came to prominence. One of their predecessors is Wayne C. Booth and his *The Rhetoric of Fiction* (Chicago: University of Chicago Press, 1961). Booth captures the novelty of attempting to put a name on what I call in general terms the author construct. "It is a curious phenomenon that we have no terms for this 'second self' or for our relationship with him. None of our terms for the various aspects of the narrator is quite accurate. 'Persona,' 'mask,' and 'narrator' are sometimes used, but they more commonly refer to the speaker in the work who is after all only one of the elements created by the implied author and who may be separated from him by large ironies" (p. 73).

36. Lamarque, p. 325.

37. WIA, pp. 118–119; QA, p. 95.

38. WIA, p. 119; QA, p. 95.

39. Alexander Nehamas, "Writer, Text, Work, Author," in Anthony J. Cascardi ed., *Literature and the Question of Philosophy* (Baltimore: Johns Hopkins University Press, 1987), p. 271.

40. Ibid., p. 288.

41. WIA, p. 119; QA, p. 95.

42. In a subsequent section of this chapter I will make clear how such a construction can actually be enabling. As we shall see, Gracia and Nehamas also see the author construct as enabling in some way.

43. DA, p. 142; MA, p. 12. Cf. Lamarque, pp. 328–331.

44. WIA, p. 102; QA, p. 78.

45. There are no arguments of any substance in DA or WIA. Perhaps they consider their claims to be so obvious as to need no supporting arguments. Derrida and others have made use of Saussure's linguistics in making arguments for similar positions.

46. Lamarque, p. 329.

47. Cf. Westphal.

48. Booth, p. 20.

49. DA, p. 148; MA, p. 17. For a similar view see Stanley Fish, *Is There a Text in This Class? The Authority of Interpretive Communities* (Cambridge, MA: Harvard University Press, 1980).

50. Cf. Walker, p. 568.

51. WIA, p. 110; QA, p. 86.

52. Nehamas (1987), p. 272.

53. Ibid., p. 273.

54. Nickolas Pappas, "Authorship and Authority," *Journal of Aesthetics and Art Criticism* 47 (1989), p. 326.

55. Cf. Robert Stecker, "Apparent, Implied, and Postulated Authors," *Philosophy and Literature* 11 (1987), p. 267.

56. Nehamas (1987), p. 285.

57. Alexander Nehamas, "The Postulated Author: Critical Monism as a Regulative Ideal," *Critical Inquiry* 8 (1981–1982), p. 145.

58. Ibid.

59. Alexander Nehamas, "What an Author Is," *The Journal of Philosophy* 83 (1986), p. 690.

60. Nehamas (1981–1982), p. 146.

61. Nehamas (1987), p. 275.

62. Cf. Jorge J.E. Gracia, *Texts: Ontological Status, Identity, Author, Audience* (Albany: SUNY Press, 1996), p. 113.

63. It is conceivable that one might argue that I am the author of such a text. I would argue that if one has merely copied the text, then one is no more the author of it than would be a photocopy machine. On the other hand, if one produced the same exact text by some grand coincidence with one's own intentions, then one would be the author of that text. For an interesting look at the controversy over the rewriting of *Don Quixote*, see Jorge Luis Borges, "Pierre Menard, Author of the *Quixote*," in Donald A. Yates and James E. Irby, eds., *Labyrinths* (New York: New Directions, 1962), pp. 36–44. See also Alfred Lessing, "What Is Wrong with a Forgery?" *Journal of Aesthetics and Art Criticism* 23 (1964), pp. 461–471.

64. Jorge J.E. Gracia, *A Theory of Textuality: The Logic and Epistemology* (Albany: SUNY Press, 1995), p. 4 (hereafter *ATT*). The intentionalist Juhl has a similar definition of "text." "To call something a poem or even a text is to say among other things that the words, phrases, lines, or sentences, of which it consists have not been arranged in this way by chance but have been produced by a person and with certain kinds of intentions" (p. 84).

65. Cf. Gracia (1996), p. 97.

66. Ibid., 100.

67. Ibid., 108.

68. Cf. *ATT*, pp. 89–96.

69. Gracia (1996), p. 133.

70. Ibid., p. 134.

71. Ibid., Cf. pp. 119–126. See also Jorge J.E. Gracia, "Can There Be Texts Without Historical Authors?" *American Philosophical Quarterly* 31 (1994), pp. 248–253.

72. Whether they should be used as texts is another question, one with an ethical dimension.

73. Gracia (1996), p. 117.

74. Nehamas (1987), p. 275.

75. Cf. Nancy Miller, "Changing the Subject: Authorship, Writing and the Reader," in Maurice Biriotti and Nicola Miller eds., *What Is an Author?* (Manchester: Manchester University Press, 1993), pp. 19-41.

76. I note that not all feminists find this answer clear, but it is the most widely accepted answer among American feminists. Cheryl Walker suggests that it has been easier for American feminists than for British feminists to deny the French author-killers, cf. p. 561. I am most indebted to Walker's article for drawing the feminist reactions to my attention. I should note that Walker herself does not go all the way in the direction of intentionalism.

77. Walker, p. 570.

78. For example, Paula Bennett *My Life a Loaded Gun: Female Creativity and Feminist Poetics* (Boston: Beacon Press, 1986) and Camille Paglia *Sexual Personae: Art and Decadence from Nefertiti to Emily Dickinson* (New York: Vintage Books, 1991). Cf. Walker, p. 561.

79. Alicia Suskin Ostriker, *Stealing the Language: The Emergence of Women's Poetry in America* (Boston: Beacon Press, 1986); Jan Montefiore, *Feminism and Poetry: Language, Experience, Identity in Women's Writing* (London: Pandora, 1987); and Cora

Kaplan, *Sea Changes: Essays on Culture and Feminism* (London: Verso, 1986). Cf. Walker, p. 561.

80. Paglia, p. 34.

81. Ibid., pp. 622–673.

82. I shall defend a type of intentionalism in chapter 3.

83. E.D. Hirsch, Jr., *Validity in Interpretation* (New Haven: Yale University Press, 1967), p. 259 (hereafter *VI*). Emphasis added.

84. *VI*, pp. 242–243. Emphasis added.

85. For Hirsch's earliest major article on the subject see E.D. Hirsch, Jr., "Objective Interpretation," *PMLA* 75 (1960), pp. 463–479.

86. E.D. Hirsch, Jr., "Transhistorical Intentions and the Persistence of Allegory," *New Literary History* 25 (1994), p. 551. Here he argues for the "persistence of intention." Even in the case of Foucault, he argues, there is an author function. For Foucault it is the reader who fulfills the author function.

87. *VI*, p. 18. Juhl would agree to a certain extent. Cf. pp. 191–192.

88. *VI*, p. 220. Emphasized parenthetical comment is mine.

89. The author construct with which Hirsch must concern himself is based very much on the historical person, and in this sense is very different form Booth's implied author.

90. E.D. Hirsch, Jr., "Counterfactuals in Interpretation," in Sanford Levinson and Steven Mailoux eds., *Interpreting Law and Literature: A Hermeneutic Reader* (Evanston, IL: Northwestern University Press, 1988), p. 58. Parenthetical comment added to reflect Hirsch's note which says he has in mind Foucault and Barthes.

91. Juhl, p. 191.

92. Juhl, p. 191.

93. Juhl, pp. 185–186. Emphasis added.

94. Indeed, as we shall see, he is not just another type of author but the basis for all our thoughts on authorship, and so is deserving of the designation "author."

95. Cf. Juhl, pp. 88–89. Despite Juhl's rejection of an author construct he is very helpful in our project of assembling the various elements that constitute the urauthor. Juhl argues throughout his book that there is a logical connection between an author's intention and a number of things on which interpretation is often based (biographical information and other external evidence, the text itself, context, use of language, and aesthetic qualities of a text). He argues that in making reference to these things, in placing our interpretive stock in them, that we are actually referring to the author's intentions.

96. Cf. Juhl, pp. 54–65. Juhl's discussion of allusion and irony sheds much light on this issue.

97. Cf. Juhl, pp. 106–112, and 66–89.

98. Cf. Juhl, pp. 90–99, and 141. For our purposes we shall consider audience as part of context, though Juhl does not specifically do so himself.

99. Cf. Juhl, pp. 103, and 261–268.

100. Juhl would argue that in appealing to any of these we are, logically speaking, appealing to the author's intentions. See notes 88–92 above.

101. Cf. Gracia (1996), p. 117.

102. Nehamas (1987), p. 275.

103. Ibid.

104. That is, for every text recognized as such and read by a reader. In some cases the text may not actually have to be read but simply recognized as a text.

105. Of course not all authors have always literally "written" their texts. The Homeric epics, for example, were produced and carried on for a time orally. When I speak of

writing, then, I mean to include all ways of composing texts. Texts can in fact be written, spoken, and even be nonphysical (i.e., mental) entities. Cf. Gracia (1996), pp. 18–26.

106. We can, of course, mistakenly begin to form an author construct for what turns out not to be a text.

107. What is conventional will vary, among other ways, according to the genre in which we place the text. For example, placing a text in the genre of poetry will usually be quite different from placing it in the genre of ordinary discourse.

108. We shall discuss this further in chapter 3.

109. One must make an effort to rid oneself of this tendency, or make an effort to guard against it. If one has trouble overcoming this natural tendency in grading there are, of course, alternatives. One alternative is to have students use ID numbers rather than names as identifiers. Handwriting and other personal eccentricities can still be a problem though.

110. Cf. Westphal.

3

A Defense of an Intentionalist Approach: Urinterpretation

INTRODUCTION

Recall that the normative approach to hermeneutics is concerned with discovering the criteria for producing correct interpretations, that is, for gaining knowledge of the meaning of a text. As we saw in chapter 1, the crucial point of disagreement among those who take a normative approach is the answer to the question: What role should the author play in interpretation? Having surveyed theories of authorship in chapter 2, we can now properly address this question.[1]

The first normative approach we shall consider greatly limits, though it does not completely exclude, the place of the author and his intention in the proper interpretation of his text. We shall find this position, as defended by Beardsley, unacceptable for several reasons. Hirsch, on the other hand, has argued that the author's intention[2] constitutes *the* criterion by which we should judge the validity of an interpretation. We shall, then, consider Hirsch's theory in detail and argue that it is correct in its general thrust, but that it is incorrect and incomplete in several respects. The major deficiency in Hirsch's position is its lack of a theory of authorship. We shall see, then, how my account of the urauthor can be used to supplement Hirsch's theory, acting as a springboard to my own intentionalist theory, urinterpretation. To be clear, the positions of Hirsch and Beardsley are not the only possible ones, but for the sake of economy, they are the only positions we shall consider in detail. One might be tempted to suggest a middle path between the two, in which both authorial intention and the text itself are given significant attention, but, in truth, both Hirsch and Beardsley already do this to some extent. Beardsley does not deny authorial intention when it is clearly manifested in the text, and Hirsch, as we shall see, does hold that authorial intention must be manifested in a way that can be supported by the text. My theory of urinterpretation also takes both authorial intention and the text itself into account. The text, however, is seen as only an important clue to the meaning that itself is dictated by the intention of the author—what the author intended to communicate by her text.

THE TEXT ITSELF

Beardsley's Position

Let us first consider the position that the text itself should govern its own interpretation, as defended by Beardsley in numerous works, in particular, "The Intentional Fallacy,"[3] and "The Authority of the Text."[4] Others have argued for this position as well, but to avoid unnecessary complications we shall take Beardsley as its representative. Indeed, we shall see from our examination of Beardsley that no variation of the "text itself" criterion will work.

As Beardsley states his case,

> The poem is not the critic's own and not the author's (it is detached from its author at birth and goes about the world beyond his powers to intend about it or control it). The poem belongs to the public. It is embodied in language, the peculiar possession of the public, and it is about the human being, an object of public knowledge.[5]

The point is, texts are produced in language that is both a public creation and public property. We can read texts, then, without reference to the author; they are written in a public medium, and so we do not need the author to decode them. Also, an author may often be unsuccessful in communicating her intention through her text. That is, her use of language may not reflect her intention. Such may often be the case, but, Beardsley argues, we do not judge the success or the meaning of a literary work by the intention of the author. A literary work is not the kind of thing we can fix by an appeal to the author. Just as we do not forgive a machine for not working by appealing to its manufacturers, so we do not forgive a poem for not working by appealing to the poet. If the text alone does not convey its meaning, then what good is it?[6] In a similar way, a joke which has to be explained (at least to its intended audience) is usually not a good joke.

Beardsley puts the matter succinctly in his principle of autonomy: Literary works are self-sufficient entities whose properties are decisive in checking judgments and interpretations.[7] According to Beardsley, we must rely on the text alone because the author's intention[8] is not a reliable indication of the text's meaning for three reasons. First, there are, at least it seems, textual meanings that do not correspond to authorial meanings. For example, "Jensen argued like a man filled with righteous indigestion."[9] This is a case of what Hirsch would call a bungled text, in which the author presumably meant to say "righteous indignation." Beardsley's point is that the text means something different from what its author meant; the text conveys the meaning that Jensen argued like a man who had heartburn, whereas the author likely meant that Jensen argued like a man filled with righteous indignation. Second, the meaning of a text can change independently of its author. For example, the meaning of a text can change after its author has died, but quite obviously the author cannot change his meaning after he has died.[10] In this way someone might interpret *Huckleberry Finn* as being about the civil rights movement of the 1960s. Third, a text can have meanings of which its author is not aware, and so it can have meanings its author did not intend.[11] For example, someone might conceivably interpret "London" as being about the oppression of workers under the system of capitalism.

We should note that textual meaning is determinate for Beardsley, not in the sense of yielding only one correct interpretation, but rather in the sense of allowing a limited array of possible correct interpretations as dictated by the text. For Beardsley, the interpretation of a text should not stay the same for all time. We should further note that Beardsley's claims are meant only to apply to the interpretation of literary texts. He does acknowledge that authorial intention is quite important in interpreting other kinds of texts, for example, a personal message or a will.[12] As I shall make clear shortly, Beardsley's arguments cannot hold for literary texts only; they apply to all texts or no texts at all. For now, however, let us see why Beardsley holds that literary interpretation should be done without consideration of authorial intention.

For Beardsley, literary texts are deemed to serve a specific purpose, what Gracia has called a cultural function.[13] Beardsley asserts that the primary purpose of literary interpretations is to help readers approach literary texts from the aesthetic point of view.[14] The aesthetic experience[15] produced by literature and aided by literary interpretation is our primary goal. Knowledge of the author cannot foster such an experience, and if it is needed in any way, this is indicative of a poor work of literary art. As Beardsley says,

The literary text, in the last analysis, is the determiner of its meaning. It has a will, or at least a way, of its own. The sense it makes along with the sounds it makes is what it offers for our aesthetic contemplation. If this contemplation is rewarding, there is no need for an author to hover about like a nervous cook, waiting to supply some condiment that was left out of the soup. And if that contemplation is not rewarding there is nothing the author can do about it, except rewrite—that is, give us another poem.[16]

The Arguments against Beardsley

Beardsley's arguments against the author, as dictating correct interpretation and in support of the text's interpretive authority, do not stand up to critical analysis. For one thing, a text can indeed have a meaning its author is not aware of but that is still the author's meaning. That is, an author can have a meaning of which she is not conscious, or not fully conscious; an intention is not necessarily a plan. Much of our daily activity is not fully conscious; much is even unconscious. Why should the case be different for what we intend to convey by texts? As Juhl says, "we are not fully aware of all that goes into nor do we have a separate act preceding such things as walking, shifting gears, raising an arm, chewing gum, eating."[17] Beardsley has assumed, without warrant, that awareness is a necessary condition for an author to have an intended meaning, but as Hirsch and others have shown, it is not.[18] As Hirsch puts says, "'unconscious meaning' refers to those meanings which are not attended to by the author but which are nevertheless present in another region of his mind."[19]

Frequently an author can become aware of his unconscious[20] meaning if it is pointed out to him. For example, in writing a satirical essay an author may have a meaning that is both shocking and enlightening, although he is only consciously aware of it as enlightening. When an interpreter points out to the author that his choice of words and imagery is frequently shocking, the author may then agree that he intended the meaning to be shocking as well.[21] The matter can be even more complex, however, in that an author may have had an unconscious intended meaning that he cannot or will not admit to, even once it is pointed out to him. In such cases the author does not necessarily have the final word.[22] The interpreter may, if she has good reason, continue to assert that such a meaning was unconsciously intended. The interpreter must offer strong support for her claim to know an author's unconscious intention, however, for without such support her claim is mere speculation, and it is safer to rely on the author's testimony or whatever other evidence is available.

Beardsley's claim that the meaning of a text can change, even when the author does not change his meaning, for example, when the author is dead, is mistaken. Unfortunately, this is not the most opportune place to explain why, because we have not yet argued for the distinction between meaning and significance needed to make the argument. In the next section of this chapter we shall examine and argue for this distinction, and in so doing lend flesh to the boneless phantom that is our argument. For the moment, let us sketch a preliminary explanation. Beardsley's claim is a rather common and widely accepted one, but it rests on a fundamental confusion between meaning and significance. The meaning of the text is a principle of stability provided by the author, while the significance of a text is a principle of change—it is meaning-as-related-to (to me, to us, to our time, etc.). It is, as we shall see, only the significance of a text that changes and not its meaning, but for the moment I am merely begging the question against Beardsley. It remains to be proved that the distinction between meaning and significance is a real and viable one. This distinction has been made most clearly by Hirsch, who developed it out of the work of Frege, Husserl, and Betti.

That there can be textual meanings that are not authorial meanings is also false, but likewise requires an argument that is better left for a subsequent section of this chapter. To take an example though, when an obviously non-native speaker of English asks me, "May I borrow your pin?" while I am holding a pen, the textual meaning appears to be quite different from the authorial meaning.[23] After all, the speaker probably meant that she wanted a writing implement, not a piercing or poking implement. Such cases also occur in writing, for instance, when through an oversight or typesetting error an important "not" is left out of a philosophical argument. Context (which is part of the urauthor) often allows us to realize that the "not" has been omitted mistakenly, and hence allows us to understand the intended meaning.

The key to refuting Beardsley's argument here has its beginnings in Hirsch who says, "meaning is an affair of consciousness and not of physical signs or things."[24] Texts are mute according to Hirsch; they say nothing unless an author speaks through them. To successfully refute Beardsley, we would have to argue for this Hirschian view in its most absolute sense. Hirsch does not do this, but stops short, granting that the text does have some authority. In a subsequent section of this chapter I shall take the argument to its logical conclusion: texts have no meaning in and of themselves; rather, they act as clues, indicating an author's meaning. Only then shall we see that Beardsley's argument does not hold.

While I have chosen not to respond in detail to all of Beardsley's arguments against the author at this point, we can nonetheless show that his criterion of the text itself as dictating its own meaning does not work. Having a historical producer, an author, is a necessary condition for being a text. As we saw in chapter 2, a text without such an author is not a text. Also, all texts have author constructs. Recognizing a text as a text logically implies recognizing it as having an author, and giving thought to an author (even in this limited way) is forming an author construct.

The text itself alone can tell us little, much less than we are inclined to think. Without at least pre-reflectively assuming a rational author who makes conventional use of the language,[25] we cannot even get off the starting block. We make such assumptions so regularly and habitually, however, that they ordinarily go unnoticed, and as a result, we tend to think texts themselves tell us more than they really do. In fact, however, a text cannot necessarily tell us whether it is indeed a text; we must refer to an author to confirm this. The text itself cannot even necessarily tell us the language in which it was written. For example, the reader of this text likely assumes that its author or translator produced the text in English. How does the reader know for certain without reference to the author? Many short texts are identical in different natural languages, and it is at least theoretically possible that long and complex texts could be similarly identical. Artificial or conventional languages could, in fact, be designed to imitate a natural language, and so cause just the kind of confusion I suggest. Consider a simple example. A friend of mine not long ago noticed a contemplative look on my face and asked what I had on my mind. I responded "*Lust.*" He immediately assumed I meant the English word "lust" and wondered why I was dwelling on such a subject. In fact, though, I meant and was considering the various uses of the German word "*Lust,*" which denotes desire but not exclusively or ordinarily of a lascivious nature.

The above example illustrates how little the text alone can necessarily tell us; we cannot even know for certain if an entity is indeed a text by an examination of the text alone, or, if it is a text, in what language it was composed. Without reference beyond the text we could not know the meaning of any text whose apparent textual meaning[26] can be taken in more than one way, and I know of no text that could not be taken in more than one way.[27] Consider for example, "Andrew is a nice guy." Does this text mean that Andrew is an agreeable fellow? Or is it a sarcastic remark that suggests he is a rotten human being? Without knowing what its speaker intended, we could take the meaning to be either of these two, and certainly many others as well.

Did Swift's *A Modest Proposal* advocate cannibalism, or was it ironic and satirical? The text alone cannot answer the question; some of Swift's contemporaries were indeed aghast at what they took to be his suggestion of cannibalism. Stylistic analysis of a text may provide some hint as to whether it is satirical or not, but it cannot give a clear answer in most cases or a definitive answer in any case.[28]

The text alone allows for a plurality of possible meanings, often notoriously including conflicting and contradictory meanings. Fortunately, we rarely, if ever, have simply the text alone. In reading a text we instinctively form an author construct (urauthor in my terms), usually making the defeasible assumption that the author was a rational person making conventional use of the language. The criterion of "the text alone" appears rather arbitrary in its application, not limiting the meaning of the text in any final way. In accord with the text itself alone, we might justifiably follow the antonym rule; after all, "bad" can sometimes mean "good," for example.[29] Why is the apparent verbal meaning of the text preferable to the antonym meaning? Verbal meaning is preferable because it generates possibilities that often strike us as possibly correct. As Knapp and Michaels say, "the verbal meaning rule limits interpreters to meanings that may go beyond the author's intention but nonetheless seem plausibly related to it."[30] We assume that the text means what it appears to until and unless some indication suggests otherwise. That is, our author construct of a given text generally starts as a rather ordinary one, and tends to grow more extraordinary with the accretion of details.

In attempting to escape the excesses of author-based interpretation, Beardsley has simply arrived at a different kind of excess. The text itself cannot limit meaning in any final way. To so limit the meaning of the text we must, as we shall see, refer to the urauthor, including the context of which it is in part constituted. To paraphrase Hirsch and Blake, the road of excess leads not to the palace of wisdom but to the dungeon of counterexcess. We must, therefore, rid author-based interpretation of its excess[31] rather than become imprisoned in the counterexcess of the text itself.

Clearly, I am not denying that we can often be quite successful in interpreting a simple text on the basis of the text alone; we do not confront texts in a state of mass confusion. As a rule, we assume that a text means what it appears to mean. We assume, for example, "He shot an elephant in his pajamas" means that the shooter, and not the beast, was wearing sleeping attire. Still, we are always open to the possibility that the text means something other than what it at first appears to mean. This is the case in ordinary discourse, and it is the case in interpreting written texts of all kinds as well.[32] We are, and must be, alert to clues from what we know of the author and the context (elements of the urauthor) that the meaning is other than what the text at first seems to suggest.

Literary Texts, Cultural Functions, and Genres

Recall that Beardsley claims that the interpretive criterion of "the text itself" is applicable only to literary texts, that the literary text has what we might call a specific cultural function, namely the production of aesthetic experience. The aesthetic experience is the product of the text alone, regardless of what its author may have meant. That is, we cannot appeal to the author to enhance an otherwise deficient aesthetic experience. There is no doubt that we can use a text to produce an aesthetic experience in this way, but what such a use of a text will generate, is a significance and not a meaning. Again, this will become clearer in the next section of this chapter.

Even without the distinction between meaning and significance in hand, however, we can still show that Beardsley is mistaken. Beardsley does admit that some nonliterary texts are dependent upon the author's intention for their proper interpretation. For example, we do not read a last will and testament for the aesthetic experience but to secure the author's intention. My claim is that if the meaning of a will is to be discovered in this way, so must the meaning of a poem or any other kind of text.[33] The argument in support of this claim is that there is no ontological distinction between groups of texts, which can dictate that all texts of a certain group must be interpreted in the same way. It is the cultural institution, not the text itself, which often demands that interpretation be dictated by textual genre.[34] Genres are not hard ontological barriers, but soft human creations—often culturally bound. The borders between genres, no matter how narrowly conceived (e.g., epic poetry and lyric poetry) are fuzzy and imprecise.[35] For practical purposes they may serve us well, but they do not yield differing yet definitive rules of interpretation. We may, for example, classify *King Lear* as a tragedy and *A Midsummer Night's Dream* as a comedy, but these classifications do not put two different and definitive sets of interpretive rules at our disposal. That is, not all tragedies and not all comedies are subject to exclusive classes of interpretive rules. As Hirsch says,

Aristotle was wrong to suppose that human productions can be classified in a definitive way like biological species, or that works of art could have intrinsic goals different from those actually aimed at by their human authors.[36]

But we may be permitted to be skeptical as long as that essence is not satisfactorily defined. According to Aristotle, the essence of any class is that system of characteristics which are shared by all its members, and which are not shared by things outside the class. . . . But in fact, nobody has ever so defined literature or any important genre within it.[37]

As Hirsch has observed, the distinctions we make among textual types or genres are not binding when it comes to interpretation. There is nothing in the nature of certain texts we call poems, for example, that compels us to group them together and interpret them in accord with the same principles. They share a family resemblance not an essence.[38] Grouping them together may be helpful in that they do share some things in common, as all plants share some things in common. Still, not all plants require the same care and environment and not all poems require the same type of interpretation. Nor should we assume that texts grouped together share compellingly distinguishing features. Such groupings are simply pragmatic; they may serve as a starting point for interpretation, but certainly not an end. As Hirsch has pointed out, no one has ever been able to successfully define literature as a whole or any genre within it in terms of a shared essence. Why then should we assume such a shared essence among members of a genre? Truly no such shared essence has ever been discovered, particularly as it would relate to interpretation, and the burden of proof rests with those who would assert it.[39] My conjecture is that examples of literature, like Wittgenstein's examples of games, share not an essence but a family resemblance.[40]

There are no sharp lines between genres, and so it is unwarranted to say that texts of type A should be interpreted in one way while texts of type B should be interpreted in another way. A given culture may have its own reasons for approaching interpretation in a given way, but the justification for those reasons is not likely to lie in textual essences (though it is a remote logical possibility that it could). Based on the evidence we have, we should interpret all texts in accord with the same basic principle. This does not mean that all texts should be interpreted in exactly the same way, but that their bedrock principle for interpretation is the same.[41] Texts certainly do differ from one another, but this difference is best accounted for by each text's own uniqueness (its intrinsic genre) rather than by membership in some broadly constructed artificial genre. While genre stipulation can be quite precise, it is incapable of doing justice to the unique character of each text; only recognizing each text as constituting its own intrinsic genre will truly do justice to any text under interpretation.

Literary texts, for example, have not always and in every culture been conceived as aesthetic (or purely aesthetic).[42] There is nothing intrinsic to them that necessarily demands aesthetic interpretation. As we shall see, the way a given culture chooses to interpret (or rather, criticize) a group of texts can affect significance but never meaning. If meaning is dictated in a definite way for one text it is dictated in the same definite way for all texts; because there is no ontological difference among texts requiring different kinds of meaning.[43] All we have are artificial distinctions among textual types that govern the kind of significance a text may have.

It stands, then, that Beardsley cannot speak of the interpretation of literary texts as being fundamentally different from the interpretation of any other kind of text.[44] Beardsley cannot with one broad stroke rule out authorial intention as a criterion in the interpretation of literary texts. All he can do, as we shall see, is espouse a preference for attending to nonauthorial significances of literary texts. Let us turn, then, to Hirsch's intentionalism with its landmark distinction between meaning and significance.

HIRSCH'S INTENTIONALISM

Meaning and Significance

The key element of Hirsch's intentionalist theory is his distinction between meaning and significance. Meaning is that which is represented by the text, what the author meant by a particular sign sequence—it is what the signs represent.[45] Simply put, meaning (as dictated by intention) is what the author wanted to communicate. Significance is meaning as-related-to some context, indeed any context beyond itself.[46] This distinction takes some getting used to; we are not ordinarily this precise in our use of the terms. We often use "meaning" where we would more precisely speak of "significance." We tend to use "significance" to connote grand importance, rather than meaning-as-related-to. Our ordinary use of these terms, however, is quite imprecise and fails to represent a distinction most would accept, the distinction between the actual meaning of the text and that actual meaning as it relates to us and our present context. Texts do not just mystically speak to our present context, but rather embody someone else's effort to communicate—the author's. As Hirsch says, "The brackets implied by the terms 'meaning' and 'significance' do in fact represent something that most of us believe we experience in verbal discourse, namely, an alien meaning, something meant by an implied author or speaker who is not ourselves."[47]

It is not our concern to settle the issue of what meaning itself is, but rather to establish a useful terminology for investigating hermeneutic concerns.[48] The words "meaning" and "significance" can be used in many ways, in addition to the ones Hirsch stipulates. To avoid equivocation and confusion, however, we shall stick with the Hirschian understandings of these words. Indeed, we shall find this very helpful.[49]

We should note that Hirsch altered the definition of "meaning" from its original form in *Validity in Interpretation* (1967) to its later form in *The Aims of Interpretation* (1976). In the earlier work, the only possible meaning was the author's meaning, but in the later work meaning becomes meaning-for-an-interpreter.[50] Hirsch himself does not believe that this change is a major one, but others have found it a substantial and weakening alteration.[51] We must agree that the conception of meaning as presented in the later work weakens Hirsch's position, although in the end he is still able to defend authorial meaning as the correct normative criterion.

Hirsch seems to have bowed to those who would repeatedly point out that we do not ordinarily use "meaning" to refer exclusively to author's meaning. While we cannot realistically hope to change the way "meaning" is ordinarily used, we can continue to insist that "meaning" be used within the context of our discussion to refer only to author's meaning. Any other meaning is, more truly speaking, significance; it is the author's meaning, or some partial understanding thereof, related to another context. To allow a text a meaning other than the author's meaning is really to allow the text to speak for itself. And that is impossible. As Hirsch says, "meaning is an affair of consciousness and not of physical signs or things."[52] That linguistic signs can somehow speak their own meaning is a mystical idea that has never been persuasively defended."[53] This of course is not to deny that meanings, inasmuch as they are dictated by intentions, can be unconscious (or not fully conscious) as well. The unconscious is itself a kind of consciousness, and, as Hirsch has shown, we can intend meanings unconsciously.

Hirsch grounds the distinction between meaning and significance in Husserlian intentionality. The distinction has its origins in Frege's famous article "Über Sinn und Bedeutung," but has its most useful development in terms of textual interpretation in Husserl's *Logische Untersuchungen*.[54] For Husserl, the relation between an act of awareness and its object is called "intention." The general term for all intentional objects, objects as related to acts of awareness, is meaning, and verbal meaning, like any other intentional object, remains the same throughout the many acts which "intend" it. A mental object, such as verbal meaning, remains the same despite our changing awareness. As

Hirsch says, "An object for the mind remains the same even though what is 'going on in the mind' is not the same. The mind's object therefore may not be equated with psychic processes as such; the mental object is self-identical over against a plurality of mental acts."[55]

All of this is clear for objects we are aware of, or "intend," through our vision. Just because I can only see the corner of a building from my position on the street does not mean that only the corner exists, or even that I believe that only the corner exists. Rather, I am aware of or "intend" the whole building.[56] Bracketing is the process by which, Husserl argued, we could eliminate what did not belong to the object of awareness and so "get back to the things themselves." Such phenomenological bracketing is a very useful way of conceiving the project of removing our own perspective in order to get to the thing itself, which for Hirsch is the author's meaning. Our acts of awareness of the author's meaning are subject to change just as our acts of awareness of a building are. After a certain early stage of our cognitive development we are no longer easily fooled by changes in the perspective of our awareness.[57] That is, for example, we "intend" the whole building despite being visually aware of only a corner of it. For Hirsch, then, we must come to approach texts in a similar way. We must learn to "intend" their meanings despite our changing angles of awareness. The meaning, just as the building, remains the same despite our changing intention or awareness of it. As Hirsch says, "Bracketing, then, is a simplified visual metaphor for our ability to demarcate not only a content but also the mental acts by which we attend to that content, apart from the rest of our experience."[58]

Husserl's intentionality, then, gives us some theoretical basis for what seems intuitively correct: the meaning of a text, the intended communication, remains the same while only our acts of awareness of it change. The meaning of a text, what the author wanted to communicate, is a constant given, and the significance of a text is that meaning as viewed through changing awareness. Meaning in this sense is ever the same, while significance is ever in flux. If the distinction between meaning and significance is accepted, then Beardsley was incorrect in asserting that the meaning of a text can change. If we use and understand the terms "meaning" and "significance" with the precision Hirsch's account makes possible, then we will conclude that the meaning of a text cannot change. It is given once and for all by the author. Beardsley can make only the obvious claim that the significance of a text can and does change.

Still, we are left with the question: How do we secure the meaning of a text? Hirsch does not advocate Husserlian bracketing per se, but rather the somewhat related process of validation. For Hirsch, interpretation aims at discovering meaning, as opposed to criticism, which aims at articulating significance. This distinction between interpretation and criticism is one we shall adopt for the purposes of our discussion.[59] Interpretation begins with a genial guess, what Schleiermacher called the "divinatory function." For Hirsch this preliminary guess is always about the genre to which the text belongs. We start with a broad conception of genre, for example, *Paradise Lost* is a poem, and narrow the genre until we have what Hirsch calls an intrinsic genre. We may decide that *Paradise Lost* is a Christian-humanist-epic, but even that is not enough.

Paradise Lost is a Christian-humanist-epic of a special kind. It is unique unto itself, having its own intrinsic genre—as do all texts.[60] Each text in effect has its own unique genre, but, for Hirsch, each text is still subject to the same fundamental norm of interpretation—authorial intention.

For Hirsch, the genre guess is followed by and works hand in hand with the process of validation.[61] Validation is simply the process in which we engage while attempting to confirm our original guess. To be sure, the original guess may often be abandoned in the process of validation, in favor of a more likely guess. Validation is the rough and winding road we take on our journey to meaning. In contrast to most journeys, however, we never know with certainty when we have reached our destination. Hirsch is quite careful in his choice of the word validation to indicate this process. As he says, "to verify is to show that a conclusion is true; to validate is to show that a conclusion is probably true on the basis of what is known."[62]

Interpretation aims at knowledge of the author's meaning, what she intended to communicate. While such knowledge can be achieved, however, it can never be known to be achieved with apodicitic certainty. As Hirsch says, "I can never know another person's intended meaning with certainty because I cannot get inside his head to compare the meaning he intends with the meaning I understand, and only by such direct comparison could I be certain that this meaning and my own are identical."[63] Lack of certainty should not deter us, however. We are faced with a similar situation in the law. To convict a defendant of murder rather than manslaughter, we must determine that the person intended to kill the victim.[64] If the defendant does not confess to his deadly intention, we must determine what that intention was on the basis of the evidence available. We do not achieve certainty, but we can reach a point at which we are comfortable with our decision.[65]

Similarly, there are ways in which we can increase the probability of our knowledge (the strength of our justification), and so achieve valid interpretation. Many interpretive hypotheses are possible on the basis of the immediately available evidence and genre guess. Validation is the process of narrowing the field of competitors until we reach only one. Because we cannot have certainty that knowledge of meaning has been achieved, that we have the truth, the only possible method of choosing between two hypotheses is to prove that one of them is false.[66] As Hirsch makes clear, this strategy bears some resemblance to Popper's conception of falsifiability. In reacting to Kuhn's claim of the incommensurability of frameworks, Popper argued that although a scientific theory could not be proven to be true, it could be proven false.[67] Such is the way we must approach interpretive hypotheses as well.

In judging among competing interpretations, we must weigh the relevant and available evidence and eliminate false interpretations. All evidence is relevant that aids us in deciding what the author could have meant. Historical and biographical information may be particularly helpful in this regard. We can set up some general guidelines for the validating process, but none of these would be infallible. Hirsch provides a preliminary sketch of some such guidelines,[68] but he recognizes, as should we, that these are but useful tools, not necessary and infallible rules. He, in fact, does not devote a substantial amount of space to such guidelines and neither shall we. While such guidelines are interesting and helpful, we need not have them in hand to proceed. In the end, the logic of validation is essentially the logic of common sense.[69]

It can happen that, for a moment, two interpretations appear equally valid on the basis of evidence. Still, unless one interpretation is a mere paraphrase of the other (and often not even then), one must in fact be more valid. Even the impasse of having two apparently equally valid interpretations can be of some value, however. The author meant what he intended to communicate and not something else, and so, if there is any conflict between the two interpretations, one must be more nearly correct. Knowing this, the apparent tie or stalemate in validity will do away with an unhealthy complacence and spur further research.[70] We should also note that a conflict between conscious and unconscious intentions is not problematic. Either the two can be combined into a harmonious whole, or one is the true intention and the other false.[71]

The process of validation is in Hirsch's terms a "survival of the fittest."[72] A validation must show that an interpretation is not just plausible, but the most plausible one available.[73] Even with this rigorous and relentless process of validation, however, we are always subject to being completely wrong.[74] The interpretive process of validation is a matter of epistemic probabilism in which apodicitic certainty is ever elusive.[75]

Author's Meaning and Correct Interpretation

In light of the difficulty of discovering the author's meaning and the impossibility of being certain that we have discovered it, why should we seek the author's meaning in interpretation? Despite the arguments of Knapp and Michaels[76] and Juhl[77] to the contrary, the choice of the author's meaning is a normative choice, a matter of ethics; it is not compelled by, although it has a basis in, logic, metaphysics, or ontology. As Hirsch says, the goals of interpretation are determined ultimately by value preferences.[78] As we shall see, there is a moral value preference in favor of seeking the author's meaning. Hirsch has argued (and I shall defend him against his critics) that the author's attempt to communicate generates an attendant obligation on the part of the interpreter to seek that meaning. To do otherwise is, potentially, to be morally at blame. We could choose a goal other than the author's meaning for interpretation, but we would have to justify it on ethical grounds and be clear to our audience that this is what we are doing. To put it correctly, we could choose to largely ignore meaning in favor of significance. As Hirsch says,

Indeed we need a norm precisely because the nature of a text is to have no meaning except which an interpreter wills into existence. We, not our texts, are the makers of the meanings we understand, a text being only an occasion for meaning, in itself an ambiguous form devoid of the consciousness where meaning abides.[79]

If interpretation is to be a worthwhile pursuit, a foundation for the *Geisteswissenschaften,* and an instrument for communicating knowledge, it must have a stable criterion for arriving at the meaning of a text. As Hirsch says,

"Without the stable determinacy of meaning there can be no knowledge in interpretation, nor any knowledge in the humanistic disciplines based upon textual interpretation."[80] The author, Hirsch correctly argues, provides such a stable criterion for the meaning of a text. It is at least possible that other stable criteria could be posited, but the author's meaning, as we shall see, remains preferable on ethical grounds: "the normative dimension of interpretation is always in the last analysis an ethical dimension."[81]

Jack W. Meiland has argued against Hirsch's position that we should choose the author's meaning as our normative criterion, pointing to what he believes to be a flaw in Hirsch's argumentation. Hirsch, he says, establishes the goal of interpretation as that of being a "cognitive discipline," one that aims at knowledge.[82] But, Meiland argues, we can set up other criteria; we can seek knowledge of things other than author's meaning, and there is no reason that we could not have a plurality of valid interpretations. As Meiland says,

[W]e do not have to aim at author's intention to make validation of interpretation possible. We can allow different interpretations to be equally valid even though they ignore the author's meaning. The author is only one interpreter of his work. He has a basic structure which may well accommodate a number of interpretations, including his own.[83]

And once one gets beyond the need to say each work must have a single meaning that is the "correct" meaning of the work, the work itself can validate interpretations and thus allow interpretation to be a cognitive discipline. . . . It is quite legitimate to think of a criterion as ruling out wrong answers, leaving all of the survivors to be equally correct. . . . The opposite of "cognitivity" is not "many things are valid" it is "everything is valid." . . . It is possible for interpretation to allow a work more than one valid meaning and at the same time remain a cognitive discipline.[84]

Meiland has misunderstood and not appreciated the subtlety of Hirsch's position. The author may be only one interpreter of her work, but it is the author's effort to communicate that gives life to her work. Her meaning is the reason for the text's existence. Although Meiland has not done so, we could theoretically supply another single normative criterion to replace the author's meaning. Yet, it would not stand, for there are ethically compelling reasons to seek only the author's meaning in interpretation. Let us, then, turn to these.

As Hirsch argues, the soul of speech, written or spoken, is communication;[85] we produce texts first and foremost to communicate meaning.[86] We may produce texts for other reasons as well (e.g., for aesthetic expression and appreciation), but these other reasons are subordinate to and dependent upon the communication of meaning. Meaning must come before significance. Meiland makes this very point himself,[87] and we shall make this argument in detail in chapter 5. The author's attempt to communicate meaning generates an attendant obligation on the part of the interpreter to seek that meaning. Hirsch gives his "fundamental ethical maxim for interpretation" as follows: "Unless there is a powerful overriding value in disregarding an author's intention (i.e. original meaning), we who interpret as a vocation should not disregard it. Mere individual preference would not be such an overriding value, nor would the mere preferences of many persons."[88]

In fact, Hirsch only posits the possibility of an "overriding value" as a kind of escape clause.[89] No such overriding value is immediately conceivable, but he allows for the possibility of its existence just to be safe. Hirsch frames the ethics of seeking authorial meaning *à la* Kant, as what we might call an "interpretive imperative": "To treat an author's words merely as grist for one's own mill is ethically analogous to using another man for one's own purposes."[90] The question is: Does the categorical imperative actually apply to an agent's words? Is to use a person's words without regard for his intention truly the same as using a person as a means only?[91] Hirsch argues that it is relevantly the same: "This imperative is transferable to the words of men because speech is an expression and extension of men in the social domain, and also because when we fail to conjoin a man's intentions to his words we lose the soul of speech, which is to convey meaning and to understand what is intended to be conveyed."[92]

Meiland has responded critically to Hirsch's imperative, particularly its Kantian foundation. His first of three arguments against the imperative is as follows: "But if there is no claim by the interpreter to be recreating the author's meaning, I do not see that any ethical precept is violated by giving a work multiple interpretations or, anyway, an interpretation different from author's meaning."[93] The problem is, though, that we expect the interpreter to be recreating the author's meaning unless she disavows such a purpose. This is our natural and ordinary presumption,[94] whether the text is a simple spoken one or a complex written one. It would be fine for an interpreter to give us something other than the author's meaning, but she owes it to us to say that is what she is doing. As an interpreter, then, she is presenting us with some significance of the text; she is actually acting as a *critic* and *not an interpreter*. Of course interpretations often present some combination of meaning and significance (that is, the activity combines both interpretation and criticism). In such cases, significance should be flagged as such to aid the audience in distinguishing it from meaning. In this way, the interpreter may be said to treat the text (and by extension its author) as an end and not a means *only*. In misrepresenting a text by giving an interpretation of it that disregards the author's intent one treats the text (and by extension the author) as a means only. This is not significantly different from lying about what a person said or otherwise misrepresenting that person. In sum, Meiland fails to recognize the interpreter's "duty to warn."

Meiland's second argument against Hirsch's interpretive imperative is that we use other artifacts[95] in ways contrary to those in which they were intended to be, so why can't we do the same with texts? As Meiland says:

[W]hy would it be ethically wrong to use a written or spoken work in a way not intended by the author when it is not ethically wrong to use some other kind of work in a way not intended by the author? Suppose a carpenter makes a chair, intending that it be used as a seat in a private home. If this chair is later purchased by a museum and used as an exhibit of craftsmanship, we would not regard the museum as being in the wrong ethically or morally.[96]

Meiland's example of the chair does not do the work he supposes it does. The intention of the carpenter is not likely to have been as specific as Meiland depicts it, but there are things that may be outside the scope of the carpenter's intention. He would not have made the chair at all, we may suppose, if he knew it would be used as part of a device in a torture chamber. There are also other artifacts similar to a chair that it would be morally wrong to use in a way other than that intended by their "authors." If, for example, I clean the greasy wheels of my car with the bedcover my grandmother made with loving hands, while a perfectly good rag was available, and with my grandmother knowing all of this, we would say I had done something ethically wrong. I would have done some harm to my grandmother by misusing the artifact she had produced. It is even clearer that I do something ethically wrong when I use someone's words for my own purposes without acknowledging that these purposes are not those of the author. In doing so I misrepresent that person. I do that person harm, and I do myself harm through the misrepresentative lie.

Meiland's third argument against Hirsch's imperative is the most interesting in that it implies that Hirsch violates the very norms he has established. Specifically, Meiland argues that Hirsch has misinterpreted and misappropriated Kant, perhaps not properly attending to the philosopher's intention. Meiland's argument is as follows:

I believe that Kant objected to the use of a person as a means on the grounds that this fundamentally restricted that person's freedom; his whole moral philosophy is, in my opinion, based on the ultimate value of freedom. But I do not think that interpreting a work in several different ways restricts the author's freedom. After all, that author has already exercised his freedom in writing his work. And it would be a restriction of the interpreter's freedom if he were not allowed to find other meanings in the work.[97]

Meiland's own interpretation of Kant is quite brief and certainly suspect. While freedom plays an important role in Kant's moral philosophy, it is, I would argue, actually rationality that is its foundation. This, of course, is not the place to settle the debate over the foundation of Kant's moral philosophy. Still, Meiland is too quick in asserting that an author's freedom is not restricted when we interpret his work in ways he did not intend. The author writes in the good faith that his words will be presented by interpreters as he intended them. His intention may be quite broad and future-directed,[98] but it is his intention nonetheless. When an interpreter uses an author's words in ways contrary to the author's intention, he may actually discourage the author from writing. Having been misinterpreted (perhaps damaging his reputation), the author may be reluctant to write more; seeing authors of the past misinterpreted, the would-be writer may never take up his craft. This certainly would be a restriction of freedom. Here we might add further to Hirsch's Kantianism by reminding the interpreter to act always on a maxim he can at the same time will to be universal law. Can the interpreter rationally will that it be universal law that an interpreter can understand and represent a text in a way that directly contradicts the intention of its author? Certainly not. Critics themselves are often quite upset when their own intentions are not properly recognized.

Plato's suspicion of the written word and what interpreter's might do with it may have been his motivation for writing dialogues. In this philosophical genre the author can hide somewhat; it is often quite difficult to tell what Plato himself thought. The Socrates character is not always a reliable guide. While Plato's dialogues are arguably the greatest works philosophy has to offer, it could still be the case that Plato's freedom was restricted in being compelled to write in that genre. Not seeking the author's meaning, then, can be, and often is, a restriction on the freedom of the author and of future authors.

Meiland suggests that the interpreter's freedom is restricted by being bound to the author's intention. Although at first this would seem to be the case, under a Kantian analysis the interpreter's freedom is not truly restricted at all. As we have argued, there is a normative demand, a duty, for the interpreter to seek meaning in accord with authorial intention. For Kant, we are most free in doing our duty, and since we have a duty to seek the author's intention, we are most free in doing so. After having discovered and acknowledged the author's intention, the interpreter has the further freedom and exercise of creativity in finding significance and articulating her criticism.[99]

In closing our discussion of author's meaning and correct interpretation, we should note that the distinction between meaning and significance is now justified. It is most appropriate to call what the author intended to communicate "meaning," and everything else as-related-to that meaning "significance."[100] Whether or not we can have meaning without and prior to significance is a concern of descriptive hermeneutics. Accordingly, we shall address it in our study of Gadamer's descriptive hermeneutics in chapter 4.

The Descriptive Aspect of Hirsch's Theory

Hirsch's defense of the author's meaning as the only acceptable normative criterion for interpretation stands unshaken. His theory as a whole, however, is not without its problems. The first problem it faces is that Hirsch's account is not purely normative, or at least is not presented that way. In *Validity in Interpretation* (1967), Hirsch was for the most part agnostic on the question of what the process of understanding in interpretation is.[101] There were some descriptive hermeneutic elements in this work, such as his analysis of the hermeneutic circle,[102] but his efforts were almost exclusively concentrated on the normative question: How do we gain knowledge of the meaning of a text? Hirsch gives a detailed discussion of the process of validating an interpretation[103] but never conceives of this process as contributing to a descriptive hermeneutics. Validation is a process of tentatively confirming an interpretive hypothesis, not a descriptive account of the process of understanding itself.

In *The Aims of Interpretation* (1976), Hirsch came to regard his earlier work on validation in a different way.

In 1967 I went almost that far when I suggested that we need to put the focus of hermeneutics on the process of validation, since we really do not understand the process of verbal understanding. . . . I have since come to think that such caution is misplaced.

The process of validation is not easily separated from the process of understanding in either theory or practice. . . . [T]he process of understanding is itself a process of validation.[104]

Hirsch's reassessment of validation is unfortunate. It is almost as if he had become greedy. Having spelled out an attractive normative account, he began to claim that the same work functioned as a descriptive account as well. Truly it does not, and certainly to attempt mixing normative and descriptive approaches to hermeneutics will stifle progress and cause confusion. The issues are too complex to handle simultaneously; they should be treated separately and with great attention. Hirsch echoes this very belief himself, ironically in the same book in which he proposed that validation was itself the process of understanding. "I propose that interpretive theories should not lump together the descriptive and normative aspects of interpretation; that theorists should disengage the descriptive dimension of hermeneutics, which concerns the nature of interpretation, from the normative dimension which concerns its goals."[105]

There may be something in the process of validation that could be helpful in describing the process of interpretive understanding itself, but that remains to be seen. As Hirsch has presented it, validation is simply a tool to be used in the normative project of seeking the meaning and correct interpretation of a text. This is how we shall understand it, and we shall leave the descriptive approach for chapter 4 and our examination of Gadamer.

There are two other important problems in Hirsch's account. The first is its lack of a theory of authorship. As we saw in chapter 2, it is important to distinguish between the historical producer of the text (what I have called the author) and the mental construct we form of the historical producer through the course of interpretation (what I have called the urauthor). The second problem is the theory's inconsistent account of meaning. Is meaning truly in the mind? Or is it somehow in the text as well, and thus subject to the rules of natural languages? The next three sections of this chapter will be devoted to these problems. The additions and corrections they require shall give birth to my own intentionalist account, urinterpretation.

As we saw through the course of our survey in chapter 2, there is an important distinction to be made between the historical producer of the text, and the author construct we form of the author in interpreting that text. Hirsch's normative approach conspicuously lacks an account of the author construct, and it was our task in chapter 2, to articulate an intentionalist author construct, the urauthor. As we shall see, Hirsch's normative approach can work only if it is based upon an author construct, one which faithfully reconstructs the author, and the urauthor is particularly well suited to be that basis.

The urauthor could be used simply to supplement Hirsch's position, but, considering Hirsch's problematic account of meaning, we shall see that the urauthor is better utilized to support my own position, urinterpretation. To be certain, urinterpretation is in its essence simply a refinement of Hirsch's intentionalism. Before turning to urinterpretation, however, let us examine Hirsch's account of meaning and formulate our own account.

TEXTS HAVE NO MEANING:[106] A DEFENSE OF HUMPTY DUMPTY

"You're holding it upside down!" Alice interrupted.

"To be sure I was!" Humpty Dumpty said gaily, as she turned it round for him. "I thought it looked a little queer. As I was saying, that *seems* to be done right—though I haven't time to look it over thoroughly just now—and that shows that there are three hundred and sixty-four days when you might get un-birthday presents—"

"Certainly," said Alice.

"And only *one* for birthday presents, you know. There's glory for you!"

"I don't know what you mean by 'glory,'" Alice said.

Humpty Dumpty smiled contemptuously. "Of course you don't—till I tell you. I meant 'there's a nice knock-down argument for you!'"

"But 'glory' doesn't mean 'a nice knock-down argument,'" Alice objected.

"When I use a word," Humpty Dumpty said in rather a scornful tone, "it means just what I choose it to mean—neither more nor less."

"The question is," said Alice, "whether you *can* make words mean different things."

"The question is," said Humpty Dumpty, "which is to be master—that's all."

Alice was too much puzzled to say anything, so after a minute Humpty Dumpty began again. "They've a temper, some of them—particularly verbs, they're the proudest—adjectives you can do anything with, but not verbs—however—I can manage the whole lot! Impenetrability! That's what I say!"

"Would you tell me, please," said Alice, "what that means?"

"Now you talk like a reasonable child," said Humpty Dumpty, looking very much pleased. "I meant by 'impenetrability' that we've had enough of that subject, and it would be just as well if you'd mention what you mean to do next, as I suppose you don't intend to stop here all the rest of your life."

"That's a great deal to make one word mean," Alice said in a thoughtful tone.

"When I make a word do a lot like that," said Humpty Dumpty, "I always pay it extra."[107]

Hirsch on Humpty[108]

Hirsch's response to Humpty Dumpty is inconsistent with his theory as a whole, and so makes the theory unacceptable. Specifically, Hirsch wavers in his account of meaning. On one hand he says that meaning is in the mind.

[M]eaning is an affair of consciousness and not of physical signs or things. . . . What has been denied here is that linguistic signs can somehow speak their own meaning—a mystical idea that has never been persuasively defended.[109]

Indeed we need a norm precisely because the nature of a text is to have no meaning except which an interpreter wills into existence. We, not our texts are the makers of the meanings we understand, a text being only an occasion for meaning, in itself an ambiguous form devoid of the consciousness where meaning abides.[110]

On the other hand, Hirsch says that meaning is partly in the text and so must conform to the conventions of language. "Although verbal meaning requires the determining will of an author or interpreter, it is nevertheless true that the norms of language exert a powerful influence and impose an unavoidable limitation on both the author and interpreter. Alice is right to say that Humpty Dumpty cannot successfully make words mean just anything he wants them to."[111]

If meaning is truly in the mind, then it need not conform to the conventions of language when that meaning is articulated. The meaning is not in the spoken or written word, but in the mind. This follows naturally if, as Hirsch and I have argued, meaning is dictated by authorial intention.[112] The words an author chooses to express the meaning in his mind are at his discretion.[113] We generally follow the conventions of language,[114] however, because this gives us the greatest probability of being understood. The text, a product in language, is only a better or worse indicator of the meaning in the mind of the author.[115] Our audience generally assumes we will be following the conventions of language; this is an ordinary starting point in the construction of an urauthor. It is usually wise, then, though not necessary, to follow those conventions. Using unconventional language, whether purposely or not, does not change the meaning if the meaning is indeed in the mind of the author.

The text itself is of restricted value in interpretation, because an interpreter can seemingly make a text say whatever she wants. As Hirsch argues, "Whenever an interpretation manages to convince another person, that in itself proves beyond doubt that the author's words can publicly imply such meaning."[116] If an interpreter can make words mean whatever she wants, why cannot an author do the same? According to Hirsch, if an interpreter could convince me that when Humpty Dumpty said "glory" he meant "a nice knock-down argument" then "glory" could imply "a nice knock-down argument." There is no reason why an interpreter could not so convince me; stranger uses of words are found in poetry. And there is no reason why an interpreter can show that a text implies anything she wishes, but an author cannot use a text to indicate any meaning he wishes. There's glory for us! Indoctrinably! When I say "Indoctrinably," of course, I mean let's take a look at an example.[117]

Poets sometimes use words in highly unconventional ways. Yet the words mean what the author intended to communicate by them. Sometimes that intended communication is suggestive and aesthetic. Witness the following poem by E.E. Cummings:

r-p-o-p-h-e-s-s-a-g-r
        r-p-o-p-h-e-s-s-a-g-r
    who
a)s w)e loo)k
upnowgath
     PPEGORHRASS
        eringint(o-
aThe):l
   eA
   !p:
S   a
        (r
rIvInG   .gRrEaPsPhOs)
         to
rea (be) rran (com) gi (e) ngly
,grasshopper;[118]

If we can accept Cummings's use of words, why not Humpty Dumpty's? The fact that Cummings is writing in the genre of poetry, and Humpty is simply engaging in ordinary discourse, does not answer the question. These genre distinctions are not hard ontological barriers but soft human creations. Indeed, as Hirsch has suggested, each text has its own intrinsic genre. Each text, though, is to be interpreted in accord with what its author intended to communicate. To say that Humpty Dumpty cannot use language the way he does because he is in the context of ordinary discourse is to miss the crucial point. Humpty's text has its own intrinsic genre, and his use of language is completely appropriate to it. If we had to characterize Humpty's intrinsic genre, we might call it poetic ordinary discourse wrapped in a riddle, but even that characterization would not be completely satisfactory. Whether Humpty Dumpty is likely to be successful in conveying his intended communication is another story, one that likely will not have a happy ending.

Hirsch's Problems with Meaning

This brings us to the issue of the bungled text. Recall that Beardsley argued that a text can mean something other than what the author intended by it because we can have textual meanings that are not verbal meanings, for example, "Jensen argued like a man filled with righteous indigestion." How can Hirsch handle such a text? Does it mean what it appears to on the text's surface—that Jensen is suffering from heartburn or some other ailment? Or does it mean what its author likely meant, i.e., intended to communicate, that he argued like a man filled with righteous indignation? Hirsch claims that there are but two alternatives: either the text represents the author's verbal meaning, or it represents no determinate meaning at all.[119]

There are two problems with Hirsch's explanation. The first is that his own tenet "meaning is an affair of consciousness" makes it irrelevant as to how a particular meaning is presented in textual form. It is simply not the case that a text with an author's meaning behind it may represent "no determinate meaning at all." According to Hirsch's own intentionalism, the text always represents or indicates the author's meaning; it only has greater or lesser or perhaps no success in communicating that meaning. Also, it is inappropriate to speak of "verbal meaning." The term "verbal meaning" implies that words and texts have meaning,[120] which, strictly speaking, if meaning is an affair of consciousness, they do not. Words and the texts they compose are simply convenient and conventional indicators of the meaning that is in the mind.

The second problem is that it is unacceptable to claim that a text can have no meaning at all connected to it. If a text has an author, then it does have a meaning behind it. That is, if an entity is truly a text then it does indicate some meaning. As we have noted, however, that meaning may not be clearly or well indicated by the text itself, the text may not serve as a very good clue to the meaning in the mind of the author. Hirsch claims that some texts represent no meaning at all. Apparently, he makes this claim as a way of dealing with texts that are badly bungled. He does not want to allow them to mean what their authors did not mean in cases where the text does not appear capable of supporting the author's intended communication. Such texts, he concludes, mean nothing at all. Again, however, meaning is in the mind; it does not depend on any particular verbal support. Whenever an author produces a text she produces meaning; it just may be difficult to gain knowledge of that meaning.

Hirsch has no clear way of distinguishing between bungled texts that can support the author's meaning and those that cannot—and so that according to him mean nothing. Since, as I have argued, any text on its own can be used to suggest any meaning by any interpreter, any text can be used by any author to indicate any meaning.[121] Humpty Dumpty can use "glory" to indicate whatever meaning he wants, but, of course, he runs the substantial risk of being misunderstood—that is his risk to take. We have little difficulty in accepting that words may be used in any number of unconventional ways in poetry, and, as I have argued, there is no hard ontological difference between a poem and any other kind of text. The rules of interpretation and the rules of language-use are not governed by genre distinctions; there is nothing in the nature of a poem that grants it permission to use language in unconventional ways, and nothing in the nature of ordinary discourse that prohibits the use of language in unconventional ways. We have simply become accustomed to seeing words used in unconventional ways in poetry, but that does not mean we cannot use them in unconventional ways in ordinary speech as Humpty Dumpty does. Hirsch's account of meaning is inconsistent and thus unsatisfactory. Let us, then, turn to an examination of what meaning is as-related-to-texts in preparation for the normative approach of urinterpretation.

Meaning as-Related-to-Texts

Meaning is what is understood when one is said to understand a text.[122] This is a definition few would find controversial. The controversial question behind it, however, is: When do we understand a text? When do we have meaning? Hirsch was on the right track in arguing that meaning is in the mind, it is what is intended by the author. His concessions to the determining power of language are unfortunate, however. I suspect that behind these concessions is Hirsch's belief that we have a duty to write in a clear and intelligible manner: "if the author has bungled his text so badly that his utterance will be misconstrued, then it serves him right when people misunderstand him."[123] We shall take up this issue shortly. For now, however, let us see where Hirsch went wrong.

The basis of Hirsch's mistake is giving determining power over meaning to the text itself, after he had actually shown that the text itself could not determine meaning. To be clear, the author remains the creator of meaning for Hirsch, but the author must respect the norms of language to some unspecified extent. The extent remains unspecified, I suspect, because Hirsch is well aware that we may often do violence to the norms of language and still succeed in communicating our meaning. If Hirsch were pushed further on this issue, he would likely say that we need to judge on a case-by-case basis. Sometimes even a slight deviation from the norms of language, or a slight but crucial error, will cause the author's communication to fail, and so leave us with no meaning at all. Take for example the case of leaving out a "not," through typographical error, in an otherwise clearly articulated argument. Sometimes the norms of language can be almost completely ignored without having the same effect. In ironic and sarcastic statements the meaning is the exact opposite of what the norms of language would seem to support. For example, "The winters in Buffalo are lovely."

All we are ever doing, however, in following the conventions of language is increasing the probability that our meaning will be communicated successfully. It is up to us, as writers, how concerned we are with accurate communication. We may choose, for example, tò produce a text quickly and with little care, thus risking miscommunication. We may also choose unconventional uses of language for stylistic or aesthetic purposes, as poets often do. In the end, then, meaning is the author's own. The text serves only to indicate it, and it is up to us, as authors, how concerned we are with communicating in a way likely to be correctly received. In some cases, there may be a duty to the audience. For example, I may be said to have a duty to my class to present my lectures in a reasonably clear fashion. Such cases are governed by the norms of duty in general; there may be a specific duty to write or speak clearly, but this must be argued for and not assumed.[124]

Knapp and Michaels have captured this point in their essay, "Against Theory 2: Hermeneutics and Deconstruction":

[F]ollowing conventions is only one way of doing what is essential, namely, giving clues to your intention. Conventions are indeed important but only because they often provide convenient ways of signaling what you intend. They don't add to, subtract from, or alter your meaning; they simply help you express the meaning you intend.[125]

We conclude, then, that texts apart from the meaning an author indicates by them mean nothing; there is no such thing as verbal meaning, only authorial meaning—which is the meaning the author intended. (We shall take up the question—Can there be intended texts?—in the next section of this chapter.) Texts are simply convenient indicators of meaning but truly speaking cannot possess meaning themselves. Further, we can choose with Humpty Dumpty to use whatever texts we wish to indicate our meaning. As Grice has said, though, we must intend an audience to recognize the intention behind our utterance.[126] Still, Grice's emphasis on audience recognition is overstated; we need not expect that all our audience will detect our intention, or that any will immediately, but only that it is in principle possible. I can intend whatever I believe it is in principle possible for my audience to understand, and there is no necessary limit on that belief though, of course, I can be mistaken in that belief.[127] The only possible limit is that I cannot intend at will any more than I can believe at will, but although that may limit a given individual, it does not in principle limit what *can* be intended.[128] A person can intend to take vitamin C to ward off a cold, and, depending on his state of mind, can even flap his arms intending to fly.[129] In the same way, Humpty Dumpty can say "glory" intending it to mean "a nice knock down argument." On the other hand, Alice, for example, could not intend glory to have the same meaning if she did not believe it was in principle possible for her audience to understand it in that way.[130]

We have, then, reduced the role of language to that of an indicator. Heidegger and Gadamer would certainly take issue with this, and we shall turn to their views in the next chapter.

URINTERPRETATION

We come now to our brief exposition of urinterpretation. This normative theory is actually just a development and refinement of Hirsch's intentionalism. Indeed, it owes much to the tradition of author-based interpretation beginning with Schleiermacher. The starting point of the theory is Hirsch's distinction between meaning and significance, as he presented that theory in *Validity in Interpretation*. I have already argued for the soundness of this distinction, and so there is no need to rehearse the relevant arguments and definitions again here.

Suffice it to say that by "meaning" we are to understand the author's intended communication, regardless of what the text may seem to say in accord with the conventions of language. By "significance" we are to understand meaning-as-related-to anything other than the text itself. Significance is the product of non-urinterpretation (i.e., criticism), which under certain circumstances may be an acceptable and quite desirable product. We shall take up the case of non-urinterpretation in chapter 5. As we shall see, urinterpretation must serve as the basis of even non-urinterpretation, and so urinterpretation is our primary normative concern.

Also essential to urinterpretation is the tenet that there is only one meaning to be sought in interpretation, that of the author—or more correctly the urauthor. (We shall discuss the urauthor shortly.) As we saw in the previous section, texts simply indicate the meaning of the author; they act as clues to that meaning. To be certain, however, without these clues we would be utterly lost. The text itself is not to be ignored, but rather is to be subjected to detailed scrutiny. The text is ordinarily the most important clue we have as to the meaning of the author, but it is not the only clue; all other elements of the urauthor can also be quite important. Recall that the urauthor is composed of relevant available biographical information, likely intentions, use of language in the text itself, information concerning the author's context and audience, and other texts of the same author inasmuch as they inform the other elements of the urauthor.

The central question for any normative theory of interpretation is: How do we gain knowledge of the meaning of a text? Urinterpretation owes much to Hirsch's intentionalism in answering this question but differs from Hirsch's theory in its use of the urauthor (as well as its account of meaning). Recall that in chapter 2 we arrived at an account of the author construct called the urauthor. That term suggests that we go back to the origins in forming this figure, that we regain as far as possible the original intention of the author. The urauthor is not the historical producer of the text, but a mental construct resembling the historical producer as closely as possible in all relevant ways. The questions we ask in forming the urauthor include: What biographical information is relevant and important? Who was the author and how did he think? What likely were his intentions in composing the text? How did he use language? What was his historical context? Who was his audience?

The urauthor is our vehicle for gaining access to the meaning, the intended communication, of the author himself. And it is this meaning we are ultimately seeking in urinterpretation. There is, however, no certainty that our urauthor is an accurate construction and no certainty that we have discovered the author's meaning through this construction. Still, we can in principle gain knowledge of the author's meaning through the urauthor even if we cannot be certain that we have. This insight and the process of validation on which it is based we take from Hirsch. The urauthor in any given case is itself open to revision, and so is the urinterpretation based on it. We are seeking the most probable and most plausible interpretation we can conceive on the basis of what we know, that is, on the basis of the urauthor we have formed. Even an urinterpretation that appears highly valid, is always subject to being completely wrong. We are always open to new evidence, and so the process of validation becomes, as Hirsch calls it, a "survival of the fittest."[131]

How much effort we put into constructing the urauthor is a function of how much evidence we have, how clear the text as indicator seems to be, and how concerned we are that our interpretation be faithful. We may, for example, put little to no effort into the construction of the urauthor of a newspaper article and a great deal of effort into the construction of the urauthor of a literary or philosophical text. Of course, we may do just the opposite as well; there may be a great deal of information available about the author of a newspaper article, and it may significantly inform our interpretation of the text. For example, after having read Pete Hamill's autobiography, *A Drinking Life*,[132] I have brought a highly developed urauthor to my interpretation of his newspaper articles. We may in fact form the urauthor of a text through interpreting other texts by the same author. The urauthor we form, then, is a coherent picture of what we have read and interpreted. An urauthor formed in this way, just as in any other way, is always subject to being inaccurate and so should always be kept open to revision.

Urinterpretation, then, involves a rigorous process of validation, assuming we are sufficiently concerned with achieving the correct interpretation. The correct interpretation is, of course, the one that reproduces the meaning of the text, i.e., the author's intended communication. Can there, however, be definitive interpretations?[133] The answer is yes, at least in a limited sense. Any interpretation that exactly and completely captures the author's intended communication would be a definitive interpretation. One problem, as we have noted, is that we are never certain that this has occurred. Another problem is that an interpretation is itself usually manifested in a text, a text that may have practical limitations to its understanding. The rules of the natural language the interpretation is presented in are likely to change over time, and what needs to be said to convey the author's meaning will vary with the audience. The elliptical aspects of the interpretation may be easily accessible to one audience but not to another.

We should conclude, then, that an interpretation can be definitive for a given audience. More importantly, however, the meaning indicated by the text of the interpretation can certainly be definitive; it can be an exact match for the author's meaning—though, as we have noted, we can never be certain of when this occurs.

The author's meaning is what she intended to communicate by her text. This raises a problem, however, because it is not clear that authors always or ever have intended texts in mind. Gracia has argued that there is in fact no such thing as an intended text.

The author may have some general intentions and some vague ideas he or she wants to convey, but those can hardly be regarded as a completely determined meaning, for those intentions and meanings could produce very different texts and, moreover, could change in the process of textual production.[134]

[O]ne may also argue that there is no such thing as the intended text for the simple reason that authors never have a clear and complete idea of the texts they intend to produce prior to the moment in which they actually produce them by writing, speaking, or thinking. . . . [T]here is never such a thing as an intended text. And this is so in turn because a text is always a result of a process of production and also does not precede such a process in any way.[135]

Gracia has made an important point, but he has also overstated his case. It is correct to say that we do not always have an intended text in the sense of one fully present to the mind before the text's actual composition. There probably is no full and complete intended text prior to the composition of any text of much length or complexity. It is difficult to imagine that Tolstoy had an intended text in any detailed sense before the actual composition of *War and Peace*, for example.

Still, it is practically possible to have an intended text for a relatively short and simple text, and theoretically possible for even a long and complex text. Take the following example: A student nervously rehearses the answer "Albany is the capital of New York," only to say, "Atlanta is the capital of New York," when her teacher calls on her. It seems that in this case we do have an intended text that is imperfectly produced; the actual text differs in a crucial way.

Gracia would likely respond that in this case we do not truly have an intended text but an actual mental text.[136] The student developed an actual mental text, "Albany is the capital of New York," and produced a different actual spoken text, "Atlanta is the capital of New York." In some sense this analysis would be correct; both texts are actual. The mental text, however, is also intended. It was intended to be produced in speech, although this intention was not realized. There is no reason a text cannot be actual in one medium, for example, the mental, and intended for another medium, for example, the spoken.[137] To be clear, however, the mental text and the spoken text are two different texts, differentiated by the media in which they are composed. What is intended, is that the mental text be duplicated as far as that is possible in the spoken word.

It is at least possible that an author could produce a written text through a series of short intended mental texts, some of these accurately reproduced in writing and some not. It is also possible that an author could have a very long and complicated mental text intended for writing. That the *Iliad*, among other works of antiquity, was carried on by oral tradition bears witness to the ability of the human mind to store long and complex texts. Neither of these possibilities does much for establishing that there need always be an intended text, however. And indeed there need not always be; it is only a possibility.

What we are concerned with in urinterpretation, however, is not intended texts but intended communications—meanings. Texts act as indicators of meanings, and so we are concerned only with what the author intended by the text. As with intended texts, intended communications may precede their texts, develop in part along with their texts, or develop somewhat contemporaneously with their texts. The author may have a meaning firmly in mind before producing the first word of the text; she may have a meaning firmly in mind before producing each part of the text; or she may develop the meaning as she is producing the text. As Stein Haugom Olsen says of texts, "Every particular element is conceived in intentional terms, i.e. under the perspective of serving an end."[138] And, as even W.K. Wimsatt admits, "it [art work] is in a sense (and this is especially true of the verbal work of art) made of intentions or intentionalistic material."[139] And, "whatever does get into a poem is presumably put there by the poet."[140] Intentions need not be well formed in advance, but they are the very "stuff" of which the text is made; they are indeed what the author "puts" in the text—that which gives the text meaning.

It can often be in the process of producing the text itself that the author's intended communication becomes most clear to him. Even then, however, the meaning itself is still prior to the text. It is only that the author's conscious awareness of his meaning comes to light in the text's production. Indeed even this may not happen. It is possible, and in fact common, for an author to produce a text, have a meaning in mind, and not be consciously aware of that meaning. Some meanings, i.e., intended communications, as Hirsch has shown, are unconscious. Some of these can be brought to the author's awareness by the interpreters of his text, and some meanings may resist being brought to awareness in this way. In the end, though, the author did have a meaning, his text serves to indicate that meaning, and it is the task of the urinterpreter to find and articulate that meaning.

CONCLUSION

Urinterpretation, then, is a workable and hopefully attractive normative approach to hermeneutics. It keeps the author's intended communication at the center of concern and provides an appropriate interpretive mechanism. Of course, just as no process of validation should be permanently brought to an end, so should no search for an interpretive theory be brought to an end. Urinterpretation is, rather, a beginning, just as every theory should be. It is a development and refinement of Hirsch in the author-based tradition initiated by Schleiermacher.

Non-urinterpretation, or criticism, that activity that aims at significance, must have its place as well. A world of only urinterpretation would be a dull and sterile one indeed. We shall take up the place of non-urinterpretation and its relation to urinterpretation in chapter 5.

Having at least temporarily settled the normative debate to our satisfaction, we turn now to the descriptive debate and its central question: What is the nature of interpretive understanding? To engage this question we shall examine Gadamer's *magnum opus Truth and Method* (*Wahrheit und Methode*). This work represents the most complete philosophical effort, thus far, to articulate a descriptive approach to hermeneutics, and so it is to it that we shall devote our attention.

NOTES

1. To be clear, the question does necessitate and include some matters of description, but it is separable from an approach that is concerned primarily with describing the process of interpretive understanding.
2. For both Hirsch and myself, when I speak of "intention" I am using an elliptical expression for "intended to *communicate* by texts."
3. W.K. Wimsatt and Monroe C. Beardsley, "The Intentional Fallacy," in *The Verbal Icon: Studies in the Meaning of Poetry* (Lexington: University of Kentucky Press, 1954), pp. 3–18.
4. Monroe C. Beardsley, "The Authority of the Text," in *The Possibility of Criticism* (Detroit: Wayne State University Press, 1970), pp. 16–37.
5. "The Intentional Fallacy," p. 5. This passage speaks of "the poem," but this is actually not problematic for our analysis. The issue of Beardsley and nonliterary texts will be addressed shortly.
6. Beardsley is not careful in his use of the words "work" and "text," but there is an important distinction to be made between the two words. See Alexander Nehamas, "Writer, Text, Work, Author," in Anthony J. Cascardi ed., *Literature and the Question of Philosophy* (Baltimore: Johns Hopkins University Press, 1987), pp. 267–291. For an improved distinction between "work" and "text" see Jorge J.E. Gracia *A Theory of Textuality: The Logic and Epistemology* (Albany: SUNY Press, 1995), pp. 59–70 (hereafter *ATT*).
7. "The Authority of the Text," p.16.
8. Presumably the only other viable criterion in Beardsley's view.
9. "The Authority of the Text," pp. 18–19.
10. Ibid., p. 19.
11. Ibid., p. 20.
12. Ibid., pp. 32 and 35–36, and "The Intentional Fallacy," p. 5. As we shall see, there is no way to discriminate neatly between texts as literary and nonliterary for the purposes of interpretation.
13. *ATT*, pp. 89–96.
14. "The Authority of the Text," p. 34.
15. For some discussion of what aesthetic experience is and how one judges a better or worse aesthetic experience, see Monroe C. Beardsley, "Aesthetic Experience Regained," *Journal of Aesthetics and Art Criticism* 28 (1969), pp. 3–11.
16. "The Authority of the Text," p. 37.
17. P.D. Juhl, *Interpretation: An Essay in the Philosophy of Literary Criticism* (Princeton, NJ: Princeton University Press, 1980), pp. 133–134.
18. E.D. Hirsch, Jr., *Validity in Interpretation* (New Haven: Yale University Press, 1967), p. 21 ff. (hereafter *VI*); *ATT*, p. 24; D.W. Hamlyn, "Unconscious Intentions," *Philosophy* 46 (1971), pp. 12–22; F. Cioffi, "Intention and Interpretation in Criticism," *Proceedings of the Aristotelian Society* 64 (1964), pp. 97–98; C. Olsen, "Knowledge of One's Own Intentional Actions," *The Philosophical Quarterly* 19 (1969).

19. Cf. *VI*, pp. 51–52. Recall that Hirsch grounds his argument for unconscious meaning in Husserlian intentionality. Meaning, for Hirsch, is an intentional object. "But an object-for-the-mind is never completely present to the mind. Husserl used the visual metaphor of horizon to indicate that beyond an object's aspects which we are attending to lie numberless further aspects of the same object which we are not attending to. In the case of verbal meanings, certain of these 'unseen' aspects may never have been attended to by anybody, including the author." "Meaning and Significance Reinterpreted," *Critical Inquiry* 11 (1984), p. 203.

20. From here on I shall use the designation "unconscious" for all degrees of unconscious meaning/intention, including those of which the author is just not fully conscious.

21. Cf. *VI*, p. 121. Here Hirsch gives an excellent example of how an author may intend to stress the similarity of two points by using parallel sentence structure, and yet be unaware of this.

22. Cf. Juhl, pp. 57 and 141. Juhl believes, as do I, that in cases in which we choose to ignore the author's testimony as to his intentions we do so because we believe we have better clues at our disposal as to those intentions than his present testimony.

23. For a similar example cf. Juhl, p. 102.

24. *VI*, p. 23.

25. For a similar view regarding an idealized conventional author see Daniel O. Nathan, "Irony, Metaphor, and the Problem of Intention," in Gary Iseminger ed., *Intention and Interpretation* (Philadelphia: Temple University Press, 1992), p. 199. On convention see, David Lewis, *Convention: A Philosophical Study* (Cambridge, MA: Harvard University Press, 1969).

26. Or, put another way, verbal meaning.

27. Along with the many other things that make textual meaning indeterminate without reference to the author, irony is always a possibility. Irony can only be conclusively ruled in or out by reference to the author or some element of the urauthor.

28. Cf. Nathan, p. 191. Nathan notes that letters to student newspapers are frequently interpreted by competent readers as serious pieces despite what we later discover to be the ironic intentions of the author. Further, I should note that any stylistic analysis that points to irony points to an author's intention as ironic and is based on context or some other part of the urauthor. That is to say, the author is inescapable in this case.

29. Steven Knapp and Walter Benn Michaels, "Against Theory 2: Hermeneutics and Deconstruction," *Critical Inquiry* 14 (1987), p. 57. I note that in some circles, "Let's do lunch," can mean "I don't care to see you again any time soon."

30. Ibid.

31. I take the excess that can be characteristic of intentionalism to be overindulgence in biography—biographicalism, one might call it. This type of excessive intentionalism is manifested in Lowes's *The Road to Xanadu*, as discussed by Wimsatt and Beardsley in "The Intentional Fallacy" and as referred to in chapters 1 and 2. Neither Hirsch nor Juhl can rightfully be faulted for this type of excess, though it has not stopped their detractors from trying. For a look at an earlier debate, focused more on the place of biographical information see, E.M.W. Tillyard and C.S. Lewis, *The Personal Heresy: A Controversy* (London: Oxford University Press, 1939).

32. For further discussion of the connection between interpreting ordinary discourse and literature see Noël Carroll, "Art, Intention, and Conversation," in Gary Iseminger ed., *Intention and Interpretation* (Philadelphia: Temple University Press, 1992), pp. 203–220.

33. My argument will ultimately be an intentionalist one, that all texts must be interpreted in accord with authorial intention. Such intention is not always or necessarily narrow and restricting, however. Some texts have intentions behind them that are broad,

future-directed, and somewhat open-ended. As we shall see, this is the case with many literary, legal, and scriptural texts.

34. It is the institution and the cultural demand placed on the interpretation of texts that so often leads to them being interpreted differently along genre lines. It is, however, nothing in the nature of the language of texts themselves that demands such interpretive splits along genre lines. Cf. Walter Benn Michaels, "Against Formalism: Chickens and Rocks," in Sanford Levinson and Steven Mailoux eds., *Interpreting Law and Literature: A Hermeneutic Reader* (Evanston, IL: Northwestern University Press, 1988), p. 224. "[W]hile there are indeed differences between poems and contracts they are institutional not formal differences. . . . Judges cannot decide that contracts are ambiguous in the same way and for the same reasons that literary critics can. But this is not because legal *language* is less tolerant of ambiguity than poetic language is; it is because the institution of the law is less tolerant of ambiguity than the institution of literary criticism is. Judges don't read the same way literary critics do."

35. *VI*, p. viii.

36. Ibid., p. 120.

37. Ibid., pp. 120–121.

38. See Ludwig Wittgenstein, *Philosophical Investigations* (New York: Macmillan Publishing Company, 1968) Third Edition trans. G.E.M. Anscombe, 66 ff. For a very useful discussion with which I am in agreement see Michael A. Simon, "When Is a Resemblance a Family Resemblance?" *Mind* 78 (1969), pp. 408–416.

39. Both sides of the argument are in danger of committing the fallacy of argument from ignorance. No essence has been discovered. Are we then to assume that one exists, or that one does not exist? In either case we must grant the possibility that the other side is correct; no definite conclusion can be drawn. Rather, it is a matter of probability. Is there a Loch Ness monster? None has been captured or reliably photographed despite persistent efforts. It seems to me that the probability that there is a Loch Ness monster is very slim, and so the burden of proof should rest with those who would claim that there is such a creature. In a similar way, the essences of literary texts and other genres have been sought with persistent efforts yielding no promising results, and so the likelihood of their existence seems quite minimal. I am willing to wager that the search for any textual genre is the search for a chimera. Even if such an essence were to be definitively articulated, it still would not necessarily imply that all texts of a certain genre must be interpreted in the same way.

40. I cannot and need not defend this conjecture within the limits of this discussion. See note 38 above.

41. As I noted above, I shall argue that this bedrock principle is authorial intention and that authorial intention is subject to idiosyncrasies, some of which are common among different textual types.

42. Cf. A.J. Close, "*Don Quixote* and the 'Intentionalist Fallacy,'" *British Journal of Aesthetics* 12 (1971), p 21. Close also argues well against the supposed distinction in the production of writing, and so ontological status, between poetry and prose. Cf. pp. 26–27.

43. Cf. Carroll.

44. As we shall see, the differences are only typical differences and ultimately depend on the nature of the authorial intention involved.

45. *VI*, p. 8.

46. E.D. Hirsch, Jr., *The Aims of Interpretation* (Chicago: University of Chicago Press, 1976), p. 8 (hereafter *Aims*).

47. Ibid., p. 6.

48. For a contrary view see Jeffrey Stout, "What Is the Meaning of a Text?" *New Literary History* 14 (1982), pp. 1–14. Stout argues that what deserves the label

"meaning" is largely a verbal disagreement, and in fact we would be better off not speaking about meanings at all.

49. We should note that, although some description is involved in the meaning/significance distinction (as was the case with our account of the author), this distinction does not involve descriptive hermeneutics. Recall that we have defined descriptive hermeneutics as the approach that is concerned with describing interpretive understanding. The distinction between meaning and significance may possibly inform a descriptive approach, but, as Hirsch articulates it, it is meant to aid in the development of a normative approach. It is meant to facilitate correct interpretation.

50. *Aims*, pp. 79–80.

51. Ibid., p. 7. See William Cain, "Authority, 'Cognitive Atheism', and the Aims of Interpretation: The Literary Theory of E.D. Hirsch," *College English* 39 (1977), p. 334 ff.

52. *VI*, p. 23.

53. Ibid.

54. For an excellent translation of Frege's article see, "On Sense and Reference," in P. Geach and M. Black eds. and trans., *Translations from the Philosophical Writings of Gottlob Frege* (Oxford: Basil Blackwell, 1952), pp. 56–78. For Husserl, see especially *Logische Untersuchungen* (Tübingen: Max Niemeyer Verlag, 1968), pp. 91–97. Cf. Dieter Munch, *Intention und Zeichen: Untersuchungen zu Franz Brentano und zu Edmund Husserls Frühwerk* (Frankfurt: am Main, 1993). For the distinction between meaning and significance see also Emilio Betti, *Die Hermeneutik als allgemeine Methodik der Geisteswissenschaften* (Tübingen: J.C.B. Mohr, 1962), pp. 27–28.

55. *VI*, p. 218.

56. *Aims*, pp. 47–48.

57. For example, we know an object continues to exist even when something blocks it from our vision.

58. *Aims*, pp. 4–5.

59. Boeckh made a very similar distinction in his *Enzyklopädie* between *Hermeneutik* and *Kritik*.

60. *VI*, p. 84.

61. This process bears some resemblance to Schleiermacher's critical function that follows his divinatory function.

62. *VI*, p. 171.

63. Ibid., p. 17.

64. This is the case except in cases in which felony murder is applicable. British law has abandoned the felony murder rule and so involved itself in some difficult cases regarding the intention of the accused. See my "Intention and Foresight in the British Law of Murder," *Sorites* 9 (1998), pp. 6–15.

65. That is, we are beyond a reasonable doubt.

66. *VI*, p. 180.

67. Karl Popper, *The Logic of Scientific Discovery* (New York: Basic Books, 1959), pp. 78–92.

68. *VI*, p. 179 ff.

69. Cf. Ibid., p.169 and p.198.

70. Ibid., p. 173.

71. Possibly the conscious intention is only a mask, hiding the true unconscious (or not fully conscious) intention.

72. *VI*, p. 169.

73. Ibid., p. 171.

74. Ibid., p. 235.

75. For an alternative to Hirsch's and my view on competing interpretations see Robert Stecker, "Incompatible Interpretations," *The Journal of Aesthetics and Art Criticism* 50 (1992), pp. 291-298.

76. Cf. Steven Knapp and Walter Benn Michaels "Against Theory," *Critical Inquiry* 8 (1982), pp. 723–742. Here they argue, "Intention cannot be added to or subtracted from meaning because meanings are always intentional; intention cannot be added to or subtracted from language because language consists of speech acts, which are also always intentional" (p. 736). Their crucial point seems to be, "what a text means and what its author intends it to mean are identical and . . . their identity robs intention of any theoretical interest" (p. 731). Knapp and Michaels see themselves as radicalizing the intentionalism of Hirsch and taking him to task for not recognizing the full thrust of intentionalism. Hirsch, however, has responded by pointing out that Knapp and Michaels have made a straw man of him, and that their claim that intention does not have any theoretical interest simply does not follow from their premise that a text necessarily means what its author intends it to mean. Cf. E.D. Hirsch, Jr., "Against Theory?" *Critical Inquiry* 9 (1983), pp. 743–747. On the subject of the straw man Hirsch says, "I am not now nor have I ever been a proponent of 'a moment of interpretation before intention is present'" (p. 744). After discussing several examples, Hirsch renews his claim for the value of intention and historical scholarship, concluding, "We do not always understand by a text what we believe an author meant in composing it. The empirical claim of Knapp and Michaels seems to me to be false" (p. 746). Knapp and Michaels at times do not exemplify the best reasoning or proper argumentation for the positions they wish to defend. Another example of this is when they claim that knowledge is true belief (Cf. p. 738). The crucial point they miss is that although meaning may, in some sense, always be the author's intended meaning, we are not guaranteed to get that meaning correct, nor does everyone always seek that meaning, in the process of interpretation. That is precisely why theory is still necessary. That is why Hirsch advocates historical scholarship and why I shall advocate use of the urauthor. Knowledge requires true belief, but also requires justification (the nature of which is a matter of some dispute). We can arrive at true belief without justification, but this is not very likely, and certainly it is not guaranteed. In a similar way, the meaning of a text may be its author's intended meaning but that alone does not guarantee that we will uncover the author's intended meaning. We may arrive at that meaning without much effort, but in many cases that is not likely. We need some method or process by which to reach it.

77. Cf. P.D. Juhl, *Interpretation: An Essay in the Philosophy of Literary Criticism* (Princeton, NJ: Princeton University Press, 1980). Juhl argues that in appealing to the various criteria other than authorial intention we are in fact appealing to the authorial intention. Juhl's argument bears some resemblance to that later offered by Knapp and Michaels but it is much more coherent and logically sound. Juhl argues that appealing to various criteria logically implies appealing to authorial intention, for we always recognize a text as having been produced by an author with definite intentions. For Juhl's argument regarding various features of the text itself including its complexity, internal evidence, and external evidence cf. pp. 66–89. For his argument regarding context and rules of language, cf. pp. 90–113. For his argument regarding aesthetic appeals, cf. pp. 114–128. In the end, Juhl has the same problem as Knapp and Michaels. He has shown that an appeal to authorial intention is, to some extent, inescapable. He has not shown that an *accurate* recovery of authorial intent is *necessary*, for it is not on logical grounds. If we are to be compelled to recover authorial intent it must be on ethical grounds. This is Hirsch's position and it is mine as well. Juhl argued that Hirsch simply begs the question in asserting his distinction between meaning and significance (pp. 31–32). As we shall see, although this distinction is at first stipulative, it becomes

justified when the seeking of authorial intention is defended as *the* ethical normative choice.

78. *Aims*, p. 75.
79. Ibid., p. 76.
80. Ibid., p. 1.
81. Ibid., p. 77.
82. Jack W. Meiland, "Interpretation as a Cognitive Discipline," *Philosophy and Literature* 2 (1978), p. 25. I would add that given this description it would better be called an epistemological discipline than a cognitive discipline.
83. Ibid., p. 30.
84. Ibid., p. 31.
85. Cf. *Aims*, p. 90.
86. This goes for literary texts as well. See Göran Hermerén, "Intention and Interpretation in Literary Criticism," *New Literary History* 7 (1975), pp. 75–77.
87. Meiland, p. 23.
88. *Aims*, p. 90.
89. Ibid., p. 90.
90. Ibid., p. 91.
91. Is this not, in some sense, a form of lying or misrepresentation?
92. *Aims*, p. 90.
93. Meiland, p. 44.
94. Juhl would say it is a logical necessity.
95. On texts as artifacts cf. *ATT*, pp. 44–52.
96. Meiland, p. 44.
97. Ibid.
98. We shall see this in particular in chapter 5 with reference to literary and legal texts.
99. More on this in chapter 5.
100. Against Stout, I would argue that this is more than a verbal disagreement.
101. "[W]e really do not understand the process of verbal understanding," as he said (at *Aims*, p. 33) of his earlier work in *Validity in Interpretation*.
102. *VI*, p. 176 ff.
103. Ibid., pp. 164–207.
104. *Aims*, p. 33.
105. Ibid., p. 75.
106. Cf. Ibid., p. 76. "[I]t is the nature of texts to have no meaning"
107. Lewis Carroll, *Through the Looking Glass* in Martin Gardner ed., *The Annotated Alice* (New York: Clarkson N. Potter, Inc., 1960), ch.6, pp. 268–270. Cf. Hirsch (1976), pp. 51-52.
108. To be clear, what we are considering here is whether the speech of Humpty Dumpty is acceptable. We are not considering Lewis Carroll's view on the subject. Carroll's view, however, was much akin to Humpty Dumpty's. See Lewis Carroll, *Symbolic Logic and The Game of Logic* (New York: Dover Publications, 1958). "I maintain that any writer of a book is fully authorized in attaching any meaning he likes to any word or phrase he intends to use" (p. 166). Cf. *The Annotated Alice*, p. 268 n. 6. It is also clear that Carroll is poking fun at the type of "egghead" Humpty Dumpty represents and also his condition of "pride before the fall." For a view to which I am sympathetic, see Keith Donnellan, "Putting Humpty Dumpty Together Again," *Philosophical Review* 77 (1968), pp. 203–215.
109. *VI*, p. 23.
110. *Aims*, p. 76.
111. *VI*, p. 27.

112. The text itself may act as an excellent clue to the intention, but nonetheless the intention is in the mind not in the text.

113. See Jonathan Bennett, "The Meaning-Nominalist Strategy," *Foundations of Language* 10 (1976), pp. 141–168.

114. Again, on convention see Lewis.

115. We could call such indication meaning, but to do so would be to equivocate on the word "meaning" and thus introduce or perpetuate confusion. "Meaning" in the sense Hirsch uses it has been justified by our analysis of authorial intention as *the* normative criterion. For another view, see Stout.

116. *VI*, p. 15.

117. My defense of Humpty Dumpty and my use of language here are not subject Wittgensteinian objections regarding private language. I am not arguing that a private language is possible. Rather, I am simply suggesting that it is possible to use language to indicate one's intentions in novel and unusual ways. Juhl does not go as far as I do along these lines, but I think he would agree that I am not positing a private language. It is in fact very difficult to commit oneself to such a thing! "I may have an idiolect in which 'bububu' can be used to mean 'If it doesn't rain I shall go for a walk.' I may even have a private language in the sense that as a matter of fact only I understand it, although others can with a little effort come to understand it as well. What perhaps I cannot have, and what Wittgenstein wanted to show to be impossible, is a private language in the sense that only I *could* understand it" (p. 145).

118. E.E. Cummings, "r-p-o-h-e-s-s-a-g-r," in *The Norton Anthology of Poetry* 3rd edition (New York: W.W. Norton & Company, 1983), p. 1044.

119. *VI*, p. 234.

120. They do not have a meaning apart from, or independent of, what the author intended. They may of course have a conventional use, but this is not meaning in the sense we have defined it. Obviously I do not subscribe to the school of thought that meaning is use.

121. Cf. Bennett's meaning-nominalism.

122. *ATT*, pp. 22 and 103.

123. *VI*, p. 234. See also p. 235.

124. Actually, I am sympathetic to the idea of such a duty, but it is beyond the scope of this project to argue for it.

125. Knapp and Michaels (1987), pp. 66–67.

126. H.P. Grice, "Meaning," *Philosophical Review* 66 (1957), p. 382. As we noted above, given that we intend to be understood and in principle can be understood, we are not positing a private language.

127. Bennett disagrees that the range of possible intentions is unbounded in the way I suggest. "In brief: free choice of meaning requires free choice of intention, which requires free choice of belief, which is impossible" (p. 166). Donnellan would also disagree.

128. At another point Bennett seems less sure as to the limits of intention and meaning. "I have implied only that meaning-limits have the same strength as belief-limits, whatever that strength is" (p. 167).

129. Cf. Donnellan, p. 212.

130. Cf. Ibid., p. 213.

131. *VI*, p. 169.

132. Pete Hamill, *A Drinking Life* (Boston: Little Brown and Company, 1994).

133. Gracia broaches this question in *ATT*, pp. 169–70.

134. Ibid., p. 113.

135. Ibid., p. 77.

136. For a discussion of mental texts see Gracia (1996), pp. 23–26.

137. This argument was originally made in my "Review of Jorge J.E. Gracia's *A Theory of Textuality: The Logic and Epistemology*," *Sorites* 3 (1995): 64–68.

138. Stein Haugom Olsen, "Interpretation and Intention," *British Journal of Aesthetics* 17 (1977), p. 215.

139. W.K. Wimsatt, "Genesis: A Fallacy Revisited," in David Newton-De Molina ed., *On Literary Intention* (Edinburgh: Edinburgh University Press, 1976), p. 116.

140. Ibid., p. 120.

4

Gadamer's Hermeneutics:
Descriptive and Normative

INTRODUCTION

In his seminal work, *Truth and Method*, Hans-Georg Gadamer presents us with a descriptive hermeneutics; his purported project is to describe what *does* occur in interpretive understanding, rather than prescribe what *should* occur (that which is the task of normative hermeneutics).[1] For Gadamer, the task of hermeneutics is to clarify the conditions under which interpretive understanding takes place, rather than to provide a methodical procedure for correct understanding. His hermeneutics "asks (to put it in Kantian terms): How is understanding possible?"[2] What is involved in the process of interpretive understanding? That this is Gadamer's project is suggested in his very definition of hermeneutics as, "the classical discipline concerned with the art of *understanding texts*."[3] Gadamer is not narrowly concerned with interpretation, but with understanding itself. The two are, for him, intimately linked, even synonymous. "It [German romanticism] has taught us that understanding and interpretation are ultimately the same thing."[4] "All understanding is interpretation."[5]

Despite the link between interpretation and understanding, Gadamer does not approach understanding in the way traditional hermeneutics approached interpretation; that is, he does not articulate a method[6] for arriving at correct understanding. His aim is not a normative one. Rather, he seeks to describe the phenomenon of interpretive understanding and is at pains to make clear that this is his project:

My real concern was and is philosophic: not what we do or what we ought to do, but what happens to us over and above our wanting and doing.[7]

Fundamentally I am not proposing a method; I am describing what is the case. That it is as I describe it cannot, I think, be seriously questioned.[8]

Hence I am trying to go beyond the concept of method held by modern science (which retains its limited justification) and to envisage in a fundamentally universal way what *always* happens.[9]

The task of hermeneutics is to clarify this miracle of understanding, which is not a mysterious communion of souls, but sharing in a common meaning.[10]

Our task, then, is to examine Gadamer's description of the process of interpretive understanding. We must not ask of this account what it does not purport to give, namely, a method of correct understanding; after all, it is providing an ontology not a methodology. Still, Gadamer's account is not purely descriptive; it does indeed have a normative agenda, which we shall examine as well.

Gadamer's descriptive account as articulated in *Truth and Method* is complex, involving many interconnected elements. For the sake of our inquiry, however, and with care to highlight by analysis, not kill by vivisection, we shall examine each of these elements alone, and then gradually in relation to their organic whole.[11] We shall begin by examining the ontology and temporality (*Zeitlichkeit*) of understanding as Gadamer develops it out of the work of Heidegger; we turn then to Gadamer's conception of truth with its connections to "play" (*Spiel*) and the aesthetic. Having examined truth, we are then prepared to focus on Gadamer's central descriptive element the "fusion of horizons" (*Horizontverschmelzung*). In connection with the fusion of horizons we shall also examine "tradition" (*Überlieferung*) and "prejudice" (*Vorurteil*). Our account of the fusion of horizons will also help clarify the crucial concept of effective history (*Wirkungsgeschichte*). The final descriptive element we shall examine is Gadamer's linguisticality (*Sprachlichkeit*), perhaps best captured in his enigmatic statement: "*Being that can be understood is language.*"[12]

THE ONTOLOGY AND TEMPORALITY OF UNDERSTANDING

The starting point of Gadamer's description of interpretive understanding is found in his appropriation of Heidegger's ontological account of understanding. For both Heidegger and Gadamer, all cognitive acts start with a pre-understanding; we never approach things without presuppositions, but rather bring our own concerns to them. Heidegger describes this pre-understanding in terms of what he calls the fore-structure of understanding, and Gadamer appropriates this fore-structure for his hermeneutics speaking of the prejudices (*Vorurteile*) with which we approach texts.[13] Let us consider Heidegger's conception of understanding, for it is the basis of Gadamer's own conception— in particular Gadamer's description of prejudice, which we shall take up in a subsequent section of this chapter.

For Heidegger, understanding has intimate connections to both *Dasein* and time; understanding is said to be part of the ontological structure of *Dasein*, and, inasmuch as being itself is time, understanding has an important temporal dimension. As we shall see, for both Heidegger and Gadamer, the gap between past and present is no "yawning abyss,"[14] and the link between the present and future is constant inasmuch as *Dasein* is always projecting its possibilities.

In Heidegger's analysis, understanding is not just one among the many activities of *Dasein*, but rather is an *existentiale* structure, one of the essential existential characteristics of *Dasein*'s being-there. As Gadamer puts it, "Heidegger's temporal analytics of Dasein has, I think, shown convincingly that understanding is not just one of the various possible behaviors of the subject but the mode of being of Dasein itself."[15] Understanding is a primary component of *Dasein*'s ontological structure. "Equiprimordial with it in constituting this Being is *understanding*. A state-of-mind always has its understanding. . . . If we interpret understanding as a fundamental *existentiale*, this indicates that this phenomenon is conceived as a basic mode of Dasein's *Being*."[16] Understanding is not something from which *Dasein* is ever independent; understanding is the way in which *Dasein* exists. For Heidegger, every attempt to understand involves interpretation (*Auslegung*), laying out what is there.[17] This can be seen at the most basic level, in that "*Dasein* is that entity which, as Being-in-the-world, is an issue for itself."[18] *Dasein* is the only being that questions its own being, that attempts to understand itself; *Dasein*, in fact, is always questioning—always projecting its own possibilities.

Why does the understanding—whatever may be the essential dimensions of that which can be disclosed in it—always press forward into possibilities? It is because the understanding has in itself the existential structure which we call "*projection*." . . . [A]ny Dasein has, as Dasein, already projected itself; and as long as it is, it is projecting. As long as it is, Dasein always has understood itself and always will understand itself in terms of possibilities.[19]

Dasein is a future-oriented being, and this is seen inasmuch as its being is constituted by understanding, which itself is structured by projection (*Entwurf*). In its attempts to understand, *Dasein* projects its own possibilities on the object of understanding; the object is not to be understood "in itself," but in terms of the possibilities *Dasein* projects upon the object. It is a fantasy to think that *Dasein* can ever understand anything "in itself" apart from *Dasein*'s own possibilities; *Dasein*'s very being and understanding are inescapably historical.

The historicality of *Dasein*'s understanding is not limited to its future oriented projection of possibilities, but is connected to its past as well. *Dasein*'s projection is "thrown" (*geworfen*) projection; *Dasein* is a "rider on the storm," thrown into a world with a past it did not create and a future over which it has limited control.[20] Its understanding is ultimately situated, ineluctably historical. Gadamer explains and endorses this Heideggerian thesis as follows.

That the structure of Dasein is thrown projection, that in realizing its own being Dasein is understanding. . . . The general structure of understanding is concretized in historical understanding, in that the concrete bonds of custom and tradition and the corresponding possibilities of one's own future become effective in understanding itself. Dasein that projects itself on its own potentiality-for-being has always already "been." This is the meaning of the existential of "thrownness."[21]

Dasein has always already "been"; it understands by projecting into the future while drawing on the past into which it was thrown. The novelty of the object of understanding is thus diminished; *Dasein* understands the object in terms of *Dasein* itself. Its understanding is, as we have said, always historical; it never understands the object of its inquiry free from its own presuppositions. Yet this is not a detriment to understanding, but a condition for its possibility. This becomes most clear in Heidegger's analysis of the hermeneutic circle.

As Gadamer explains, "Heidegger's thesis was that being itself is time."[22] This implies, of course, that the being of *Dasein* is temporal. We have, in fact, already seen this to the extent that *Dasein's* ontological mode of being is understanding, and understanding is thrown projection. Gadamer explains correctly that, "Heidegger derives the circular structure of understanding from the temporality of *Dasein*."[23] The analysis of understanding or interpretation in terms of the hermeneutic circle was not an original Heideggerian contribution. (Schleiermacher, among others, had earlier made such analysis.) Heidegger's analysis is original, however, in that he does not view the circle as needing to be broken, but rather claims that the circle is most truly complete in understanding.

Dasein's own mode of understanding, quite apart from textual interpretation per se, is a constant shifting back and forth between part and whole. This shifting is also characteristic of the structure of the hermeneutic circle—we must understand the whole in terms of its parts, but to understand the parts we must understand the whole. Some have argued that the circular movement of part and whole cannot lead us to the meaning of the text; the circle must be broken in some way.[24] As Heidegger argues, however, this back and forth motion between part and whole is characteristic of *Dasein*'s understanding; in true understanding the circle is not broken but most fully realized.

Heidegger describes *Dasein*'s apprehension of whole and parts in terms of the fore-structure of understanding which consists of: fore-having (*Vorhabe*), fore-sight (*Vorsicht*), and fore-conception (*Vorgriff*).[25]

In every case this interpretation is grounded in *something we have in advance*—in a *fore-having*. . . . In every case interpretation is grounded in *something we see in advance*—in a *fore-sight*. This fore-sight 'takes the first cut' out of what has been taken into our fore-having, and it does so with a view to a definite way in which this can be interpreted. Anything understood which is held in our fore-having and towards which we set our sights 'foresightedly,' becomes conceptualizable through the interpretation. In such an interpretation, the way in which the entity we are interpreting is to be conceived can be drawn from the entity itself, or the interpretation can force the entity into concepts to which it is opposed in its manner of Being. In either case, the interpretation has already decided for a definite way of conceiving it, either with finality or with reservations; it is grounded in *something we grasp in advance*—in a *fore-conception*.[26]

The fore-structure of understanding, consisting of fore-having, fore-sight, and fore-conception, confirms that there is no neutral vantage point from which to approach a text or any other object of understanding. *Dasein* always forms some conception of the whole and parts as a result of its situatedness; *Dasein*'s understanding is always contextual thrown projection.

The fore-structure of understanding implies the seeming paradox that, for *Dasein* to understand it must already understand what is to be understood.[27] Heidegger would claim, however, that this is not paradoxical or, if it is, the logic that disparagingly calls it paradoxical cannot accurately capture reality. The circle of understanding is, he claims, intimately related to the nature of *Dasein* itself.

What is decisive is not to get out of the circle but to come into it in the right way. This circle of understanding is not an orbit in which any random kind of knowledge may move; it is the expression of the existential *fore-structure* of Dasein itself. It is not to be reduced to the level of a vicious circle, or even of a circle which is merely tolerated. In the circle is hidden a positive possibility of the most primordial kind of knowing.[28]

The 'circle' in understanding belongs to the structure of meaning, and the latter phenomenon is rooted in the existential constitution of Dasein—that is, in the understanding which interprets. An entity for which, as Being-in-the-world, its Being is itself an issue, has, ontologically, a circular structure.[29]

The circle of understanding, then, is reflective of the very being of *Dasein*, or at least so it is claimed. To be clear, Heidegger's account of the circle is a matter of descriptive, not normative, hermeneutics; Gadamer is quick to point out that Heidegger's account of the hermeneutic circle places no necessary demands on the interpreter, but is a description of what *is* in every act of interpretation. "What Heidegger is saying here is not, in the first instance, a demand issued to the practice of understanding, rather it *describes* the form in which the interpretation which produces understanding is accomplished."[30]

What assessment shall we make of this ontology and temporality of understanding? There is certainly something correct in the analysis of *Dasein* in terms of understanding (though one might wish for greater support for the Heideggerian arguments). There is also some appeal to explaining the hermeneutic circle in terms of the nature of human being. Though the circle defies logic, it still seems to represent the process of understanding quite accurately. The connections that Heidegger and Gadamer see between the being of *Dasein* and the being of the circle are tenuous however. The circular structure of *Dasein* as Being-in-the-world, having itself as an issue, is a substantively different circularity from that of the hermeneutic circle. The two circles deal with quite different matters, and there is no reason why *Dasein*, as the being that questions its own being, should embrace an inescapable circularity in textual understanding, or otherwise. We may make sense of *Dasein*'s tendency to do so in light of this, but it does not mean that this is what *Dasein* should do, must do, or always does.

Perhaps the strongest and most controversial claim that begins to unfold here is the historicality of understanding; it is argued that because of *Dasein*'s thrown projection there is no presuppositionless understanding. *Dasein*, as a future-oriented being, is always projecting its own possibilities upon the objects of its understanding. Gadamer will further claim that recapturing the understanding of a historical past is not only undesirable but also fundamentally impossible. The past, then, is not to be dreaded as a "yawning abyss," but to be appropriated in our present understanding. We shall discuss this historicism in some detail when we examine the concepts of "fusion of horizons" and effective history. But that must wait—let us first turn to an examination of Gadamer's conception of truth.

TRUTH AND PLAY

The title of Gadamer's *magnum opus Truth and Method* leads us to ask: What is the relationship between truth and method? In describing hermeneutic experience Gadamer dismisses the search for a methodology of correct understanding, which had characterized most previous endeavors in their attempts to find truth. As he says: "The hermeneutic phenomenon is basically not a problem of method at all. It is not concerned with a method of understanding by means of which texts are subjected to scientific investigation like all other objects of experience."[31] Earlier hermeneutics, Romantic hermeneutics in particular, saw methodology as *the* means for reaching truth. In contrast, Gadamer not only rejects methodology[32] as the means for reaching interpretive truth, but rejects all traditional conceptions of truth as well. As Joel Weinsheimer says, for Gadamer, "truth cannot be equated with methodical proof"[33] and "truth cannot be limited to what is confirmable by method."[34]

For Gadamer, interpretive truth is not something to be sought actively through method, though one does seek it through dialogue. Still, there is something undeniably passive[35] about Gadamer's conception of truth; truth discloses itself to us. As he says, "Truth is the disclosure of being that is given with the historicity of Dasein.[36] . . . [I]t [work of art or text] expresses something in such a way that what is said is like a discovery, a *disclosure* of something previously concealed."[37] This conception of truth is clearly an appropriation of Heidegger's conception of truth as disclosure (*Erschlossenheit* and, later, *Un-verborgenheit*), as articulated in *Being and Time* and some of his later works.[38] Let us briefly consider Heidegger's conception of truth, as it will shed light on the role of truth in Gadamer's hermeneutics.

In *Being and Time* Heidegger looks back to the beginnings of Western thought to discover what exactly truth *is*. Traditional accounts of truth, he thinks, have offered a criterion for truth rather than an explanation of the meaning or essence of truth, and in this sense, the Being of truth has been forgotten. In order to pose the question of Being adequately, Heidegger thus explores the Being of truth. Heidegger does not accept correspondence, coherence, or pragmatics as the ultimate ground of truth. He, in fact, focuses his criticism on the correspondence theory, calling it the traditional account, finding its definition of truth, as *adaequatio intellectus et rei* (agreement of mind and things), to be unsatisfactory. This definition, he believes, locates truth in propositions and really does not capture any complete or genuine agreement. When I say, for example, "The dog is on the leash," the proposition and its psychical representation in my mind contain no actual dog and no actual leash. How, then, can the actual state of affairs and the proposition agree when they are of such disparate natures? As Heidegger says:

With regard to what do *intellectus* and *res* agree? In their kind of Being and their essential content do they give us anything at all with regard to which they can agree? If it is impossible for *intellectus* and *res* to be equal because they are not of the same species, are they then perhaps similar? . . . [I]t becomes plain that to clarify the structure of truth it is not enough simply to presuppose this relational totality, but we must go back and inquire into the context of Being which provides the support for this totality as such.[39]

Going back to the Greeks, Heidegger conceives truth as *aletheia* (Αληθεια)— disclosure or uncovering. The traditional definition of truth as *adaequatio intellectus et rei* simply would not do, but could be appropriated primordially under the most fundamental conception of truth as uncovering. The proposition conceived as true is, for Heidegger, only a derivative form of truth. The Greek word *aletheia* holds the key to the essence of truth; truth is not ultimately correspondence to fact/thing but an uncovering, an un-concealment, a disclosure of Being.

Truth (uncoveredness) is something that must always first be wrested from entities. Entities get snatched out of their hiddenness. The factical uncoveredness of anything is always, as it were, a kind of *robbery*. Is it accidental that when the Greeks express themselves as to the essence of truth, they use a *privative* expression—A-ληθεια?[40]

Heidegger illustrates this conception of truth with the example of a picture hanging askew. "'[T]he picture on the wall is hanging askew.' This assertion demonstrates itself when the man who makes it, turns round and perceives the picture hanging askew on the wall."[41] There is a place, though not a primary place, for propositional truth, as a derivative of truth as the disclosure of Being. "In proposing our 'definition' of 'truth' we have not *shaken off* the tradition, but we have *appropriated* it primordially."[42] Further, Heidegger asserts that truth refers not to the thing but to *Dasein*; it is an existential of *Dasein* and does not exist independently of *Dasein*. Still *Dasein* is not free from error. *Dasein* is both in truth and untruth; remember, truth must be wrested, even robbed. "*Because Dasein is essentially falling, its state of Being is such that it is in 'untruth.'*"[43] "To be closed off and covered up belongs to Dasein's *facticity*. In its full existential-ontological meaning, the proposition that 'Dasein is in the truth' states equiprimordially that 'Dasein is in untruth.'"[44]

In "On the Essence of Truth" Heidegger holds to his description of truth as offered in *Being and Time*, but adds the striking claim that the essence of truth is freedom.[45] How is it that truth and freedom are related? For Heidegger, it is freedom that allows beings to be, which allows beings to disclose themselves. "Freedom for what is opened up in an open region lets beings be the beings they are. Freedom now reveals itself as letting beings be."[46] Heidegger does not mean for this to be a completely passive occurrence; in letting beings be, the subject is still somehow active. "To let be is to engage oneself with beings."[47] "[F]reedom is engagement in the disclosure of beings as such."[48]

In "Plato's Doctrine of Truth," Heidegger continues to hold to the basic conception of truth as given in *Being and Time*, adding an explanation of how the original conception of truth as disclosure was lost. In his interpretation of the allegory of the cave, Heidegger locates the shift in the conception of truth as disclosure (Αληθεια, *Un-verborgenheit*) to the conception of truth as correctness (*orthotes, Richtigkeit*). It is not that Plato begins to speak of *orthotes* rather than *aletheia*, but that under Heidegger's interpretation this is what Plato means. "The ambiguity is clearly obvious in the fact that Αληθεια is mentioned and treated while at the same time *orthotes* is meant and set as a standard—and all in the same train of thought."[49] Despite the continuity from *Being and Time* through these two essays, Heidegger did later amend and retract significant parts of his conception of truth in "The End of Philosophy and the Task of Thinking." We shall reserve our discussion of this essay for our criticism of Gadamer's Heideggerian conception of truth.

Let us return now to Gadamer's conception of truth. Play (*Spiel*) is the essential link between truth as disclosure and textual interpretation.[50] Gadamer claims that play is not the kind of activity we ordinarily assume it is; it is not we as players who are in control of play, "all playing is a being-played."[51] The German word *Spiel*, which is translated as "play," is a richer word than this translation may suggest; *Spiel* means not only play, but game and drama—and originally dance as well. It is perhaps in the game and in dance that the role of the participants is most clear. The game has certain rules, certain restrictions, but aside from these *it* is the one who is in control, as players struggle against, or perhaps with, the greater entity that is the game itself. As Gadamer says, "In order for there to be a game, there always has to be, not necessarily literally another player, but something else with which the player plays and which automatically responds to his move with a countermove. . . . [B]all games will be with us forever because the ball is freely mobile in every direction, appearing to do surprising things of its own accord."[52] Dance captures our role in play as well. Though we may perceive ourselves as dancing, we are (Gadamer might say) more truly *being danced*—swept up in the greater entity that is the dance. The realization of the player or dancer is that she is not ultimately in control; play plays itself. "The players are not the subjects of play; instead play merely reaches presentation (*Darstellung*) through the players."[53]

The connection between play and truth as disclosure is a subordination to an entity greater than oneself. In both play and seeking interpretive truth it is easy to believe that one is in greater control than one actually is. The point of Gadamer's analysis of play is to demonstrate that in actuality, "The player experiences the game as a reality that surpasses him."[54] If she is honest, the player must admit that the game itself has the greater power. Such is the case with the power and truth of the text or artwork as well. Gadamer speaks of play in terms of truth as disclosure to make this point, "In being presented in play, what *is* emerges. It produces and brings to light what is otherwise constantly hidden and withdrawn."[55]

For Gadamer, the experience of an artwork or text is quite similar to that of play; we submit to its greater power. While truth is not necessarily an issue in play, it is (for Gadamer) *the* issue in our experience of the artwork or text. "[W]hat we experience in a work of art and what invites our attention is how true it is."[56] Against our ordinary conception, however, Gadamer argues that though we must seek truth in the artwork or text through dialogue, *its* truth seizes us. This disclosure is an action of the subject matter (*Tun der Sache selbst*). The artwork or text makes an immediate truth claim, one that we give at least the benefit of the doubt. We must assume that the artwork or text is possibly true and that it has something to say to us.[57] More often, however, the immediacy with which the truth of the artwork or text seizes us is such that we are overcome; we do not decide to accept it provisionally but are involuntarily swept up in it. Gadamer likens this experience to our experience of the beautiful.[58]

Someone who understands is always already drawn into an event through which meaning asserts itself. So it is well founded for us to use the same concept of play for the hermeneutical phenomenon as for the experience of the beautiful. When we understand a text, what is meaningful in it captivates us just as the beautiful captivates us. It has asserted itself and captivated us before we can come to ourselves and be in a position to test the claim to meaning that it makes. What we encounter in the experience of the beautiful and in understanding the meaning of tradition really has something of the truth of play about it. In understanding we are drawn into an event of truth and arrive, as it were, too late, if we want to know what we are supposed to believe.[59]

Through his analysis and application of play and truth as disclosure to textual interpretation, Gadamer has tried to subvert the status quo. He has effected a Copernican revolution of sorts; no longer does the interpreter seize the truth of the meaning in the text, but rather the interpreter is seized by the truth. As he says, "Hermeneutics . . . is not 'knowledge as domination'—i.e., an appropriation as taking possession; rather, it consists in subordinating ourselves to the text's claim to dominate our minds."[60]

The concept of dialogue (*Gespräch*), of question and answer,[61] is central to Gadamer's account of textual interpretation. It is, first, the text that poses a question to the interpreter. The text, as dominant, asserts its truth claim and elicits a response—the question calls for an answer. The interpreter, too, poses questions to the text and can find truth and meaning in the text only inasmuch as she questions it. The questions the interpreter asks are in essence constituted by her presuppositions. The interpreter as thrown and situated is never without her presuppositions, and it is these that determine her questions—and that bring the text to life. The text, even in seizing and questioning the interpreter, is seizing her as situated and replete with presuppositions. The textual understanding that results from a dialogue of question and answer between text and reader is always in the end substantive agreement with others (*Verständigung*) on truth in regard to a subject matter.[62] As we shall see, such understanding eschews historical reconstruction and embraces a "prejudiced" understanding through a "fusion of horizons." We shall take this up in the next section, but now let us turn a critical eye to Gadamer's connection between play and truth in textual interpretation.

We must ask of Gadamer's description of truth: Is it true? Although truth as disclosure is a powerful way of understanding some of our experience of truth, it is actually only a metaphorical explanation of a limited range of experience. It explains what the experience of learning the truth is sometimes like rather than what truth itself *is*. I would argue that only when the experience is such that my expectations are thwarted, that is, when I have an experience in one sense of *Erfahrung*,[63] do I experience truth as disclosure. Only then do I feel as though the truth of Being is making itself manifest to me. Even then, however, this experience (*Erfahrung*) is contingent upon my expectations, and may not even be revealed to me directly. The same truth may be experienced as a grand disclosure of Being by one person, and just another banal correspondence to fact by another person. Heidegger recognizes this to some extent in saying that, "In a large measure uncoveredness gets appropriated not by one's own uncovering, but rather by hearsay of something that has been said."[64] Often we do not experience the disclosure of truth about a subject matter but are the beneficiaries of truth disclosed to others.

Another problem with Gadamer's appropriation of the Heideggerian conception of truth is that this conception does not supply us with a sufficient condition for truth.[65] We can have an experience of disclosure that leads us not to truth but to untruth. It is not uncommon to believe that truth has been revealed, only to discover later that what was revealed or disclosed was not the truth at all. Who has not, at one time or another, believed himself to have the truth or meaning of a text only to believe later that original truth or meaning to be completely mistaken?[66] In "The End of Philosophy and the Task of Thinking" Heidegger himself concedes that he was mistaken in so strictly equating truth with *aletheia*.

Why is *aletheia* not translated with the usual name, with the word "truth"? The answer must be: Insofar as truth is understood in the traditional "natural" sense as the correspondence of knowledge with beings, demonstrated in beings, but also insofar as truth is interpreted as the certainty of the knowledge of Being, *aletheia*, unconcealment in the sense of the opening, may not be equated with truth. Rather, *aletheia*, unconcealment thought as opening, first grants the possibility of truth. For truth itself, just as Being and thinking, can be what it is only in the element of the opening. Evidence, certainty in every degree, every kind of verification of *veritas* already move *with* that *veritas* in the realm of the prevalent opening. *Aletheia*, unconcealment thought as the opening of presence, is *not yet truth*.[67]

In any case, one thing becomes clear: to raise the question of *aletheia*, of unconcealment as such, is not the same as raising the question of truth. For this reason, *it was inadequate and misleading to call aletheia in the sense of opening, truth.*[68]

In addition, Heidegger's interpretation of the allegory of the cave was not well-grounded historically. Plato was not the first to use *aletheia* in the sense of correctness, *orthotes*; this usage dates back at least as far as Homer. Heidegger himself admits this:

The natural concept of truth does not mean unconcealment, not in the philosophy of the Greeks either. It is often and justifiably pointed out that the word *alethes* is already used by Homer only in the *verba dicendi*, in statement and thus in the sense of correctness and reliability, not in the sense of unconcealment. . . . In the scope of this question, we must acknowledge the fact that *aletheia*, unconcealment in the sense of the opening of presence, was originally experienced only as *orthotes*, as the correctness of representations and statements. But then the assertion about the essential transformation of truth, that is, from unconcealment to correctness, is also untenable.[69]

Having criticized Gadamer's conception of truth, let us turn to his account of play, which has some merit, but which fails to make a legitimate connection to textual interpretation. A game is something that, in a very real sense, exists only in being played. We can have a detailed account of the rules of baseball, but without playing it, there is, in some sense, no game of baseball. On the other hand, the text exists in and of itself once the author has produced it; it does not need to be interpreted in the same way that the game needs to be played. The interpreter is not passive in the way the player is; the player becomes a subordinate element in the greater entity that is the game, but the interpreter is not similarly obliged to become a passive participant in the text. The text does not need the interpreter, and when the interpreter comes to it she comes as an active seeker.

That the artwork or text seizes us with a truth claim, as does the immediacy of the beautiful, is false.[70] Japanese music and cheap romance novels make no immediate truth claim on me whatsoever. Japanese music is so foreign in its aesthetic ideals that, if not placed in the proper context, it would be difficult for me to recognize it as art at all. I have no doubt that I could come to appreciate this art if I were properly trained to hear its beauty and "truth," but without such training it makes no immediate truth claim on me. My immediate reaction to a cheap romance novel is not that it is making some truth claim to which I must subordinate myself, but that it is trash that is not worth my time. These examples may at first seem contrived. Japanese music may be said to be outside my tradition, but in an important way it is not. If I know of it and am confronted with it, then it becomes part of my tradition. Cheap romance novels are not true art it may be claimed, but that is not a problem. Gadamer describes all textual understanding, not just that of textual art, as a being seized by truth. "When we understand a text, what is meaningful in it captivates us."[71] This is the case, for Gadamer, whether the text is a novel or a legal statute. While there is no doubt that our experience of a text or work of art can be that of being seized by an immediate truth claim, it need not be. This is so in very much the same way that we can experience truth as disclosure, but we would be mistaken to characterize truth itself as disclosure.

Even if we moderate Gadamer's claim, such that textual interpretation does not involve being seized by truth as by beauty, but simply involves the preconception of completion (*Vorgriff der Vollkommenheit*), it is still too strong. On Lawrence K. Schmidt's interpretation, this preconception of completion means that: "the interpreter must initially presuppose 1) that the contents of a text are not incoherent or self-contradictory (the immanent unity) and 2) that what the text expresses relating to a topic does not conflict with what is true concerning this topic, or in other words, that the text speaks the truth (the transcendent unity)."[72]

While this may be a useful way to approach many texts, there is no necessity to it. I may usually assume that a text is coherent, even when it at first does not appear to be. This is a useful way of trying to make sense of a text, but there is nothing necessary about it. I can, if I choose, approach a text with the idea in mind that it is incoherent or even self-contradictory—particularly if I do not hold its author in high regard. There is even less necessity in approaching a text as if what it had to say about its topic or subject matter (*Sache selbst*) were true. This is certainly a charitable and potentially productive state of mind in which to approach some texts, but with others it would be completely inappropriate. For example, a prosecuting attorney who examines the text of the testimony of the accused must surely approach it as untrue with respect to what it says about the crime committed (the *Sache selbst*, in this case). The prosecutor must approach the text as if what it says is false, at least to some extent; he must exercise a hermeneutic of suspicion.

There are serious problems with Gadamer's conception of truth and, in turn, the description of interpretive understanding that depends on it. Still, we should not be deterred from examining his description as a whole, which, though flawed, certainly contains some insight and is instructive as to where our descriptive efforts should be focused. Let us turn now to Gadamer's central descriptive element, the "fusion of horizons."

THE FUSION OF HORIZONS, PREJUDICE, AND TRADITION

Gadamer employs the concept of "fusion of horizons" (*Horizont-verschmelzung*) to describe our understanding of things past, including, and perhaps most importantly, texts. His essential claim is that historical reproduction is impossible, that we understand the past in terms of the present; past and present "fuse" in our understanding. Gadamer is here very much under the sway of Heidegger, who temporalized understanding and asserted that past meanings cannot be reproduced in the present because the past is ontologically alien to the present. Differences in time are differences in being[73]; a past meaning cannot be reproduced in the present because by simply being in the present it would be different and so would be a different meaning.

It is not, however, just a problem of differences in being resulting from differences in time. Gadamer appropriates Heidegger's fore-structure of understanding in his own terms, arguing that each present is laden with presuppositions, and it is within the context of these inescapable presuppositions that we must interpret the past. We thus comprehend the past in terms of our present, not in terms of the past that was its present, and so our understanding of the past is not as that past understood itself. "Part of real understanding, however, is that we regain the concepts of a historical past in such a way that they also include our own comprehension of them. Above I called this 'the fusion of horizons.'"[74]

The term "horizon," used earlier and differently by Nietzsche and Husserl,[75] is meant to suggest our situatedness and contextuality.[76] Gadamer defines a horizon as, "the range of vision that includes everything that can be seen from a particular vantage point."[77] That the horizon includes "everything" that can be seen suggests that, although there is much to be seen, this is "everything" for the horizon and not "everything" that can be understood. To truly have or acquire the horizon we must come to know not only what seems nearby, but also that which is far off at the edge of the horizon. "To acquire a horizon means that one learns to look beyond what is close at hand—not in order to look away from it but to see it better, within a larger whole and in truer proportion."[78] The horizon of the present is continually in flux as the present slips away into the past. There is no sharp division between the horizon of the present and that of the past. And, as we have seen, the horizon of the past can only be understood in terms of the present.[79] As Gadamer says, "There is no more an isolated horizon of the present in itself than there are historical horizons which have to be acquired. *Rather, understanding is always the fusion of these horizons supposedly existing by themselves.*"[80]

It is, then, in the fusion of horizons that we come to understand. The objects of our understanding, texts for example, are endowed with their very meanings through the fusion of horizons. The concerns and presuppositions of our present horizon fuse with the text of the past to make it speak in a meaningful way. Such understanding is productive not reproductive; it brings the text to life in a new way and makes it speak to our present concerns. Gadamer's account here is ostensibly descriptive and not normative. He is not saying that this is the way textual understanding *should* be practiced, but that this *is* the way textual understanding always occurs. "Not just occasionally but always, the meaning of a text goes beyond its author. That is why understanding is not merely a reproductive but always a productive activity as well."[81]

The projects of historically reproducing the author's intention or understanding, for example, would actually be impossible. We are still historically situated even when we make our concern the past intention or understanding of an author. Our account of authorial intention or understanding, then, will inevitably be no more than one historical perspective on them. This descriptive account should not go without challenge, but we shall defer that challenge for the moment. We should also note that, although Gadamer's account here is purportedly descriptive, it does have some normative spirit. Gadamer does not think that a historical reproduction would be particularly valuable even if it could be achieved; it would be a case of simply passing on "dead meaning." "[T]he text . . . *if it is to be understood properly*—i.e., according to the claim it makes—must be understood at every moment, in every concrete situation, in a new and different way. Understanding here is always application."[82] To understand why each present horizon is alien to the past, we must come to terms with Gadamer's conceptions of "prejudice" and "tradition."

For Gadamer, no understanding takes place without presuppositions. Following Heidegger, he would assert that it is part of *Dasein*'s ontological structure that it projects itself in its possibilities in understanding.[83] The very historicity of *Dasein*'s being entails that it has certain presuppositions, certain prejudices (*Vorurteile*[84]), which it makes use of in understanding. In speaking of our prejudices, Gadamer says, "They constitute, then, the horizon of a particular present, for they represent that beyond which it is impossible to see."[85] The term "prejudice" (*Vorurteil*) has come in recent times to have almost universally negative connotations associated with it. This was not always the case, however, and Gadamer attempts a rehabilitation of prejudice in his effort to describe understanding. The word "prejudice" (*Vorurteil*) is actually pretty innocuous, meaning simply to judge before hand, and, in this sense, a prejudice may be either correct or incorrect. Gadamer traces the negative connotations of the word prejudice to the Enlightenment. As he says, "[T]he fundamental prejudice of the Enlightenment is the prejudice against prejudice itself."[86] "Actually 'prejudice' means a judgment that is rendered before all the elements that determine a situation have been finally examined."[87] "The overcoming of all prejudices, this global demand of the Enlightenment, will itself prove to be a prejudice, and removing it opens the way to an appropriate understanding of the finitude which dominates not only our humanity but also our historical consciousness."[88]

Prejudice, then, as Gadamer understands it, is actually a necessary, i.e., inescapable, condition for all understanding. We cannot come to understand anything without making some prior judgment about it and without operating under certain given presuppositions. There is some kinship here to Heidegger's analysis of the hermeneutic circle; we understand the part in terms of the whole and the whole in terms of the part. This circle is not broken, but most fully realized in understanding. In a similar way, we do not understand by ridding ourselves of prejudices, but rather by bringing our prejudices to bear on the object we attempt to understand. We cannot exercise understanding in any other way. Still, some prejudices are correct and lead to understanding while others are incorrect and lead to misunderstanding.

Gadamer's point, then, is that while prejudices are a necessary condition for understanding, the prejudices we have are subject to revision and dismissal. Such revision and dismissal, however, are no easy tasks. Our prejudices are not always immediately apparent to us, and the "tyranny of hidden prejudices"[89] can cause us to misunderstand. "The prejudices and fore-meanings that occupy the interpreter's consciousness are not at his free disposal."[90] It is not, in fact, until we attempt to understand that our prejudices may come out of hiding and be subject to revision. As Gadamer says, "He [the interpreter] cannot separate in advance the productive prejudices that enable understanding from the prejudices that hinder it and lead to misunderstandings. Rather, this separation must take place in the process of understanding itself."[91]

Even productive ("true") prejudice is rather stealthy; it operates with force but goes unnoticed. Prejudice likes to hide, carrying out its task and passing itself off as self-evident knowledge. It is only when prejudice is challenged that it can be seen as such; it is only when an opposing point of view is brought to bear that our presuppositions lose the guise of self-evident knowledge and are exposed for what they are, prejudices. As Gadamer says,

It is impossible to make ourselves aware of a prejudice while it is constantly operating unnoticed, but only when it is, so to speak, provoked. . . . In fact our own prejudice is properly brought into play by being put at risk. Only by being given full play is it able to experience the other's claim to truth and make it possible for him to have full play himself.[92]

It is crucial, then, to be open to the claim of the other as expressed in his text and in dialogue. Only by such an openness can one hope to rid oneself of prejudices which lead to misunderstanding. Such prejudices are more easily detected than are correct prejudices confirmed. We can subject our prejudices to the test of falsifiability in light of what the other says, but merely passing this test does not confirm that they are correct. As Gadamer says, "The important thing is to be aware of one's own bias, so that the text can present itself in all its otherness and thus assert its own truth against one's own fore-meanings."[93] "True prejudices must still finally be justified by rational knowledge, even though the task can never be fully completed."[94]

Tradition (*Überlieferung*) is a vital part of Gadamer's description of interpretive understanding. Tradition is something both outside of us and, at the same time, something in which we are contained, and this can be seen through the connections between prejudice and tradition. On the one hand, as Georgia Warnke explains, "Gadamer argues, that because of our historicity we can never transcend the prejudices of the tradition to which we belong and evaluate them according to independent criteria of reason."[95] This is why, though we must justify our prejudices, we can never fully justify them; it is far easier to falsify them. On the other hand, Gadamer says, "It is the tyranny of hidden prejudices that makes us deaf to what speaks to us in tradition."[96] This statement suggests that our prejudices are separate and distinct from tradition. The conflict could be resolved by arguing that there are certain prejudices that belong to the tradition as a whole and certain other prejudices that are unique to some present horizon.

Tradition is essentially a handing down of issues and concerns that have developed over the course of time. With respect to texts,[97] this means that we never confront a text as if it were completely fresh and new. Any traditionary text will have a history of interpretations that will be passed on with it in and that we thus confront in interpreting the text. As Gadamer says, "Literature is a function of being intellectually preserved and handed down, and therefore brings its hidden history into every age."[98]

Tradition can contain both familiar and alien elements. On the one hand Gadamer says, "we are always situated within traditions . . . we do not conceive of what tradition says as something other, something alien. It is always part of us."[99] This is certainly the case some or most of the time, just as our prejudices are frequently embedded within our tradition. On the other hand, we do sometimes encounter what is passed on to us through tradition as something alien. Prejudice can, then, make us deaf to what speaks to us in tradition, or it can urge us to re-form tradition. As Gadamer says, "Every age has to understand a transmitted text in its own way, for the text belongs to the whole tradition whose content interests the age and in which it seeks to understand itself. The real meaning of a text . . . is always co-determined also by the historical situation of the interpreter and hence by the totality of the objective course of history."[100]

There is, then, some freedom within tradition, though tradition always maintains some regulative force. We can never break out of tradition but we can break with it on certain issues by emphasizing other elements of the tradition,[101] and in a sense, re-forming the tradition. As Gadamer says, "Tradition is not simply a permanent precondition; rather, we produce it ourselves inasmuch as we understand, participate in the evolution of tradition, and hence further determine it ourselves."[102] There is, therefore, freedom for knowledge within tradition, and not only that, but tradition is actually what allows for and generates knowledge. "To be situated within a tradition does not limit the freedom of knowledge but makes it possible."[103] "[I]t still is part of the nature of man to be able to break with tradition, to criticize and dissolve it."[104] The recurring theme here is that temporal distance (*Zeitenabstand*) is not something to be overcome but rather is a condition for the possibility of knowledge. As Gadamer says, "In fact the important thing is to recognize temporal distance as a positive and productive condition enabling understanding. It is not a yawning abyss but is filled with the continuity of custom and tradition, in the light of which everything handed down presents itself to us."[105]

To understand we must, then, orient ourselves within our horizon in such a way that we can hear the truth that tradition speaks to us. It is only then that we truly understand; it is only then that we effect a fruitful "fusion of horizons." In making productive use of the past through tradition we come to agreement both with the past and with each other within our tradition and horizon. In this way understanding is most fully achieved.

Another related way in which we make productive use of the past is through what Gadamer calls effective-history (*Wirkungsgeschichte*). We shall turn our attention to this important descriptive element in the next section of this chapter. For now, however, let us turn a critical eye to Gadamer's conception of the "fusion of horizons."

Gadamer does not provide adequate support for his claim that understanding must take place through a fusion of horizons and that historical reconstruction is impossible. He argues that because our present horizon is laden with presuppositions and prejudices that are different from those of a given historical past, we cannot recreate the understanding of the past. Rather than attempt such a futile project, we are to bring about new and productive understanding through a fusion of past and present horizons.[106] Gadamer has not adequately demonstrated, however, why our present presuppositions and prejudices preclude historical reconstruction. Quite obviously they are an obstacle, but it is not obvious that they are an insurmountable obstacle. Different causes, after all, can produce the same effect.[107] The use of eyeglasses by someone with poor sight can cause the effect of seeing an object just as clearly as can someone with perfect vision. Similarly, there is no logical impossibility precluding the reproduction of a past meaning or understanding. Often all we do know is the past. When we look at the stars in the night sky we know them as they were, not as they are. We can even know the ancient history of a star through scientific examination of the light it has thrown into our present. Gadamer has not shown why it is not, at least in principle, possible to counteract our present prejudices[108] and so know the past as it was. He has not shown that the project of seeking authorial intention is impossible, but, at most, has shown it to be a very difficult project and one in which he finds little value.

Gadamer has not provided a sufficient argument for why we could not factor our present presuppositions and prejudices into the equation in attempting a historical reconstruction. As Hirsch has pointed out, Gadamer might argue in Heideggerian terms that being itself is time, differences in time represent differences in being, and so an understanding at a later time represents a different understanding.[109] This argument may be correct, but even if it is, it does not do the work it is supposed to do. The differences in being that are produced by differences in time need not be essential. Two understandings can differ in being and time and so be extensionally different while being intensionally the same.[110] Put another way, we can certainly have two tokens of the same type. Of course without making strenuous effort at historical reconstruction, the understandings are likely to be intensionally different as well, but as I have argued, this need not be the case. In any event, we can picture the understanding as one we strive toward, though we may never attain it or even know for certain if we have.[111]

Even if Gadamer were to accept our argument that accurate historical reconstruction is possible, he still would not find this practice valuable. He would consider such reproductive understanding to be sterile and undesirable, arguing that only through productive understanding in the "fusion of horizons" is true and valuable understanding achieved. As he says, "it is universally true of texts that only in the process of understanding them is the dead trace of meaning transformed back into living meaning."[112] Historical reproduction would simply be issuing forth a "dead trace" of meaning. This claim is actually a normative one; Gadamer does indeed have an agenda for correct interpretation. A correct interpretation, for him, would not be one that simply reproduces what the author meant. We shall not dispute his normative claim here, however, but defer that task for a later section.

EFFECTIVE HISTORY

Gadamer's descriptive concept *Wirkungsgeschichte* has caused some problem for translators but its sense is perhaps best rendered as "effective history" or alternatively "history of effect."[113] For Gadamer, the meaning of a text is its effective history, its history of effects on *Dasein*. That is to say, the text's meaning is the history of its many interpretations. One could, for Gadamer, even say that the text itself is its history of effects, or its collection of interpretations. Texts are their interpretations and not simply the objects of interpretation.[114] As Gadamer says,

> The true historical object is not an object at all, but the unity of the one and the other, a relationship that constitutes both the reality of history and the reality of historical understanding. A hermeneutics adequate to the subject matter would have to demonstrate the reality and efficacy of history within understanding itself. I shall refer to this as "history of effect." *Understanding is, essentially, a historically effected event.*[115]

Understanding, as Gadamer describes it, is effective historical understanding. We do not understand by merely reproducing some past meaning but rather by contributing to the text—by adding to its effects—through our interpretation. Approaching a text in this way requires a certain disposition, a historically effected consciousness (*Wirkungsgeschichtliches Bewusstsein*), which is primarily consciousness of the hermeneutical situation itself.[116] This consciousness is a being-aware-of the need to effect and be effected by the text.

The dynamic goes both ways.[117] Historically effected consciousness is open to whatever may occur in interpretation, bringing no dogmatic expectations and putting forth no interpretations dogmatically. Rather, it is always open to experience (*Erfahrung*); it is willing to have its expectations thwarted. As Gadamer says, "Understanding, then, does not consist in a technical virtuosity of 'understanding' everything written. Rather, it is a genuine experience (Erfahrung)—i.e., an encounter with something that asserts itself as truth."[118]

Effective history and historically effected consciousness are intimately linked to Gadamer's description of the fusion of horizons. In understanding, the boundaries between present and past horizons melt away, and what is produced is a new interpretation. The fusion of horizons demonstrates that we are not concerned with meaning as some past relic but as a novel creation.[119] In understanding, we effect the object of our understanding. As Gadamer says,

[H]istorically effected consciousness is something other than inquiry into the history of a particular work's effect—as it were, the trace a work leaves behind. It is, rather, a consciousness of the work itself, and hence itself has an effect. The purpose of the whole account of the formation and fusion of horizons was to show how historically effected consciousness operates.[120]

Through the fusion of horizons and effective history, then, each interpretation is a new and vital one. For Gadamer this does not imply an insidious relativism, but rather "It is enough to say that we understand in a *different way, if we understand at all.*"[121] That is, to truly understand one must understand differently. The sign of understanding is not repetition; even a parrot can repeat without understanding. Rather, it is clear that one understands when one appropriates what is given and makes something new and useful of it. When we understand something its truth speaks to us, but the truth of the object of understanding speaks into ever-changing conditions. The understanding must, therefore, be ever-changing in order for it to be understanding at all.

Understanding for Gadamer involves application (*Anwendung, Applikation*) and participation (*Teilnehmen, Teilhaben*). That is, the interpreter participates in forming the meaning of a text by applying it to her own circumstances.[122] Gadamer denies the separability of what Hirsch calls "meaning" and "significance." For Gadamer it is impossible to have meaning apart from significance; only in applying the text to one's own circumstances—generating significance—does one find meaning at all.

Application does not mean first understanding a given universal in itself and then afterward applying it to a concrete case. It is the very understanding of the universal—the text—itself. Understanding proves to be a kind of effect and knows itself as such.[123]

Gadamer likens the application characteristic of hermeneutics to that of Aristotelian ethics.[124] For Aristotle there is no moral knowledge in abstraction from practice. The good is not simply relative, but it is dependent upon the situation of the moral agent. We must, therefore, be trained in the virtues (e.g., courage and temperance) in order to do the virtuous thing in a given situation.

We must come to rely on *phronesis*, a practical moral knowledge, rather than on *episteme*. In the same way, Gadamer argues, there is no knowledge of the meaning of the text itself to be sought; there is only the meaning of the text for our particular situation.

Understanding requires not only application to our situation but participation as well. Participation has both active and passive dimensions. We must submit to the given state of affairs that is the text, just as in a game we must submit to the rules, but we must also actively make a contribution—we must add something to the given state of affairs.[125] This is much as the player contributes to the game, making it always a different game. For Gadamer, this is not a subjective or relativizing process, but is, in fact, the only way in which we can interpret. Interpretation is and must be novel in just the way that a game is always novel. As he says, "*Understanding is to be thought of less as a subjective act than as participating in an event of tradition*, a process of transmission in which past and present are constantly mediated. This is what must be validated by hermeneutic theory, which is far too dominated by the idea of a procedure, a method."[126]

There is much that is unsatisfactory in Gadamer's account of effective history, and much that takes him into the realm of the normative. Gadamer has a problem with textual identity. He likens a text to a game or a festival that is always the same and is yet always different, but, as Wachterhauser has noted, the festival is not necessarily the same festival year after year—it is the same in name only.[127] In the same way we could say that a game of baseball is the same in name only every time it is played. That is, although the rules remain the same, the action is invariably different. In contrast, there is something permanent about a text; once produced by the author, it truly remains the same (barring any textual corruption). It is only our interpretations of it that can change. The normative question that Gadamer broaches here is: *Should* our interpretations of a text always change? We shall address this further in a subsequent section of this chapter.

For Gadamer our interpretations change of necessity: we understand in a different way if we understand at all. Is this true, however? It is true in only the trivial sense that some unimportant, i.e., accidental, elements of our understanding are apt to change, e.g., the time and place of that understanding. What is far more important, however, is that the essence of our understanding remains the same as previous correct understanding if we can be said to understand at all. Take the simple text, "three goats plus four goats equals seven goats."[128] It would be impossible to understand this text in a way different from that in which it was intended and still understand it. With changes in the language through time this text might become more difficult to understand, but to truly understand it we would have to understand it as it was intended. The same could be said of more complex texts as well.[129] If we do not preserve the essence of our understanding, we open the door to interpretive relativism, a fate Gadamer wishes to avoid. Reading becomes an act of creation like writing, and, as Stanley Rosen aptly puts it, "If reading is writing, then writing is scribbling."[130]

Gadamer's description of application and its implicit denial of the distinction between "meaning" and "significance" is also unsatisfactory. Again, that understanding involves some application to my own circumstances is necessarily true in only the most trivial sense. Inasmuch as I am the subject of my own understanding that understanding will be personal, but this does not preclude bracketing my personal circumstances in the service of understanding the text apart from those circumstances. Granted, this is no easy task and it may not be our usual way of understanding,[131] but (as Hirsch and I have argued) it may be preferable. What Gadamer describes in terms of effective history and application is what is ordinarily the case, not what is of necessity the case or what *should* be the case. We shall discuss this issue again in a subsequent section of this chapter devoted to Gadamer's normativism. For now, however, let us turn to an examination of a final descriptive concept, linguisticality.

LINGUISTICALITY

For Gadamer, a descriptive account of hermeneutics must of necessity examine the place of language. Gadamer argues that understanding is not impeded by language, but actually takes place in language; understanding does not come prior to words only to be lowered and made deficient through verbal expression. To the contrary, "the way understanding occurs—whether in the case of a text or a dialogue with another person who raises an issue with us—is the coming-into-language of the thing itself (*Zur-sprache-kommen der Sache selbst*)."[132] The linguisticality (*Sprachlichkeit*) of understanding is such that reality finds its truest expression in language. It goes beyond mere expression, however, in that part of the Being of things is their very expression in language. As Gadamer says, "we must recognize that all understanding is interwoven with concepts and reject any theory that does not accept the intimate unity of word and subject matter."[133] Language, therefore, is what makes understanding possible despite our contextuality and situatedness. It is what makes our connection with each other and with the past possible, "*the fusion of horizons that takes place in understanding is actually the achievement of language.*"[134]

What makes understanding through language possible is the connection of language to reason. All language is, in a sense, a mirror reflecting reason, and in this way it is the vehicle of mutual understanding. "Language is the language of reason itself."[135] We can have a vast plurality of human languages, all capturing reality, because all language is intimately connected to reason itself, "behind all the relativities of language and convention there is something in common which is no longer language, but which looks to an ever-possible verbalization, and for which the well-tried word 'reason' is, perhaps, not the worst."[136]

The link between language and understanding is of such a nature that Gadamer has proclaimed, "Being that can be understood is language (*Sein, das verstanden werden kann, ist Sprache*)."[137] This profound and cryptic statement demands attention. It means that what *can* be understood is the being that is produced by a writer or speaker; what *can* be understood "offers itself to be understood"[138] in language. The operative word in Gadamer's dictum is *can*; he is not suggesting that through language we *can* understand everything. Quite to the contrary, he is implying that, that which *is can* never be completely understood.[139] And, as Schmidt explains, "what can be understood and communicated are not entities but language alone."[140] Language, however, is the key to a tremendous wealth of understanding and so it should be used accordingly. "The principle of hermeneutics simply means that we should try to understand everything that *can* be understood. This is what I meant by the sentence: 'Being that can be understood is language.'"[141]

In language human beings do not create reality, but rather reality manifests itself. There is a coming-into-language of the subject matter (*Zur-sprache-kommen der Sache selbst*); it is in language that the Being of the subject matter discloses itself to us. The Being or reality that becomes manifest is not some imperfect copy of a Platonic form. Language is not some distorted reflection of Being, but, in part, is determinate of Being. "[T]hat which comes into language is not something which is pregiven before language; rather, the word gives its own determinateness."[142] All experience is linguistic for Gadamer, even when the words to capture it are not at our fingertips or perhaps not even yet in the language. In experience, "We seek the right word—i.e., the word that really belongs to the thing—so that in it the thing comes into language."[143] Word and thing are united. Neither one is primary; they codetermine one another for Gadamer. As Schmidt says, "In the completion of experience the correct word which expresses the object is discovered in as much as the experience is understood. Neither word nor object is known before the other."[144]

As the analogy of play demonstrates, understanding, for Gadamer, involves submission. We submit ourselves to the truth claim of the artwork or text, and we also submit ourselves to the determining power of language.[145] Language has us in its thrall, moving us through a world of meaning we did not create.[146] The statement "Being that can be understood is language" reflects this. We are subject to language in terms of what we *can* understand. We come to understanding through substantive agreement (*Verständigung*) with others, and such agreement is reached through dialogue (*Gespräch*) and conversation: "language is by nature the language of conversation; it fully realizes itself only in the process of coming to an understanding."[147] Conversation, however, is not something the participants control entirely; every conversation has its own guiding spirit and operates through the power of language. As Gadamer says:

We say that we "conduct" a conversation, but the more genuine a conversation is, the less its conduct lies within the will of either partner. Thus a genuine conversation is never the one that we wanted to conduct. Rather, it is generally more correct to say that we fall into conversation, or even that we become involved in it.[148]

In the final analysis, "language is a medium where I and world meet or, rather, manifest their original belonging together."[149] It is in language that we come to know and understand the world, and language does not merely designate but codetermines the objects of our world. As Gadamer says, "Whoever has language 'has' the world."[150]

Despite our attempts to clarify Gadamer's concept of linguisticality, much remains cryptic and indeed false. Not all experience is linguistic. Gadamer himself notes the criticism of Habermas that the experience of domination and the experience of work are nonlinguistic.[151] Habermas also points out, as Gadamer notes, that there is a prelinguistic experience of the world. Piaget demonstrated this through his research in early cognitive development. Gestures, facial expressions, tears, and laughter all appear to generate understanding through experience without the aid of the linguistic.[152] As Schmidt acknowledges, in *Truth and Method* Gadamer firmly states that the only experience of a subject matter (*Sache selbst*) is through language because it is only by and through language that man has a world.[153] Subsequently, however, Gadamer shifted ground claiming that there could be prelinguistic experiences but that these could not be communicated.[154] With this qualification Gadamer's dictum now becomes: Being, which can be understood and that implies communicated, is language.[155] This modified claim, however, is no more defensible than it was in its original form. Certainly we can communicate outside of and before language; facial expressions and bodily movements often communicate more than words. Infants communicate their needs through cries and facial expressions well before they acquire language.

There is something merely metaphorical about Gadamer's conception of linguisticality. Yes, sometimes we seem to experience a word as codetermining Being, but this is not always the case and it is not an accurate description of reality. Quite often we are sensitive to how poorly language captures reality or reflects our understanding.[156] We search for the right word and even having found the best possible word, we are dissatisfied. Nor does language truly sweep us up in the way Gadamer claims. We have all had the experience of a conversation seeming to have a spirit of its own, to be controlling us as the participants, but again, what we have here in Gadamer is an imperfect metaphor. It describes poetically some part of our experience, while ignoring the rest—it describes a part without harmony to the whole.

AN EVALUATION OF GADAMER'S DESCRIPTION

Having completed our survey of Gadamer's descriptive hermeneutics, we must ask: What has it contributed? Though this is low praise, perhaps Gadamer's most important achievement in the descriptive hermeneutics of *Truth and Method* is to have carried the project out so thoroughly. Although Heidegger had made some inroads to *describing* interpretive understanding, Gadamer was the first to do an exhaustive descriptive study of it. In his study Gadamer has demonstrated the importance of inquiring into the nature of interpretive understanding itself. Simply determining the criteria for correct interpretation is not the whole hermeneutic picture. Indeed, there are problems and difficulties in carrying out the normative project of "method" that Gadamer rightly criticizes. He has made clear the difficulty (he would say impossibility) of historical reconstruction due to our presuppositions and prejudices.

Gadamer has also made abundantly clear the importance of interpretation that goes beyond the author and historical reconstruction.[157] Through his discussion of effective history, Gadamer has shown that we must invigorate a text with a new understanding if we hope to keep it alive and interesting. We should also note that through his emphasis on the role of language in interpretive understanding, Gadamer has drawn attention to a previously underexplored area. Deconstruction, which has taken up exploration in this area, is not his heir but his rival.[158] Much work must still be done in answering the questions Gadamer has raised.

Gadamer's descriptive account is, unfortunately, fraught with problems; in nearly every area it is overstated and highly metaphorical.[159] He has, for the most part, failed to describe interpretive understanding accurately. His insights and images are, however, quite keen and serve their purpose, at least inasmuch as they spur others into taking up the task of descriptive hermeneutics. Another serious problem with Gadamer's account is that it does not stay purely descriptive but drifts far into the normative. We shall take up Gadamer's normativism in the next section of this chapter.

We have noted our criticisms of Gadamer's description throughout, and so there is no need to reiterate them in detail here. Let us simply note some of the major problems. Gadamer's description of the ontology and temporality of understanding is largely an appropriation of Heidegger's analytic of *Dasein* in *Being and Time*. To this extent it requires that we accept much Heideggerian doctrine, something that many will be unwilling to do—at least without further arguments in support of it. Gadamer's account of truth, based on Heidegger's conception of truth as disclosure, is also problematic. That truth *is* a disclosure of Being and that in interpretation the truth of the text seizes us are metaphorical descriptions that can account for only a limited range of the phenomena they purport to describe. Gadamer's account of understanding as a "fusion of horizons" in which historical reconstruction is impossible has again overstated the case. Ignored is the logical possibility that a past historical understanding could be recreated in a way different from that in which the original understanding was created; different causes can have the same effect. Gadamer also says nothing of degrees of reproducibility. Just because exactly reproducing a past historical understanding of a long and complex text is difficult, does not mean that we cannot to a greater or lesser extent approach exact reproduction.

Gadamer's description of understanding in terms of effective history, that understanding always requires application, is also troublesome. The extent to which I *must* apply the meaning of a text to my own situation and so "understand differently" is negligible, as is readily apparent in the case of short and simple texts. Gadamer's description of the role of language in understanding is quite cryptic, and, in what it does say clearly, is overstated. His description of our passivity in relation to language is again metaphorically accurate for a limited range of cases. In addition, we often do understand Being apart from, before, and other than language.

In my estimate, a rehabilitation of Gadamer's descriptions would not be a worthwhile endeavor, at least within the limited scope of the current study. Gadamer does, however, raise the important question of how to describe hermeneutic understanding. Also of true importance, Gadamer highlights the value of creative interpretation, that which surpasses historical reconstruction and enlivens the text—spurring the progress of ideas. We shall conclude the present study with an attempt to "harmonize" this kind of interpretation (criticism or non-urinterpretation) with what we have called urinterpretation. Before taking up that task, however, we must complete our study of Gadamer by briefly examining his normativism.

GADAMER'S NORMATIVISM

As we have noted throughout our discussion of Gadamer's descriptive hermeneutics, his account is *not* purely descriptive but drifts into the realm of the normative; Gadamer is, in fact, concerned with articulating the criteria for correct interpretation. What exactly Gadamer's normative criteria are, however, is not completely clear. Even Gadamer's followers and those well acquainted with his work do not agree on this matter. It is not that they do not agree as to whether Gadamer is correct, but rather, they do not agree as to what he said, what he put forward as the criteria for correct interpretation.[160]

We shall begin by considering two candidates for Gadamer's normative criterion: (1) the text is the measure: there must be a harmony of part and whole, and (2) accord with tradition. Finding these to be unsatisfactory, we shall then consider a third possible criterion, legitimizing one's prejudices (*Vorurteile*) and so arriving at an enlightening (*einleuchtende*) perspective (*Ansicht*) on the subject matter (*Sache selbst*). We shall find that this is Gadamer's criterion, but that it does not stand up to critical analysis. Although Gadamer claims that, "The naive belief in the objectivity of historical method was a delusion. But what replaces it is not a simple relativism,"[161] we shall see that, in accepting Gadamer's account, even if relativism does not necessarily follow, the door to it is left wide open. In closing, we will examine other ways in which Gadamer involves himself in normative issues.

The first candidate for Gadamer's normative criterion may be put thus: the text is the measure. For Gadamer a text means whatever an interpreter takes it to mean, with some limitations. As Wachterhauser says, "A text means whatever it can be construed to say with two important qualifications: Gadamer rules out self-contradictory interpretations and interpretations that do not account for all the recognizable features of the text."[162] Wachterhauser seems to be taking the preconception of completion (*Vorgriff der Vollkommenheit*) as Gadamer's normative criterion. He is not alone in this,[163] and Gadamer himself does say, "The harmony of all the details with the whole is the criterion of correct understanding. The failure to achieve this harmony means that understanding has failed."[164] This preconception of completion is what saves interpretation from arbitrariness; we cannot make the text say just anything but only what can fit consistently with the rest of the text. Each part must fit harmoniously with each other part and with the whole.

If this is Gadamer's normative criterion, he assumes without warrant that a text necessarily forms a complete and coherent whole. Texts in which all the parts fit harmoniously with each other and the whole are more likely to be the exception, not the rule. Even if Gadamer were warranted in making this assumption, his "text itself" argument would not stand. As we saw in chapter 3, without recourse to the author, we can make a text "say" whatever we wish. It is only the author who can[165] limit the otherwise endless possibilities of what the text "says." If this were his established criterion, relativism would not necessarily follow but it would be heartily invited.

Also contained within this criterion of "the text is the measure," as dictated by the preconception of completion, is the guide that an interpretation should not be self-contradictory.[166] This follows from the other assumptions that a text has a completeness (*Vollkommenheit*) and that there should be harmony between part and whole. As I have suggested, however, a text need not necessarily be complete and coherent, nor must there be harmony between all the parts and the whole. Texts are imperfect human creations, and our interpretations of them must sometimes reflect the contradictions within them. Derrida and the deconstructionists have made this quite clear by placing emphasis on the tension within texts. We should note that although, given this criterion, Gadamer can be seen as ruling out self-contradictory interpretations; he does not hold that one or both of two mutually exclusive or contradictory interpretations must be unacceptable. Such mutually exclusive interpretations are not precluded by and indeed are somewhat likely within a text's effective history. In embracing both of two mutually exclusive or contradictory interpretations, however, Gadamer is in effect embracing relativism. There is no practical limit on what a text can be construed as saying, if it can be construed as saying each of two separate and contradictory things.

Although, given some of what Gadamer says, it would be sensible to take the preconception of completion as his truth criterion, very likely it is not. Rather, the preconception is a part of Gadamer's *description* of interpretive understanding. The two fundamental assumptions of the preconception are: (1) that the contents of a text are not incoherent or self-contradictory and (2) that what the text expresses with respect to a certain topic (*Sache selbst*), does not conflict with what is true concerning this topic.[167] As Schmidt argues, however, Gadamer does not claim that what a text says *must* always be coherent and true, but that our starting point *is* always the assumption that such is the case. The function of the preconception of completion is that it allows one to question one's own prejudices regarding the subject matter by opposing them to what the text says. "The point is not that a text always speaks the truth but that one has to initially assume its truth in order to possibly oppose its judgment to one's own opinion."[168] Schmidt is correct in arguing that the preconception of completion is a descriptive rather than a normative element of Gadamer's hermeneutics but goes too far in describing the preconception as a *necessary* part of interpretation. It may often be beneficial to assume that what a text says is coherent and true, but there may well be times when I can and should assume just the opposite. Hoy takes a position on the preconception similar to Schmidt's, but without the emphasis on necessity. "[I]t is a heuristic recommendation to the interpreter, suggesting that it will be more useful to go along with the text as far as possible than to dismiss the text's truth claims as outdated or its arguments as primitive."[169] This puts the matter correctly.

Having seen that the "text is the measure" candidate cannot function as a viable normative criterion, and in fact is not Gadamer's normative criterion, let us turn to the second candidate—tradition (*Überlieferung*). Some have also interpreted Gadamer as making use of tradition as a normative criterion governing correct interpretation.[170] Under this interpretation, Gadamer is perhaps sensitive to the deficiency of the "text is the measure" criterion, and so proposes a supplement. As we have seen, even contradictory interpretations for a given text can be generated given this criterion alone. Perhaps to avoid arbitrariness and relativism, then, Gadamer posits a second normative criterion, that of tradition. As he says,

> There cannot, therefore, be any single interpretation that is correct "in itself," precisely because every interpretation is concerned with the text itself. The historical life of tradition depends on being constantly assimilated and interpreted. An interpretation that was correct in itself would be a foolish ideal that mistook the nature of tradition. Every interpretation has to adapt itself to the hermeneutical situation to which it belongs.[171]

The interpreter who is in accord with tradition, who assimilates to the current hermeneutical situation, gives a correct interpretation. We can, therefore, have contradictory interpretations but not at a given point in time within a tradition. As Hirsch understands Gadamer's position here, "The determinate meaning of a text at a given point in time is what a present culture would generally take that meaning to be."[172] An appeal to tradition would not successfully avoid relativism, however; the best it could hope for is to limit the range of correct interpretations for some narrow and fleeting moment in time. As Hirsch says, "tradition cannot really function as a stable, normative concept, since it is in fact a changing, descriptive concept."[173] Even if we were content with the stability that tradition could provide in avoiding relativism for the moment, that stability would prove to be an illusion. There is no guaranteed uniformity of agreement or opinion among members of a tradition as to what a text means at any given moment. To think otherwise is to commit the fallacy of homogenous present-day perspective.[174] As Hirsch says, "The saving concepts of *Mitsein* and *Tradition* are mirages. Even though there are always shared elements in a culture which constitute its very substance, *all* men in a culture do not share the same general perspective on life, the same assumptions; they do not always speak in the same idiom."[175] When disagreements arise at a given moment between heirs of a tradition, there would be, for Gadamer, no hierarchical figure to whom we could appeal. Neither the author nor anyone else is accepted as such a figure, and as a result there does not seem to be a way to resolve the disagreement. The criterion of tradition would not save Gadamer's theory from relativism.

Though tradition would not succeed as a normative criterion, it is not likely that Gadamer intended it as such. Some of what he says might well lead one to think that accord with tradition is a normative matter, but in fact it is a descriptive one. Gadamer is describing the role tradition plays in our coming to understand a text. Schmidt argues that tradition is important because it provides us with prejudices (*Vorurteile*) that have been preserved through time and through numerous fusions of horizons. Such prejudices are, he claims, likely to be legitimate.[176] Hoy has a similar take on tradition. "Gadamer is frequently misread as saying that an interpretation must stay in contact with that tradition and that 'nontraditional' readings are therefore wrong. This interpretation of

Gadamer mistakes a *descriptive* claim about the nature of understanding for a *normative* one about what an understanding ought to do. What Gadamer in fact maintains is that often an interpretation will correct the traditional way of reading a text."[177] Again, Hoy puts the matter correctly.

Neither the candidate of "the text is the measure" nor the candidate of tradition is, or could function appropriately as, Gadamer's normative criterion. Let us, then, consider a third candidate. Schmidt argues that, for Gadamer, one understands a text correctly when one legitimizes one's prejudices (*Vorurteile*) and so arrives at an enlightening (*einleuchtende*) perspective (*Ansicht*) on the subject matter (*Sache selbst*).[178] Prejudices may be either correct or incorrect, though one does not know which until one brings them to bear in interpretation. As we saw, Schmidt argues that it is the function of the preconception of completion to allow those prejudices to be challenged, and so, if need be, corrected. Legitimate prejudices are those founded on the subject matter and not mere opinion.[179] Indeed Gadamer tells us that, "the goal of all attempts to reach an understanding is agreement concerning the subject matter."[180] How then does one come to give an interpretation that is based on legitimate prejudices and so gives an enlightening perspective on the subject matter?[181]

Although one must actively challenge one's prejudices by bringing them to bear in interpretation, there is still something passive about reaching the correct understanding. The subject matter is primary and comes to express itself. As Schmidt says, "the *correct* word or words which articulate the perspective of the *Sache selbst* in a particular human language have their justification in the power of the *Sache selbst* to express itself as the *Einleuchtende* (enlightening)."[182] The *Einleuchtende* is that which shines forth as true. Here we see the underlying passivity of Gadamer's hermeneutics and the relevance of his conception of truth as disclosure. "This self-presentation of the *Sache selbst* is what Heidegger termed *aletheia*."[183]

The *Sache selbst* that shines forth is not, however, absolute in its power. With changes in the linguistic view (*Sprachansicht*), the subject matter may demand a different expression. Still, within each linguistic view the interpretation that is the result of the enlightening perspective on the subject matter, that in which the subject matter shines forth and presents itself, is correct. As Schmidt says, "The *Sache selbst* is only partially expressed in its *Ansicht* yet as completely as the *Ansicht* allows and the *Sache selbst* does not change."[184] Again there is a connection to Gadamer's conception of truth and its ties to the beautiful. "Gadamer's reference to the classical metaphysical theories of the beautiful and the light was meant to demonstrate that the *Einleuchtende* does not require a further testing. . . . The experience of the *einleuchtende Ansicht* requires no further justification; it is enlightening."[185] Schmidt concludes, then, that for Gadamer the experience of the enlightening guarantees that the interpretation is correct.

Schmidt has, I would contend, successfully articulated Gadamer's normative criterion. Given the mistakes made by others and the difficulty in piecing together what Gadamer has said, this is no small achievement. Schmidt goes beyond just articulating this criterion, however, and endorses it. For Schmidt, to ask what one should believe is to presume that what was experienced was not enlightening.[186] When one experiences the enlightening one knows it is true, and indeed it is. I cannot share his endorsement. As Grondin has argued, not every enlightening interpretation is correct; the enlightening and the beautifully said may conceal a falsity. The experience of truth is always only probable and so requires further dialogue.[187] As I argued against the conception of truth as disclosure, not everything which "discloses" itself to us is true. Even if everything that *genuinely* disclosed itself to us were true, we would still be left with the problem of not knowing for certain when something had *genuinely* disclosed itself to us. Further, even if this problem were somehow resolved, relativism would still loom over Gadamer's theory. The idea of a linguistic view causes some trouble. How long does a linguistic view last? Who belongs to the same view? In what sense do different languages constitute different views?[188] If an interpretation is only correct within a given linguistic view we will then have a vast plurality of correct interpretations. Relativism will not follow of necessity, but it would be difficult to avoid. The linguistic view as a normative criterion has many of the same problems that tradition, as a normative criterion, would have.

If we do not accept Gadamer's normative criterion as explicated by Schmidt, are there any other viable alternatives? Weinsheimer asserts that, for Gadamer, "Whether an interpretation is true is a matter of taste."[189] I would contend that, although we could argue for some objective grounding of taste, this criterion is certain to allow for a vast plurality of "true" interpretations, likely including contradictory ones. And so this criterion will lead to interpretive relativism. Inasmuch as Gadamer wants to avoid relativism and inasmuch as I have argued against relativism, I do not accept that this is Gadamer's normative criterion nor, in any case, do I accept it as valid. We conclude, then, that Schmidt has correctly identified Gadamer's normative criterion, and that, although it is more tenable than other proposed Gadamerian criteria, it too fails.

Aside from offering a criterion for correct interpretation, Gadamer strays from the descriptive into the normative in other ways as well. In his description of understanding as involving application Gadamer raises a normative issue. As Hirsch says, "The fundamental distinction overlooked by Gadamer is that between the meaning of a text and the significance of that meaning to a present situation."[190] It would be more correct, however, to say not that he overlooks the distinction but that he does not believe it exists. Interpretive understanding, as Gadamer describes it, always involves application to our present situation—it always already involves what Hirsch calls significance. Gadamer has overstated the terms of his description and consequently has obscured an important normative issue. It may well be that we ordinarily apply what we are trying to understand to our own situation, but this does not mean that we necessarily do so. Our understanding is not as necessarily historical as Gadamer argues; we can understand the past without applying it to the present. Particularly when we see some value in understanding apart from application—in seeking meaning apart from significance—we can bracket our current situation and understand the text's meaning as it is in itself.

While it is a formidable task to show that we can bracket in understanding in the way I suggest, the consequences of not doing so suggest that bracketing is indeed possible. We postulate that a text remains identical through time,[191] and our argument takes the form of a *reductio ad absurdum*. If we cannot bracket and thus find the meaning itself we cannot establish textual identity, there must be textual identity, and so bracketing must be possible. Gadamer insists that application is a necessary part of understanding because we can never understand a text apart from our own situatedness; we cannot bracket our situation and understand the text's meaning apart from its application. The result is that every understanding of a given text is a different understanding. Gadamer likens this to an annual festival that is always the same yet always different.[192] As Wachterhauser has pointed out, however, this festival is really the same in name only. Is a text, then, the same in name only across its many interpretations? Two texts can of course be identical in terms of the marks on the page that represent them and still be different texts. Is it the case, then, that every time we interpret a text we create a new text? Although some literary theorists[193] would embrace the idea that we create a new text with each interpretation, Gadamer would not. As he says, "We saw that to understand a text always means to apply it to ourselves and to know that, even if it must always be understood in different ways, it is still the same text presenting itself to us in these different ways."[194] Gadamer cannot maintain both that understanding necessarily implies application and that texts maintain their identity across interpretations. Giving up textual identity implies an extreme relativism that Gadamer would not accept, and so the only tenable option is to admit that understanding is possible apart from application. Across our various interpretations some core part of our understanding is independent of any application to our own situation. It is, of course, possible that one would opt for defending the theory that each interpretation generates a new text, but that is not an option Gadamer would take. And so we will not consider it further.

Gadamer's remarks on the nature of writing, though descriptive in nature, have clear normative import.

[A]ll writing is a kind of alienated speech, and its signs need to be transformed back into speech and meaning. Because the meaning has undergone a kind of self-alienation through being written down, this transformation back is the real hermeneutical task.[195]

What is fixed in writing has detached itself from the contingency of its origin and its author and made itself free for new relationships. *Normative* concepts such as the author's meaning or the original reader's understanding in fact represent only an empty space that is filled from time to time in understanding.[196]

Gadamer's claim that writing is self-alienating speech, and so is detached from its author, bears a strong resemblance to the positions of Foucault and Barthes. As we argued in detail in chapter 2, however, such a conception of writing is flawed. It treats a text as if it did not have an author, and a text without an author is no text at all. Gadamer's descriptive claim that writing is self-alienation is once again an overstated claim, and in this case it supports a normative claim—that texts mean what they appear to say apart from their authors—which is false.

PROSPECTUS

Having examined both the normative and descriptive approaches to hermeneutics, we turn now to the task of harmonizing them. Should one approach have priority over the other? Can the two coexist in a single interpretive effort? What ethical considerations do we need to be aware of?

NOTES

1. Cf. Jean Grondin, "Hermeneutics and Relativism," in Kathleen Wright ed., *Festivals of Interpretation: Essays on Hans-Georg Gadamer's Work* (Albany: SUNY Press, 1990), p. 44.

2. Hans Georg Gadamer, *Truth and Method* (New York: Continuum, 1989) Second Edition. Trans. Joel Weinsheimer and Donald G. Marshall, p. xxx (hereafter *TM*).

3. *TM*, p. 164; *Wahrheit und Methode* (Tübingen: J.C.B. Mohr, 1972) 3. Auflage, p. 157 (hereafter *WM*). Emphasis added.

4. *TM*, p. 388; *WM*, p. 366.

5. *TM*, p. 389; *WM*, p. 366.

6. For an excellent discussion of Gadamer on method and its limits see Joel C. Weinsheimer, *Gadamer's Hermeneutics: A Reading of Truth and Method* (New Haven: Yale University Press, 1985), pp. 4–59. "Gadamer's central thesis [is]: truth cannot be limited to what is confirmable by method" (p. 41). See also Jean Grondin, *Introduction to Philosophical Hermeneutics* (New Haven: Yale University Press, 1994). "Gadamer first retorted that he never intended any sharp opposition between truth and method. Certainly truth can be achieved by way of method. What he considered dubious was merely the claim on the part of modern methodical consciousness to a monopoly, its dogmatic assertion that there can be no truth outside of method" (p. 132). In addition, see Lawrence K. Schmidt, *The Epistemology of Hans-Georg Gadamer: An Analysis of the Legitimization of Vorurteile* (Frankfurt: Peter D. Lang, 1985). (hereafter *The Epistemology of Hans-Georg Gadamer*). "Gadamer's thesis is that the use of any method can only occur within the historically determined situation and that this situation is prior to and so prevents any claim to absolute objectivity by a method" (p. 152).

7. *TM*, p. xxviii. Emphasis added.

8. *TM*, p. 512, supplement "Hermeneutics and Historicism." Emphasis in the original, except for on the words "describing" and "describe"; *WM*, p. 483, "Hermeneutik und Historismus."

9. *TM*, p. 512, supplement "Hermeneutics and Historicism"; *WM*, p. 484, "Hermeneutik und Historismus." Emphasis in the original.

10. *TM*, p. 292; *WM*, p. 276. This is said in reference to Schleiermacher's Romantic hermeneutics.

11. While I shall respect Gadamer's approach, which rejects propositional logic in favor of the logic of question and answer characteristic of dialogue, I do not find that he has argued for it sufficiently. Grondin summarizes Gadamer's position well when he says, "Against the primacy of propositional logic, which conceives—or, rather, misconceives—understanding as something at our disposal, Gadamer elaborates a logic of question and answer that understands understanding as participation—participation in meaning, a tradition, and ultimately a dialogue" (p. 119). As Schmidt points out, "It is historical life, not logical consistency, which is the final arbiter and ground of truth. That is Gadamer's thesis" (p. 59).

12. *TM*, p. 474; *WM*, p. 450. Emphasis in the original.

13. Cf. *TM*, pp. 269–270; *WM*, pp. 254–255; and Lawrence K. Schmidt, "Introduction: Between Certainty and Relativism," in *The Specter of Relativism: Truth, Dialogue, and Phronesis in Philosophical Hermeneutics* (Evanston, IL: Northwestern University Press, 1995), p. 4. See also Lawrence K. Schmidt, "The Enlightening Perspective: A Hermeneutic Truth Criterion," *Southwest Philosophical Studies* 10 (1988), p. 84.

14. *TM*, p. 297; *WM*, p. 281.

15. *TM*, p. xxx.

16. Martin Heidegger, *Being and Time* (San Francisco: HarperCollins, 1962), trans. John Macquarrie and Edward Robinson, p. 182 (hereafter *BT*). Heidegger, *Sein und Zeit* (Tübingen: Max Niemeyer Verlag, 1967) 11. Auflage, pp. 142–143 (hereafter *SZ*). Emphasis in the original.

17. For Heidegger there is no understanding without interpretation. Interpretation does not necessarily add to understanding, but rather clarifies (*auslegen*) what is to be understood. Cf. *BT*, pp. 188–189; *SZ*, p. 148. For someone who disagrees see Stanley Rosen, "Horizontverschmelzung," in Lewis Edwin Hahn ed., *The Philosophy of Hans-Georg Gadamer* (La Salle, IL: Open Court, 1997), p. 211. Rosen suggests that to interpret we must first understand.

18. *BT*, p. 182; *SZ*, p. 143, "Dasein ist Seiendes, dem als In-der-Welt-sein um es selbst geht."

19. *BT*, pp. 184–185; *SZ*, p. 145. Emphasis in the original.

20. This is perhaps more characteristic of the later Heidegger's understanding of *Dasein*.

21. *TM*, p. 264; *WM*, p. 249.

22. *TM*, p. 257; *WM*, p. 243.

23. *TM*, p. 266; *WM*, p. 250.

24. Jorge J.E. Gracia, *A Theory of Textuality: The Logic and Epistemology* (Albany: SUNY Press, 1995), pp. 189–214. Gracia argues that we learn the meaning of a text on the basis of expected behavior taken in context (hereafter *ATT*).

25. Heidegger's description of the fore-structure of understanding is brief and difficult to grasp. Fortunately, an intimate acquaintance with it is not necessary in order to grasp Gadamer's conception of prejudice, which is far more central to our concerns in this study. However, those who seek further explanation of Heidegger's fore-structure would do well to consult Michael Gelven, *A Commentary on Heidegger's Being and Time* Revised Edition (Dekalb, IL: Northern Illinois University Press, 1989), pp. 95–97. Here Gelven gives a lucid exposition and example of the fore-structure as applied to car trouble. Gelven also points out that in *BT* section 63 Heidegger uses the fore-structure in the interpretation of the question of Being.

26. *BT*, p. 191; *SZ*, p. 150. Emphasis in the original.

27. "Any interpretation which is to contribute understanding, must already have understood what is to be interpreted" (*BT*, p. 194; *SZ*, p. 152).

28. *BT*, p. 195; *SZ*, p. 153. Emphasis in the original.

29. *BT*, p. 195; *SZ*, p. 153.

30. Hans-Georg Gadamer, "On the Circle of Understanding" in John M. Connolly and Thomas Keutner ed., *Hermeneutics Versus Science?: Three German Views* (Notre Dame, IN: Notre Dame University Press, 1988), p. 71. Emphasis added. Gadamer, "Vom Zirkel des Verstehens," in *Kleine Schriften vol. IV Variationen* (Tübingen: J.C.B. Mohr, 1977), p. 56.

31. *TM*, p. xxi; *WM*, p. xxvii.

32. Cf. Weinsheimer, pp. 1–59.

33. Ibid., p. 19.

34. Ibid., p. 41. Grondin explains the relationship between truth and method similarly, though more adequately recognizing that the two are not diametrically opposed.

"Gadamer first retorted that he never intended any sharp opposition between truth and method. Certainly truth can be achieved by way of method. What he considered dubious was merely the claim on the part of modern methodical consciousness to a monopoly, its dogmatic assertion that there can be no truth outside of method" (p. 132).

35. Heidegger resists labeling the experience of truth as passive; letting disclosure occur, he thinks, is actually quite active. Cf. Martin Heidegger, "On the Essence of Truth," in David Farrell Krell ed., *Martin Heidegger: Basic Writings* (New York: Harper and Row, Publishers, 1977), pp. 117–141; "Vom Wesen der Wahrheit," in *Wegmarken* (Frankfurt am Main: Vittorio Klostermann Verlag, 1967), pp. 73–97. "[T]o let beings be—does not refer to neglect and indifference but rather the opposite. To let be is to engage oneself with beings" (p. 127). Despite Heidegger's protests, there is something undeniably passive about the role of the subject in this conception of truth. This becomes all the more clear, as we shall see, in Gadamer's appropriation of truth as disclosure. Cf. Lawrence K. Schmidt, "Recalling the Hermeneutic Circle," *Philosophy Today* 40 (1996), p. 270. "Into this openness the truth shines forth as enlightening. In accepting this truth the conversants may be said to be more passive and the subject matter to be more active" (p. 270).

36. *TM*, p. 529, supplement "Hermeneutics and Historicism"; *WM*, p. 500, "Hermeneutik und Historismus."

37. Hans-Georg Gadamer, *Philosophical Hermeneutics* (Berkeley: University of California Press, 1976), trans. and ed. David Linge, "Aesthetics and Hermeneutics," p. 101. Emphasis added. Gadamer, "Ästhetik und Hermeneutik," *Kleine Schriften II Interpretationen* (Tübingen: J.C.B. Mohr, 1967), p. 6.

38. *BT*, pp. 256–273; *SZ*, pp. 212–230. Heidegger also discusses his conception of truth in some of his later essays, and we shall consider these as well. Cf. "On the Essence of Truth." "Plato's Doctrine of Truth," in William Barrett and Henry D. Aiken eds., *Philosophy in the Twentieth Century* vol. 3 (New York: Random House, 1962), pp. 251–270; *Platons Lehre von der Wahrheit. Mit einen Brief über den "Humanismus"* (Bern: A. Francke, 1947). Cf. "The End of Philosophy and the Task of Thinking," in David Farrell Krell ed., *Martin Heidegger: Basic Writings* (New York: Harper and Row, 1977), pp. 373–392; *Zur Sache des Denkens* (Tübingen: Max Niemeyer Verlag, 1969), pp. 61–80.

39. *BT*, pp. 258–259; *SZ*, p. 216. Emphasis in the original.

40. *BT*, p. 265; *SZ*, p. 222. Emphasis in the original.

41. *BT*, p. 260; *SZ*, p. 217.

42. *BT*, p. 262; *SZ*, p. 220. Emphasis in the original.

43. *BT*, p. 264; *SZ*, p. 222. Emphasis in the original.

44. *BT*, p. 265; *SZ*, p. 222. Emphasis in the original.

45. "On the Essence of Truth," p. 125.

46. Ibid., p. 127.

47. Ibid.

48. Ibid., p. 128.

49. "Plato's Doctrine of Truth," pp. 265–266.

50. Cf. *The Epistemology of Hans-Georg Gadamer*, p. 235.

51. *TM*, p. 106; *WM*, pp. 101–102.

52. *TM*, pp. 105–106; *WM*, p. 101.

53. *TM*, p. 103; *WM*, p. 98.

54. *TM*, p. 109; *WM*, p. 104.

55. *TM*, p. 112; *WM*, p. 107. Emphasis added.

56. *TM*, p. 114; *WM*, p. 109.

57. Georgia Warnke, *Gadamer: Hermeneutics, Tradition and Reason* (Stanford, CA: Stanford University Press, 1987), p. 86.

58. Cf. Jean Grondin, *Hermeneutische Wahrheit? Zum Wahrheitsbegriff Hans-Georg Gadamers* (Königsten/Ts.: Verlag Anton Hain Meisenheim, Forum Academicum, 1982), pp. 91–92. Grondin argues correctly that Gadamer accepts Heidegger's conception of truth but adds to it Platonic and Neo-Platonic conceptions of the beautiful.

59. *TM*, p. 490; *WM*, p. 465.

60. *TM*, p. 311; *WM*, p. 295. For a predecessor to this account see Augustine, *On Free Will*, Bk. II.

61. Cf. *TM*, p. 370; *WM*, p. 352. Gadamer endorses Collingwood's claim that, "We can understand a text only when we have understood the question to which it is an answer."

62. Warnke, p. 11.

63. *Erfahrung* can mean experience in which expectation is thwarted. Gadamer is fond of using *Erfahrung* in this Hegelian sense. Cf. Hans-Georg Gadamer, "Reply to Robert Sokolowski," in Lewis Edwin Hahn ed., *The Philosophy of Hans-Georg Gadamer* (La Salle, IL: Open Court, 1997), pp. 235–236. "To have an experience means to have a new experience. An experience which confirms itself is not experienced as such" (p. 235). *Erfahrung* can also be used in a more ordinary sense. It is, though, to be distinguished from *Erlebnis*, "lived" experience—that which is gone through. There is, of course, some debate as to the precise distinction between *Erfahrung* and *Erlebnis*, but this is certainly no place to attempt settling the debate.

64. *BT*, p. 266; *SZ*, p. 224.

65. Cf. Karl-Otto Apel, "Regulative Ideas or Truth Happening?: An Attempt to Answer the Question of the Conditions of the Possibility of Valid Understanding," in Lewis Edwin Hahn ed., *The Philosophy of Hans-Georg Gadamer* (La Salle, IL: Open Court, 1997), p. 71. We should note that it was Ernst Tugendhat who first argued so forcefully for this.

66. Correspondence and coherence theories of truth have their problems as well. One is subject to error with them too, but when one is wrong it is more clearly the fault of the agent rather than the theory. Inasmuch as disclosure is ineluctably bound to the agent, it cannot account for error in the same way.

67. "The End of Philosophy and the Task of Thinking," pp. 388–389. Emphasis added on "not yet truth." Cf. Apel, p. 72.

68. "The End of Philosophy and the Task of Thinking," p. 389. Emphasis added on the final sentence. Cf. Apel, p. 72.

69. "The End of Philosophy and the Task of Thinking," pp. 389–390. Cf. Apel, pp. 72–73.

70. At least if it is taken, as it seems meant, in universal terms.

71. *TM*, p. 490; *WM*, p. 465.

72. Lawrence K. Schmidt, "When the Text Speaks the Truth: The Preconception of Completion," *The Southern Journal of Philosophy* 25 (1987), pp. 396–397.

73. E.D. Hirsch, Jr., *Validity in Interpretation* (New Haven: Yale University Press, 1967), p. 256 (hereafter *VI*). Even if Hirsch is mistaken about Heidegger's view here, Heidegger does commit himself to another view that can be refuted. Namely, he implicitly rejects the view that understanding is ever really a matter of reproduction. Thanks to David Weberman for this point.

74. *TM*, p. 374; *WM*, p. 356.

75. Cf. *TM*, p. 302; *WM*, p. 286.

76. Cf. Weinsheimer, "Horizon is another way of describing context. It includes everything of which one is not immediately aware and of which one must in fact remain unaware if there is to be a focus of attention; but one's horizon is also the context in terms of which the object of attention is understood" (p. 157).

77. *TM*, p. 302; *WM*, p. 286.

78. *TM*, p. 305; *WM*, pp. 288–289.

79. Cf. Jan Edward Garrett, "Hans-Georg Gadamer on 'Fusion of Horizons,'" *Man and World* 11 (1978), pp. 392–398.

80. *TM*, p. 306; *WM*, p. 289. Emphasis in the original.

81. *TM*, p. 296; *WM*, p. 280.

82. *TM*, p. 309; *WM*, p. 292. Emphasis added. At most, Gadamer sees the reconstruction of authorial intention as an auxiliary operation, a *Hilfsoperation*. Thanks to David Weberman for this point.

83. Cf. Weinsheimer, "Being thrown means that prejudice is not merely prior to consciousness but is its condition. We understand our world before we begin to think about it; such pre-understanding gives rise to thought and always conditions it" (pp. 10–11).

84. Gadamer sometimes speaks of *Voreingenommenheiten* rather than *Vorurteile*. This has the advantage of acknowledging our situatedness is not always expressed in explicit judgments, but often comes in the form of opaque commitments to practices and assumptions. Thanks to David Weberman for this point.

85. *TM*, p. 306; *WM*, p. 289.

86. *TM*, p. 270; *WM*, p. 255.

87. *TM*, p. 270; *WM*, p. 255.

88. *TM*, p. 276; *WM*, p. 260.

89. *TM*, p. 270; *WM*, p. 254.

90. *TM*, p. 295; *WM*, p. 279. Cf. Schmidt, *The Epistemology of Hans-Georg Gadamer*, p. 90. Schmidt speaks of unconscious *Vorurteile*.

91. *TM*, pp. 295–296; *WM*, p. 279.

92. *TM*, p. 299; *WM*, p. 283.

93. *TM*, p. 269; *WM*, pp. 253–254.

94. *TM*, p. 273; *WM*, p. 257.

95. Warnke, p. 91.

96. *TM*, p. 270; *WM*, p. 254.

97. Cf. Schmidt, *The Epistemology of Hans-Georg Gadamer*, "Of all that constitutes *Überlieferung*, the written word has a priority, since it transcends the particular circumstances of its creation" (p. 149).

98. *TM*, p. 161; *WM*, p. 154.

99. *TM*, p. 282; *WM*, p. 266.

100. *TM*, p. 296; *WM*, p. 280.

101. Warnke, p. 103.

102. *TM*, p. 293; *WM*, p. 277.

103. *TM*, p. 361; *WM*, p. 343.

104. *TM*, p. xxxvii.

105. *TM*, p. 297; *WM*, p. 281.

106. This is the point at which Hirsch and Gadamer make their fundamental break. Hirsch sees historical reconstruction as very difficult but not impossible. It is still quite worthwhile even if we cannot be certain that it has been achieved. Gadamer sees historical reconstruction as impossible and so not worthwhile.

107. Cf. *ATT*, pp. 104–105.

108. Habermas, too, believes that we can counteract our prejudices. Reflective consciousness can escape the historical conditioning of understanding. For a discussion of the early exchanges between Gadamer and Habermas see David Couzens Hoy, *The Critical Circle: Literature, History, and Philosophical Hermeneutics* (Berkeley: University of California Press, 1978).

109. *VI*, p. 256.

110. *ATT*, pp. 104–105.

111. Cf. *VI*, p. 169.

112. *TM*, p. 164; *WM*, p. 156.

113. Cf. Joel Weinsheimer and Donald G. Marshall, "Translator's Preface," *TM*, p. xv. Cf. Warnke, pp. 79–81. Cf. Weinsheimer, *Gadamer's Hermeneutics*, p. x.

114. Cf. Brice Wachterhauser, "Interpreting Texts: Objectivity or Participation?" *Man and World* 19 (1986), p. 444.

115. *TM*, pp. 299–300; *WM*, p. 283. Emphasis added.

116. *TM*, p. 301; *WM*, p. 285.

117. It is often noted that *Wirkungsgeschichtliches Bewusstsein* is more being than consciousness. The interpreter is not aware of all the *Vorurteile* which effect him. Cf. *The Epistemology of Hans-Georg Gadamer*, p. 208.

118. *TM*, p. 489; *WM*, p. 463.

119. This is not to say that Gadamer dismisses all traditional ways of coming to understand a text or that he cares not at all for historical understanding. The human sciences "must endeavor to acquire as much historical self-transparency as possible" (*TM*, p. xxiv). Of course he would hold that this self-transparency can never be complete. Cf. *The Epistemology of Hans-Georg Gadamer*, p. 74.

120. *TM*, p. 341; *WM*, p. 324.

121. *TM*, p. 297; *WM*, p. 280.

122. The question of whether all applications are equally acceptable is a normative concern that we shall take up in the section to follow on Gadamer's normativism. Schmidt argues that applications are legitimate or illegitimate based on the *Vorurteile* that help to produce them. Cf. *The Epistemology of Hans-Georg Gadamer*, pp. 87 and 113.

123. *TM*, p. 341; *WM*, p. 323.

124. *TM*, pp. 312–324; *WM*, pp. 295–307.

125. I owe this point to Wachterhauser, p. 445.

126. *TM*, p. 290; *WM*, pp. 274–275. Emphasis in the original.

127. Wachterhauser, p. 454.

128. Carl Page, "Historicistic Finitude and Philosophical Hermeneutics," in Lewis Edwin Hahn ed., *The Philosophy of Hans-Georg Gadamer* (La Salle, IL: Open Court, 1997), p. 380. Page makes the point that mathematical knowledge serves well as a counterexample to attempts to reduce the activity of understanding to its contingent circumstances.

129. Demonstrating this through examples would take us too far afield. In fact, though, this has already been established in principle by the arguments of chapter 3.

130. Rosen, p. 212.

131. Page agrees that there is no necessity in Gadamer's claim that we must always understand in a different way. "A single example of insight, a single *unzietgemässige Betrachtung*, ruins philosophical historicism's deflationary program" (p. 380). On the other hand, Hirsch has come to moderate his own stance on application and significance. Cf. "Meaning and Significance Reinterpreted," *Critical Inquiry* 11 (1984), p. 210.

132. *TM*, p. 378; *WM*, p. 360.

133. *TM*, p. 403; *WM*, p. 381.

134. *TM*, p. 378; *WM*, p. 359. Emphasis in the original.

135. *TM*, p. 401; *WM*, p. 379.

136. *TM*, p. 547, supplement 2, "To What Extent Does Language Perform Thought?"

137. *TM*, p. 474; *WM*, p. 450.

138. *TM*, p. 475; *WM*, p. 450.

139. Hans-Georg Gadamer, "Text and Interpretation," in Brice R. Wachterhauser ed., *Hermeneutics and Modern Philosophy* (Albany: SUNY Press, 1986) p. 382; "Text und Interpretation," in Phillipe Forget ed., *Text und Interpretation* (München: Wilhelm Fink

Verlag, 1984), p. 29. I believe he means it cannot be understood either in itself or apart from language.

140. *The Epistemology of Hans-Georg Gadamer*, p. 145.

141. *Philosophical Hermeneutics*, "On the Scope and Function of Hermeneutical Reflection," p. 31. Emphasis added.

142. *TM*, p. 475; *WM*, p. 450.

143. *TM*, p. 417; *WM*, p. 394.

144. *The Epistemology of Hans-Georg Gadamer*, p. 153.

145. The connections among play, truth as disclosure, and textual interpretation are further clarified here. Cf. Weinsheimer, "As light becomes visible itself only when it makes something else visible, so being manifests itself (and is) only in the historical process of disclosing beings that can be understood—that is, in language. This process is the continuing event of truth, *aletheia*, the self-revelation of being that speaks directly to historical men living in diverse times and places. . . . Being presents itself in the light of words which reflect it as it truly is, just as beauty is revealed in what makes it beautiful" (p. 257).

146. Language, according to Gadamer, transcends all its individual usages. The doctrine of the "ideality of the word" holds that words have an objective range of meanings independent of the acts in which they originate. Thanks to David Weberman for discussion on this point.

147. *TM*, p. 446; *WM*, p. 422.

148. *TM*, p. 383; *WM*, p. 361.

149. *TM*, p. 474; *WM*, p. 449.

150. *TM*, p. 453; *WM*, p. 429.

151. *TM*, p. 546, supplement 2, "To What Extent Does Language Perform Thought?" Jürgen Habermas, "The Hermeneutic Claim to Universality," trans. Josef Bleicher, in Josef Bleicher ed., *Contemporary Hermeneutics: Hermeneutics as Method, Philosophy and Culture* (London: Routledge and Kegan Paul, 1980), pp. 181–211.

152. *TM*, p. 547, supplement 2, "To What Extent Does Language Perform Thought?" Gadamer and Heidegger could, and perhaps do, claim that facial and bodily expression is a kind of language. But this would be strange and would make the umbrella of language far too broad.

153. *The Epistemology of Hans-Georg Gadamer*, p.176.

154. Hans-Georg Gadamer, "Replik," in Jürgen Habermas et al. eds., *Hermeneutik und Ideologiekritik* (Frankfurt am Main: Suhrkamp, 1971), p. 291. Cf. *The Epistemology of Hans-Georg Gadamer*, p. 176.

155. *The Epistemology of Hans-Georg Gadamer*, pp. 176–177.

156. Gadamer has (somewhat recently) admitted that this is quite common. Cf. "Reply to Carl Page," in Lewis Edwin Hahn ed., *The Philosophy of Hans-Georg Gadamer* (La Salle, IL: Open Court, 1997), pp. 385–387. "That constitutes the real question of hermeneutic experience: that the words we seek and find, be it in our daily dealings, be it in a thoughtful conversation, are never able to convey exactly what we wanted to say" (p. 386).

157. This is what I have called criticism or non-urinterpretation. We shall look at it in detail in chapter 5.

158. Cf. D. Michelfelder and R.E. Palmer eds., *Dialogue and Deconstruction: The Gadamer-Derrida Encounter* (Albany: SUNY Press, 1989).

159. Please do not misunderstand; I do not disapprove of metaphors. (In fact, I think they're the cat's meow!) I simply do not find metaphor a sufficient ground for the argument here.

160. This, I would suggest, is the result of Gadamer's own lack of clarity and tendency to overcomplicate matters. Cf. *Philosophische Lehrjahre: Eine Rückschau* (Frankfurt am

Main: Klostermann, 1977). In reference to his early teaching career Gadamer says, "My friends had even invented a new scientific unit: it was called a 'Gad' and designated a certain measure of unnecessary complexity" (p. 46). Cf. Weinsheimer, p. x, who adds, "Even *Truth and Method*, it is not disrespectful to say, is perhaps too complex by a Gad or two." Considering the difficulty that even Gadamer's students and followers have had in identifying his criterion for correct interpretation, I would suggest that *Truth and Method* is actually a Gad or two, or three *too* complex—at least with respect to this issue.

161. Hans-Georg Gadamer, "Wahrheit in den Geisteswissenschaften," *Kleine Schriften I Philosophie, Hermeneutik*, p. 42 (Cf. Warnke trans. p. 81).

162. Wachterhauser, pp. 449–450.

163. Karl-Otto Apel, *Transformation der Philosophie*. 2 vols. (Frankfurt am Main: Suhrkamp, 1973), pp. I: 47, and II: 216–217. Apel also takes the preconception of completion to be Gadamer's normative criterion. For a discussion of this see *The Epistemology of Hans-Georg Gadamer*, pp. 54–56.

164. *TM*, p. 291; *WM*, p. 275.

165. In an ethical way.

166. Cf. Wachterhauser, p. 449. Cf. *The Epistemology of Hans-Georg Gadamer*, p. 46.

167. *The Epistemology of Hans-Georg Gadamer*, p. 47.

168. Ibid., p. 52.

169. David C. Hoy, "Interpreting the Law: Hermeneutical and Poststructuralist Perspectives," in Sanford Levinson and Steven Mailoux eds., *Interpreting Law and Literature: A Hermeneutic Reader* (Evanston, IL: Northwestern University Press, 1988) p. 325.

170. *VI*, p. 257. Habermas has also taken Gadamer to be asserting accord with tradition as a normative criterion. For a discussion of this see *The Epistemology of Hans-Georg Gadamer*, pp. 37–41.

171. *TM*, p. 397; *WM*, p. 375. Emphasis added.

172. *VI*, p. 250.

173. Ibid.

174. E.D. Hirsch, Jr., *The Aims of Interpretation* (Chicago: University of Chicago Press, 1976), p. 41.

175. *VI*, p. 257.

176. *The Epistemology of Hans-Georg Gadamer*, p. 77.

177. Hoy (1988), p. 320. Emphasis added.

178. *The Epistemology of Hans-Georg Gadamer*, p. 189.

179. Ibid., pp. 158–159.

180. *TM*, p. 292; *WM*, p. 276.

181. Gadamer begs the question in assuming that it is always, or even most commonly, the subject matter that interests us most. We frequently read texts not so much because we are interested in the subject matter, as we do because we are intrigued by the author. As Tolstoy says of his reading Maupassant, "What sort of man are you? Wherein are you different from all the people I know, and what can you tell me that is new, about how we must look at this life of ours?" *Writings on Art* (London: Oxford University Press, 1924), p. 64. Cf. Francis Sparshott, "The Case of the Unreliable Author," *Philosophy and Literature* 10 (1986), p. 146.

182. *The Epistemology of Hans-Georg Gadamer*, p. 178.

183. Ibid., p. 180.

184. Ibid., p. 196.

185. Ibid., p. 220.

186. Ibid.

187. Grondin, *Hermeneutische Wahrheit?*, pp. 165–166, 191–192.

188. *The Epistemology of Hans-Georg Gadamer*, p. 236. Schmidt raises these questions himself in closing his study. He does not answer them but suggests they are important for the continuing discussion of philosophical hermeneutics.

189. Weinsheimer, p. 111.

190. *VI*, p. 255.

191. Some might disagree. Cf. David Weberman, "The Nonfixity of the Historical Past," *Review of Metaphyscics* 50 (1997), pp. 749–768.

192. *TM*, pp. 122–123; WM, p. 117. Wachterhauser makes a similar argument, and I am indebted to him for it. Cf. pp. 452–453.

193. Stanley Fish, *Is There a Text in This Class? The Authority of Interpretive Communities* (Cambridge, MA: Harvard University Press, 1980), and Wolfgang Iser, "The Reading Process: A Phenomenological Approach," in Jane P. Tompkins ed., *Reader Response Criticism* (Baltimore: Johns Hopkins University Press, 1980), pp. 50–69.

194. *TM*, p. 398; *WM*, p. 375.

195. *TM*, p. 393; *WM*, p. 371.

196. *TM*, p. 395; *WM*, p. 373. Emphasis added.

5

Conclusions and Implications

INTRODUCTION

We shall close the present study by reaching conclusions regarding the normative and descriptive approaches, as well as urinterpretation and non-urinterpretation. We shall find that the normative and descriptive approaches need not be at odds; they can, and indeed should, be taken separately on the theoretical level. This analysis will act as a springboard to our conclusion that urinterpretation and non-urinterpretation can coexist within the same hermeneutic examination. We shall then consider the implications of our account for the interpretation of philosophical, literary, and legal texts.

As we argued in chapter 3, the meaning of a text is what its author intended to communicate.[1] Sometimes authors attempt to simply communicate their thoughts, and other times they attempt to communicate more. An author may, for example, attempt to communicate, i.e., to bring about, an aesthetic experience.[2] We should also note that authorial intentions are not constricted or dictated by textual genres; it is a mistake to interpret all texts of a given genre in the same way. As we saw in chapter 3, each text is best approached as having its own intrinsic genre. Placing a text in a broad genre, for example poetry, may provide some important initial insights as to how best to learn its meaning, but coming to know the text's intrinsic genre, what exactly the author intended to communicate by it, is the key to unlocking the text's meaning. An author's intentions may be specific or vague, firmly grounded in the present or open to future applications,[3] productive of logical reasoning or of aesthetic experience. The list of possibilities is nearly endless. Each text is a unique production, yet we can speak with profit about some of the similarities within genres, of ways in which texts of a given genre should typically be approached. To be clear, we are simply drawing out the implications of our account and can offer only a beginning in each case. And certainly it would be desirable to consider a number of other textual types as well.[4] We are, however, constricted by the scope and limitations of the current project.

THE NORMATIVE AND DESCRIPTIVE APPROACHES

As we argued in chapter 1, and as our study has demonstrated, we can separate the normative and descriptive approaches on the theoretical level, that is, we can consider each separately. The reason for doing so is to facilitate work on each. Since the two are potentially separable, pragmatically speaking we lessen the difficulty of our overall task by approaching it in terms of two smaller and simpler tasks as opposed to one larger and more complex task.

As we saw in chapter 3, Hirsch is largely normative in his approach to hermeneutics. While there is a descriptive dimension to Hirsch's account, for the most part he is concerned with articulating his normative criterion for correct interpretation. We can, without much difficulty, remove the descriptive dimension from Hirsch's account, leaving it intact and indeed improving it. Further, our account of urinterpretation is an example of a purely normative approach to hermeneutics. As we saw in chapter 4, Gadamer is largely concerned with the descriptive approach to hermeneutics, with describing what occurs in interpretive understanding. Still, his account in *Truth and Method* includes a prominent normative dimension as well. This does not suggest, however, that a theory of descriptive hermeneutics cannot be articulated in isolation from a theory of normative hermeneutics. Indeed, one could remove the normative dimension from Gadamer's account and have just such a purely descriptive theory.

This study has defended a particular normative approach, urinterpretation, the central claim of which is that the meaning of a text is the author's intended communication. Importantly, it is not the author as person with whom we are concerned but the author as a particular mental construct, the urauthor, and it is through our conception of the urauthor that we seek meaning. This study has not provided, nor has it attempted to provide, a theory of descriptive hermeneutics, but has, instead, examined Gadamer's descriptive hermeneutics and offered pointed criticism of it. We shall leave for another time and for those more inclined to it, the project of rehabilitating descriptive hermeneutics. Let us offer one suggestion, however. This project may prove to be better pursued by cognitive psychologists and psycholinguists than by philosophers.[5] Gadamer, as a philosopher, has raised a wealth of descriptive issues and pioneered this uncharted territory, but it may well be prudent to see what other disciplines can contribute to a description of what occurs in interpretive understanding.

INTERPRETATION AND CRITICISM

As we suggested in chapter 3, we can speak of interpretation as the activity concerned with seeking the meaning rather than the significance of a text. The normative approach urinterpretation is, as we have argued, the correct way of seeking meaning.[6] Criticism is the activity that seeks the significance rather than the meaning of a text; it is a very broad and encompassing term. As Stein Haugom Olsen says, "criticism is an amorphous concept covering many types of different interest."[7] Non-urinterpretation, as articulated in chapter 3, is a catch-all for approaches that do not fit the mold of urinterpretation, including those approaches that by design seek significance and those that seek meaning but result instead in significance. To simplify matters, for the remainder of this study we shall, for the most part, leave aside the terminology of urinterpretation and non-urinterpretation and speak instead in terms of interpretation and criticism.

A single hermeneutic examination may often include both interpretation and criticism, and so let us examine the relationship between interpretation and criticism both in theory and in practice. Interpretation must have a certain primacy over criticism. As Olsen says, "In so far as any further comments on a literary work must be based on its proper understanding, interpretation must be said to be prior to criticism; considered as one of its parts, it is the most basic part."[8] There is some logical justification for this position, though the ultimate justification is an ethical one. Logically speaking there is reason to think that we must interpret a text, and so understand its meaning, before we can generate its significance. That is, how can we know the significance of a text if we do not know its meaning? There can, however, be a dialectical relationship between interpretation and criticism. A partial interpretation yielding a partial meaning may give way to criticism yielding significance, which may in turn lead back to further interpretation, and so on. This is somewhat akin to the description of the hermeneutic circle, which depicts understanding as mediating between part and whole.

Though there is a logical primacy of interpretation over criticism, it is not necessary in one important respect. As Juhl has argued against Hirsch's distinction between meaning and significance, "[A] critic who interprets a work as meaning something other than what the author intended is not as a rule relating the meaning which the author intended to something else; nor does his interpretation appear to presuppose any claim about what the author meant."[9] Juhl is correct to point out that criticism may in fact be based on something other than the author's intended communication, the meaning. Such criticism must be based on something, however; we cannot have significance with no ground in anything else. Even if what the significance is rooted in is not the author's meaning, it is rooted in something—some pseudo-meaning. Further, what such a hermeneutic examination generates is not meaning, as we have defined it, but rather significance. An interpretation does not need to be successful or accurate to be the basis for criticism. As we have argued above, some partial interpretation may precipitate a dialectic with criticism. There is also no logical reason that a complete misunderstanding could not precipitate such a dialectic or simply serve as the basis for criticism. The value of such criticism and the significance it generates would certainly be suspect, however.

This brings us to the ethical primacy of interpretation over criticism. In order to generate genuine significance through criticism, we must take care to understand the meaning of a text correctly through interpretation. As Hirsch explains the process, "A responsible interpreter (a) tries to understand the original meaning; (b) tries to *accommodate* that meaning to present circumstances; (c) tries to distinguish between an accommodation that remains true to the spirit of the original and one that does not."[10] As we shall see, one way of determining if a criticism is faithful to the meaning is to ask hypothetically: Would the author intend that sort of meaning in the present world?[11] We shall examine the place of such counterfactuals in our discussion of legal texts and, to a lesser extent, in our discussion of literary texts.

Without taking care to base our criticism on interpretation, we risk misrepresenting the author and deceiving our audience. Nazi philosophers notoriously produced such criticism of Nietzsche in support of their anti-Semitic final solution. Not all criticism based on misinterpretation need be so virulent, however. Most of us have had the experience of misunderstanding a text while generating significance through criticism that was of real personal value. On discovering that our interpretation was anachronistic or in some other way did not capture the meaning of the text, we were somewhat saddened that the personal significance we had generated no longer seemed to hold as well. Still, we can hold on to those significances if we do not put them forth to others or ourselves as stemming from the meaning of the text. A text of any sort can often be a valuable and productive heuristic aid even when misinterpreted. The trouble with this, as we have noted, lies in the ethical transgression of misrepresenting the author and deceiving the audience. If this transgression is avoided, no harm and frequently some good is done.[12]

That interpretation has a certain primacy over criticism does not imply that criticism does not have eminent value and importance. In a very real sense interpretation is just a beginning, although it is an essential beginning. Interpretation that captures the meaning of the text serves as the launchpad for productive criticism. Often the meaning of a text in and of itself is no longer of great interest. The significance that may take off from the meaning, however, may be quite interesting, important, and relevant. As Jeffrey Stout says, "Good commentary is whatever serves our interests and purposes."[13] Criticism is what keeps a text "alive" and spurs the further progress of ideas. In this way interpretation and criticism can peacefully coexist; in this way, to use our earlier terminology, urinterpretation and non-urinterpretation can coexist within the same hermeneutic examination. Let us turn now to a brief survey of interpretation and criticism in philosophical, literary, and legal texts.

PHILOSOPHICAL TEXTS

It is the intention of the author and not the genre of the text that determines correct interpretation. Authors of texts of a particular genre may often have intentions of the same general kind, for example specific rather than vague intentions. Still, it is in each case the author's intention and not the text's genre that determines correct interpretation. With this caveat in mind, however, we can still benefit from discussing the implications of our account for particular genres as they are typically conceived. Our remarks, then, are generalizations and not strict guidelines for interpreting texts along genre lines. We begin with the group of texts classified as philosophical.

A philosophical text is generally an attempt to communicate the thoughts of an author on a given subject (or subjects) of philosophical concern. What is of philosophical concern and even what philosophy itself is, are matters of debate, and this is not the place to settle them. Still, certain texts, for example Aristotle's

Metaphysics and Kant's *Critique of Pure Reason*, are undeniably philosophical.[14] Though philosophical texts may at times be purposely vague and broadly suggestive, they are usually meant to be representations of the thoughts of their authors. In fact, after having articulated her views a philosopher may actually pause to make her intentions clear.[15] As is the case with all criticism, one can make creative use of a philosophical text by generating significance. One should, and indeed must, however, acknowledge to one's audience that this is what one is doing. The value of such criticism can be great, but it can easily be overvalued as well. Readers of philosophy can draw their own significance from a text and will perhaps profit from this exercise more than if a significance were given to them through the work of another. The audience of a philosophical text is usually more in need of an interpretation than a criticism.

Few contemporary readers of Aristotle's *Metaphysics*, for example, will have the full training and background necessary to accurately obtain the meaning of the text. They will need the help of an interpreter who can, for example, place the text in context and clarify the important Greek terms. Once the readers have the meaning through the interpretation of an expert, they can responsibly produce their own criticism of the text. Of course the expert interpreter may have some valuable criticism to offer as well, but his most valuable contribution will usually be his interpretation of the text. We must also confront the fact that many or most hermeneutic examinations combine interpretation and criticism. This can be a precarious mix because it is often unclear to the audience, as well as to the interpreter, which part is interpretation and which part is criticism—that is, what is the meaning of the text and what is its significance. An interpreter must be very careful to keep the interpretive and critical aspects of his presentation distinct—first of all in his own mind, so that he may keep them distinct for his audience as well. Even with such effort, however, there is no guarantee that the interpretive and critical efforts will be kept fully separate for either the interpreter or his audience.

Although it may appear dull and sterile, a purely interpretive account may be a desirable solution. After having laid out the interpretive account, we are then prepared to offer criticism based on the meaning of the text. Of course one can always offer criticism that is not faithful to or derived from the meaning of the text, but one should be careful to acknowledge it as such.

The case of Plato is an interesting one in that he wrote dialogues rather than treatises, articles, or the like. In most philosophical texts the voice of the philosopher as author is generally clear. There may be some vagueness, ambiguity, even irony, but the project of constructing the urauthor is not an unusually daunting one. Not so in the case of Plato. By writing dialogues Plato has somewhat obscured his own voice—very likely because of his fear of the way in which the written word could be abused. Hence we get the fallacy of "Plato said." Plato never literally "said" anything in his dialogues, and in fact the name Plato is mentioned only three times in the entire Platonic corpus.[16] Of course Plato may "say" something through the characters of his dialogues, but there is no character Plato, and there is some difficulty in determining what Plato the author meant or said. This is certainly not an insurmountable difficulty, but it makes interpreting a Platonic text more like interpreting a literary text than is the case with most other philosophical texts. That is, interpreting Plato is in one way more akin to interpreting Shakespeare than Kant.

Kant's dry philosophical prose has none of the attempts to hide that are characteristic of Plato's dialogues. Nonetheless, it is not always clear what Kant meant; it takes hard work and attentive scholarship to interpret Kant correctly. Problems result when, for example, such hard work and attentive scholarship are bypassed in the name of "hermeneutical violence," as in the case of Heidegger who believed that some "hermeneutical violence" was necessary in ferreting out what the author left unsaid. The ethical problem with this approach is that very often an author leaves something unsaid because she does not mean it. For example, in his *Kant and the Problem of Metaphysics* Heidegger, with some effort, concludes that the real meaning of the *Critique of Pure Reason* is that it opens up the question of the finitude of man as the initial approach at Being.[17] This may well be a significance of the first *Critique*, especially in light of the third *Critique* and Heidegger's own work, but it is not, most would agree, the meaning of the text. Heidegger's ethical transgressions here include the misrepresentation of Kant and the deception of his audience. If Heidegger clearly acknowledged that what he was offering was not the meaning of the text but a significance, he would have been free from blame. By not doing so, however, he has wronged Kant and deceived his audience.[18]

In teaching philosophy we encounter many of the same problems as we do in writing. The audience, however, is likely to be quite different, and this may justify some practices in teaching that would be unethical in most writing. In teaching philosophy we are charged with making the subject matter interesting and accessible to students. This may, at times, include simplifications and applications of a text that would otherwise be unwarranted, but even those should not in general go without disclaimer. As teachers we should advise our students that at times we will be presenting simplifications that do not fit in all ways with the original. Sometimes we should make this point about a specific simplification, connection, or application we are making. We should also be clear about this for and to ourselves. When teaching Plato, for example, I do not believe that I know his meaning in every case, but part of the value of the Platonic dialogues is their significance. They remain important philosophical and pedagogical texts in part due to the extent to which they urge us to challenge our beliefs and force us to think.

LITERARY TEXTS

Criticism is an essential operation in keeping literary texts[19] fresh, alive, and read with each passing generation and era. In large measure this task of criticism falls on the shoulders of the teacher.[20] Shakespeare's *Macbeth*, for example, is foreign, odd, and inaccessible to the average high school student, and it is the job of the teacher to bring the text to life. Part of this will include interpretation, making the meaning clear through historical background and clarification of early modern English, but the more vital task is demonstrating the relevance of the text to our own time—showing that what Shakespeare wrote was indeed timeless. This need not be at odds with the meaning the author intends, however. As Hirsch says of Shakespeare's Sonnet 55 ("Not marble, nor the gilded monuments / Of princes, shall outlive this powerful rhyme."[21]), "The author's intention in this poem (and this is characteristic of literature, law, and religion) includes an intention to communicate effectively into the future."[22] This underscores the point that authors of literary texts may have intentions of various types. (Consider the case of Hermann Hesse, who makes clear that his *Steppenwolf* has been widely misinterpreted as a pessimistic book.[23]) An author's intention may be specific or vague, firmly grounded in the present or open to future applications, productive of logical reasoning or of aesthetic experience. The possibilities are nearly endless. As A.J. Close says, "Intentions in literature . . . include such non-tangible 'aims' as the cerebral Jamesian interest in presenting the ambiguous complexities of a moral issue or Quevedo's delight in the dramatic dissonances of a conceit."[24] Whatever the author intended to communicate is, as we have argued, the meaning of the text.

A literary text, as an effort to communicate, is a speech act.[25] As a speech act, the literary text involves an illocutionary act and a perlocutionary act. An illocutionary act has a certain conventional force and to be successful must secure uptake, bringing about an understanding of the meaning and the force of the locution.[26] This is to be distinguished from producing effects, which is characteristic of the perlocutionary act. A perlocutionary act is what we bring about or achieve by saying something, such as convincing, persuading, deterring, and surprising.[27] Often, then, the author of a literary text will intend a certain perloctutionary effect, and inasmuch as this is what she intends it is part of the meaning to be sought. Authors of literary texts are often concerned with producing aesthetic experiences in their audiences, and such experiences can be the intended perlocutionary effects of their texts. One may even, to some extent, judge the success of a literary work by the extent to which its perlocutionary effect is achieved. As Currie says, "success in the aesthetic sense is a matter of perlocutionary effect, not of illocutionary uptake."[28]

As was the case with teaching a philosophical text, in teaching a literary text we should indicate when what we are presenting is significance rather than meaning. In a written hermeneutic examination, criticism and interpretation will often be interwoven. This, too, should be properly indicated. There is an ethical transgression involved in presenting a significance of a text as if it were the meaning of the text; the author is misrepresented and the audience deceived. The author of a literary text may have broad, suggestive, and inclusive intentions, but surely these have their limits. Where the limits are is a difficult question to answer, and to some extent must be answered on a case-by-case basis.[29] Hirsch himself has come to express a similar view. As he says of future-directed intentions, their "purpose could embrace an indefinite number of future applications that no human being could foresee in precise detail."[30] We must approach such future-directed intentions on an individual basis. There will be cases in which a given interpretation no longer bears any resemblance to the author's intention, and such interpretations are not to be accepted. "The genuine difficulty of the problem presents itself when future fulfillments depart further and further from what one might originally have expected."[31]

Let us consider briefly the value of criticism which departs from what the author intended to communicate. Feminist, Marxist, and Freudian criticisms are often of this kind. As long as such hermeneutic examinations are indicated as criticism rather than interpretation, they need not misrepresent the author or deceive the audience, and, in fact, they may be quite valuable in stirring ideas. We are often, however, the best producers of criticism and significance ourselves, as T.S. Eliot would confirm.[32] Most of us have, for example, found personal significance in a work of literature we later discovered we had misinterpreted. This should not, however, profoundly devalue the significance we had formerly found in the text. The significance I find in *King Lear* may well have a more profound effect on me than that which is found by a noted Shakespeare scholar. His interpretation is likely to be better than mine, based as it would be on a superior knowledge of Shakespeare and all that relevantly concerns him, but in what sense could his criticism be said to be better than mine? Other readers of Shakespeare might find it more appealing and engaging, but this is a matter of taste. Whereas interpretation is rigorously objective and can be judged by objective standards, criticism is less rigorously objective and can, to some extent, be judged by subjective standards.

It is possible, we should note, for a literary text to lose its appeal through time—though there seems little danger of this in the case of Shakespeare. In such a case, however, what shall we do? Shall we offer ever more creative criticisms of the work, departing further and further from its meaning? Perhaps not. Perhaps we should draw the line and recognize that at some point a given literary text may lose its appeal, that its meaning may no longer be of much interest no matter how far criticism departs from that meaning. Hirsch has suggested that in such cases we should "introduce truer and more valuable works into the traditional literary canon to replace those that are outdated."[33] I quite agree, and we face a similar situation with legal texts.

LEGAL TEXTS

There is a temptation to see legal hermeneutics as an enterprise distinct from hermeneutics in general. However, such is not the case. The meaning of a text is what its author intended to communicate, and this holds for texts of all genres. One thing, though, does distinguish legal interpretation, there is usually, i.e., under ordinary circumstances, more at stake in the interpretation of legal texts[34] than in the interpretation of most other texts. Although, as I have argued, it is unethical to misrepresent the author of a philosophical or literary text, rarely does any unjust punishment or social upheaval result from such a transgression. On the other hand, misinterpreting a law can lead to weighty and considerable injustices.

Legal texts have some common ground with many literary texts, in that they are often intended to be somewhat open-ended and inclusive, allowing for future developments. We must be careful to observe the distinction between meaning and significance in interpreting the law. In addition we must be careful to keep two questions distinct: (1)What does the law mean? and (2)Is it a good law? The conflation of these two questions has caused much confusion among legal theorists.[35] The semantic intentions of legal texts are often spare rather than rich, that is, legal authors often intend to use a term in the right way whatever that turns out to be. To be certain, though, semantic intentions can also be rich, i.e., in accord with paradigmatic examples or particular definitions or descriptions.[36] That is, an author may intend a law to be applied in a very specific and constricted way. Under the interpretive account we have offered, the meaning of the legal text is what the author intended to communicate by it, and so we must deal with legal texts on a case-by-case basis. Some will prove to be open and others constricted. Whether or not a given law is a good one is a separate matter. We shall make this point more clearly in our discussion. To be clear, we shall not attempt to interpret any particular legal texts. Rather, we shall simply draw out the implications of our interpretive theory by briefly examining wills, ordinances, and the Constitution.

An intentionalist approach to the interpretation of a last will and testament is unlikely to encounter much disapproval. We readily recognize that the author, usually one person, produces the text to declare his final wishes and bequeath his property. When a man declares in his will that all of his wealth should pass to his mistress rather than to his wife and children, his text means just that. His desire to have that state of affairs realized is what the author intends to communicate; whether this state of affairs should be realized is a separate issue. We can expect that the man's wife and children will challenge his final wishes and perhaps see to it that they are not fulfilled. Other circumstances might also lead us to conclude that although we can understand what the author of a will intended, we will not honor those intentions—for example, when a will is revised by someone not of sound mind.

An intentionalist approach to the interpretation of a living will is also unlikely to encounter disapproval. Indeed, such interpretation is standard practice. The text of the living will means what the author intended to communicate by it. If the author of the text indicates that under no circumstances should artificial respiration, nutrition, or hydration be used to continue his life, then that is what the text means. There may, however, be conditions under which we would not honor this legal text. If, for example, the author had an excellent prognosis for recovery but was severely depressed, we might well challenge the decision to honor his living will. What a legal text means and whether it is a good one—one that should be honored—are two separate issues. Inasmuch as living wills are often vague, not covering every possible scenario in specific detail, they help to illustrate the importance of counterfactuals in legal interpretation. Although the author of a text did not address a given issue we must sometimes counterfactually imagine what he would have said had he addressed it. When a living will is not clear as to how its author would have addressed a given situation, family members are left with the task of producing a counterfactual interpretation—with deciding how the author would have wanted things handled.

To examine the implications of our account further let us examine the case of ordinances. To do this we shall consider a variation of an often-used example.[37]

A five member town council enacts an ordinance declaring that no vehicles are allowed in the park. What does the text of the ordinance mean? Is it a good ordinance? The ordinance means what the authors, in this case the members of the council, intended to communicate. If they intended to communicate a ban on automobiles then this is what it means. If they intended to communicate a ban on mopeds, roller blades, baby carriages, military tank displays, futuristic hovercrafts, and anything else that acts as a means of transportation, then this is what it means. If they intended to communicate a ban on only green Fords then this is what it means. In short, the text means whatever they intended to communicate by it—a ban of whatever kind. What about cases they did not consider? Perhaps, in fact, they did not consider whether skateboards are included in their ban on vehicles. Here we must appeal to counterfactual intentions, what the members of the legislature would have determined ought to be done about an application not in mind at the time of enactment.[38] If they had considered the case of skateboards, would the members of the council have included them in the ban? If the answer is yes, then that is what the text means and they are banned; if the answer is no, then that is what the text means and they are not banned. To be clear, what we are talking about here is what the text means—what is banned by the law it enacts. We are not saying whether or not it is a good law, one that should be enacted. For example, if we discovered that the council members intended to ban only green Fords, we would not likely consider this a good law. Such a law, then, should be amended or repealed. That, however, is another issue. Not everything that we would judge to be good, fair, or just is in accord with the laws as they are. Nor can a given law necessarily make a neat accommodation of a present circumstance. Sometimes a law must be changed.

What if the members of the council disagree? The answer is that their disagreement is settled by majority rule; the text means what its majority intended it to mean. If a majority intended to ban only automobiles, while a minority intended to ban skateboards as well, then only automobiles are banned. What if there is no majority in a given case? Then we have what Alexander calls "failed law." Failed law "occur[s] when the legislating authorities individually intend different applications and thus mean different things, despite having agreed on the language of their legislative text."[39] The agreement signified by the majority is actually illusory. Had the members made their language more specific there would be no majority and hence no law. Such a case of failed law, then, should be amended or repealed. We should note that there is an important type of case that may appear to be failed law but actually is not. If the members of the legislature recognized that they differed in their intentions regarding specific applications but nonetheless chose the general language of "No vehicles are allowed in the park" with the intent that future legislative decisions or judicial interpretations would determine the proper scope of applications, then we do not have failed law. To the contrary, we simply have a law with spare semantic intentions.

Let us now very briefly consider the implications of our account for the interpretation of the Constitution. As with any other text, the Constitution means what its authors intended to communicate by it, but one serious difficulty that constitutional interpretation faces is that it is often difficult to know what the authors, the framers of the Constitution, intended. Another serious difficulty is that there may be reason to think that what a group of men intended over two centuries ago should no longer be followed in every detail. As Walter Benn Michaels says, though, "this is an objection to constitutional government, not to intentionalist interpretation. Intentionalists are free to think that the Constitution should be jettisoned as they are free to think of it as a sacred text."[40]

We must, then, keep our two questions clear: (1)What does the legal text mean? (2)Is it a good law? Consider, for example, what is covered by the free speech guaranteed by the First Amendment. The authors of the Constitution did not specifically mention cyberspace communications, but their intention may have been sufficiently open-ended so as to encompass them. If they had considered the counterfactual situation in which cyberspace communications exist, they may have been willing to extend freedom of speech to this domain. If they would have extended free speech to cyberspace communications then this is part of what the text means, and once we know what the text means then we are in a position to judge whether or not it is a good law. As it turns out, however, the First Amendment Free Speech Clause may not have been originally intended in the abstract way in which we tend to conceive it.[41] In fact, one could argue that in the case of the First Amendment, and the Constitution in general, there is much evidence that the framers' intentions were generally rich rather than spare.[42] It is not our purpose here to settle the issue of the proper interpretation of the First Amendment or any other part of the Constitution. Such a task would be worthy of a volume of its own.

Sometimes a law as it stands cannot be construed correctly so as to include a current circumstance, yet our feeling is that the law must be made to accommodate it. Such may well have been the case in *Brown v. Board of Education*. In this landmark case the court overturned *Plessy v. Ferguson*, eliminating the doctrine of separate but equal and segregated schools by appealing to the Fourteenth Amendment, yet it is far from clear that the intentions of the authors of the Fourteenth Amendment would have supported such an action. As Gregory Bassham points out, "The fact, for example, that many influential congressional supporters of the Fourteenth Amendment stressed that the amendment was not intended to guarantee equal political rights for blacks is weighty evidence that, *pace* Dworkin, no broad principle of 'equal citizenship' was intended."[43]

Whether or not the Fourteenth Amendment was misinterpreted in the *Brown* case is a weighty and complex historical issue, and so we cannot hope to settle it here.[44] Still, we can use the case to remind ourselves of the two distinct questions involved in legal interpretation. First, what does the text of the law mean? The text means whatever its authors intended to communicate by it. If the authors of the Fourteenth Amendment did not intend, actually or counterfactually, that segregation should be abolished, then it should not have been abolished under that law. Second, is it a good law? Should segregation have been abolished? Yes, most certainly. If the Fourteenth Amendment could have been shown to be proper grounds for such action, then it is a good law in that respect. If the amendment could not have been shown to be proper grounds for that action, then the law was deficient in at least that respect. What is good, fair, and just is not always constitutional. In such cases we are left with the problem of not having a law to enact what we know is right. The solution, however, should not be in every case to find such a present circumstance to be covered by the law. To the contrary, when the meaning of the law as given by its authors cannot truly apply to it, either the law should be rewritten or a new law should be enacted. Thomas Jefferson once remarked that it would not be an altogether bad thing to have a revolution every twenty years. On the Constitution itself Jefferson said, "I had rather ask an enlargement of power for the nation, where it is found necessary, than to assume it by construction which would make our powers boundless. Our peculiar security is in a written Constitution. Let us not make of it a blank check by construction."[45]

Neither the Constitution nor any government should be allowed to become too stale or too powerful. If an intentionalist interpretation of the Constitution no longer suits our needs we are left with two options. We can abandon the Constitution or we can ferret out its significance for our time. Abandoning the Constitution is a genuine consideration, just as is dropping a literary classic from the canon. As Hirsch has said, "Better to change the literary canon or repeal the law than bring interpretation and the law into disrepute."[46] On purely practical grounds it does not seem wise to abandon the Constitution at this time, however, and so we are left with the task of finding its significance.

Our laws are not the inspired words of a deity, but rather, pragmatic human creations. If they no longer suit us though we wish to continue to use them, we must either rewrite them or add to them. One way in which we can add to laws is through new interpretations—actually criticisms—offered by judges. We cannot, however, afford to play fast and loose with the law, twisting its words and stretching its meaning. The reality of such practice is frightening indeed. Consider that Justice William O. Douglas is reputed to have said of the Supreme Court during the Warren era, "With five votes, we can do anything." In the theoretical arena, Ronald Dworkin interprets the Constitution in terms of abstract general injunctions such as "act fairly."[47] His motivation in such interpretation is to mold the Constitution so as to fit contemporary society. Interestingly, even Dworkin ties his account to the intentions of the framers, arguing that their use of highly abstract language provides "very strong positive evidence" that the principles they intended to enact were equally abstract.[48] As Bassham points out, however, Dworkin is guilty of "attributing to the framers abstract intentions across the board, while ignoring clear evidence that their true intentions may in many cases have been relatively specific."[49] Such practice, though often done with noble purposes, is subject to abuse. Of course not every case involves either the best intention or leads to the worst abuse.

In *Original Intent and the Constitution* Bassham has defended the pragmatic approach of Benjamin Cardozo that is characterized by three central themes.

(1) a rejection of "foundationalist" interpretive theories in favor of a more ad hoc, eclectic approach that emphasizes the complexity and situatedness of constitutional decisionmaking; (2) a claim that, in constitutional law as in law generally, judges must give due weight to considerations of institutional competence and such rule-of-law

virtues as stability and predictability; and (3) an insistence, rooted in what Cardozo saw as the core democratic aspirations of American society, that in the relatively few cases in which a judge may be warranted in making new law for a new day, his task is "to objectify in law, not [his] own aspirations and convictions and philosophies, but the aspirations, convictions, and philosophies of the men and women of [his] time.[50]

I must agree with Bassham that if we are going to continue to use the Constitution we must take such a pragmatic approach to it. We must, however, be clear that this is in fact what we are doing. Only criticism yielding significance makes the Constitution a viable document. Interpretation that would yield the meaning of the Constitution in accord with the original intent of the authors might well make the text seem one to which we would no longer want to submit. Many of the gains made in civil rights do not accord with what were likely the rich semantic intentions of the authors of the Constitution.

In the ideal situation an intentionalist approach would be taken to a given legal text, just as with any other kind of text. In the case of the Constitution, as in the case of any body of law that has become dated, a pragmatic approach of highlighting significance is to be recommended if we are to continue to use the law. We must, however, be clear to ourselves and to the public at large that this is the approach we are taking. We must not misrepresent our current use of the Constitution as being faithful to the intent of its authors. With this precaution taken, it certainly is often more pragmatic to continue using an existing law than to draft, ratify, and implement a new one.

CONCLUSION

As we have seen, the normative and descriptive approaches can and should coexist, and both interpretation and criticism have a place in our hermeneutic examinations. Though interpretation should not be done in strict accord with genre considerations, it is still instructive to consider what is typical in the interpretation of various genres. We have briefly examined the cases of philosophical, literary, and legal texts to make our point. A more detailed examination of these and a further examination of other textual types would be a worthy endeavor but would take us beyond the scope of this volume.

NOTES

1. This is as opposed to significance, meaning as-related-to some context.
2. We shall discuss this in terms of perlocutionary acts in a subsequent section of this chapter on literary texts.
3. Cf. E.D. Hirsch, Jr., "Meaning and Significance Reinterpreted," *Critical Inquiry* 11 (1984), p. 206. Here Hirsch speaks of future-directed intentions, which may include future applications.
4. Scriptural and sacred texts are, for example, fascinating objects of inquiry.
5. E.D. Hirsch, Jr. made this suggestion to me in correspondence. See for an example of such efforts, P.N. Johnson-Laird, *Mental Models: Toward a Cognitive Science of Language, Inference, and Consciousness* (Cambridge, MA: Harvard University Press, 1983). For a similar view see Göran Hermerén, "Intention and Interpretation in Literary

Criticism," *New Literary History* 7 (1975), p. 81. As an alternative to Gadamer's phenomenology see Wolfgang Iser, "The Reading Process: A Phenomenological Approach," in Jane P. Tompkins ed., *Reader Response Criticism* (Baltimore: Johns Hopkins University Press, 1980), pp. 50–69.

6. Cf. Jeffrey Stout, "What is the Meaning of a Text?" *New Literary History* 14 (1982), "We say that such texts possess inexhaustible meaning. I would rather say that they never manage to exhaust our interest" (p. 8). Although Stout is not an intentionalist and does not even think we should speak of meaning, the significance of his statement is appropriate for our consideration.

7. Stein Haugom Olsen, "Interpretation and Intention," *British Journal of Aesthetics* 17 (1977), p. 210.

8. Ibid.

9. P.D. Juhl, *Interpretation: An Essay in the Philosophy of Literary Criticism* (Princeton, NJ: Princeton University Press, 1980), p. 43.

10. E.D. Hirsch, Jr., "Counterfactuals in Interpretation," in Sanford Levinson and Steven Mailoux eds., *Interpreting Law and Literature: A Hermeneutic Reader* (Evanston, IL: Northwestern University Press, 1988), p. 61.

11. Cf. Hirsch (1988), pp. 61–62.

12. Cf. Stout, p. 10 for a similar view, though based on different reasons, that we should be careful in specifying what we mean by the term "meaning."

13. Ibid., p. 6. He later adds, "Meanings, if they exist, could turn out to be the *least* interesting thing about texts" (p. 7).

14. Jorge J.E. Gracia, *A Theory of Textuality: The Logic and Epistemology* (Albany: SUNY Press, 1995), pp. 90–91 (hereafter *ATT*). Gracia also further explains that philosophical texts generally come in five forms: treatise, commentary, article, lecture, and oral discussion frequently presented in writing as a dialogue.

15. For an example of this see John Corcoran, "Argumentations and Logic," *Argumentations* 3 (1989), p. 20.

16. *Apology* 34a1 and 38b6; *Phaedo* 59b10.

17. Edwin Alexander, "Hermeneutical Violence: Heidegger's Kant-Interpretation," *Philosophy Today* 25 (1981), p. 289.

18. Although he later corrected himself to some extent, Heidegger is also guilty of misrepresenting Plato, "convicting" him as the first philosopher to conceive of truth as correspondence. See the discussion of truth in chapter 4.

19. As was the case with philosophical texts, it is not easy to say what exactly a literary text is—or what literature itself is. This is not a problem for our account, however, but actually supports it. Recall that we argued in chapter 3 that genres do not represent hard ontological barriers. Still, some texts are undeniably literary, for example *Hamlet* and *Paradise Lost*.

20. The task also belongs to the writer of criticism, and we shall discuss this shortly.

21. William Shakespeare, Sonnet 55, in *The Norton Anthology of Poetry,* 3rd edition (New York: W.W. Norton & Company, 1983), pp. 187–188.

22. Hirsch (1984), p. 205.

23. Hermann Hesse, *Steppenwolf* (New York: Henry Holt and Company, 1990), "Author's Note—1961," pp. v–vi.

24. A.J. Close, "*Don Quixote* and the 'Intentionalist Fallacy,'" *The British Journal of Aesthetics* 12 (1972), p. 23.

25. I cannot argue at length for this assertion within the scope of this project. For a defense of this position see Juhl, pp. 218–219. See also Hirsch (1988), p. 64.

26. J.L. Austin, *How to Do Things with Words*, 2nd edition (Cambridge, MA: Harvard University Press, 1962), pp. 116–117.

27. Austin, p. 109.

28. Gregory Currie, "What Is Fiction?" *The Journal of Aesthetics and Art Criticism* 43 (1985), p. 391. Cf. Close, "The recognition that poets, novelists, and dramatists intend to arrest our attention, and engage our interest, in certain ways is basic to our response to literature" (p. 36).

29. Cf. Hirsch (1988), pp. 62–63. Hirsch argues that a counterfactual conditional does have a truth value, and so thinking in terms of counterfactuals is a valuable way of determining if an interpretation is a valid accommodation of the past to the present. Hirsch discusses counterfactual interpretations of Blake's "London." We shall discuss counterfactuals in greater detail in the next section of this chapter on legal texts.

30. Hirsch (1984), p. 206.

31. Ibid., p. 207.

32. T.S. Eliot, *The Frontiers of Criticism* (University of Minnesota: Gideon D. Seymour Memorial Lecture Series, 1956). "I suspect, in fact, that a good deal of the value of an interpretation is—that it should be my own interpretation" (pp. 15–16). We should note that Eliot here uses the word "interpretation" where we would use the word "criticism."

33. Hirsch (1984), p. 219.

34. What makes something a legal text is not completely clear, though perhaps it is somewhat clearer than is the case with philosophical or literary texts. This is not a problem for our account in that we have already argued that texts are not to be interpreted along genre lines but in accord with authorial intentions. We shall not attempt to examine every type of text that could be considered a legal text, but will restrict ourselves to a brief discussion of wills, ordinances, and the Constitution. For an interesting intentionalist take on the interpretation of contracts see Walter Benn Michaels, "Against Formalism: Chickens and Rocks," in Sanford Levinson and Steven Mailoux eds., *Interpreting Law and Literature: A Hermeneutic Reader* (Evanston, IL: Northwestern University Press, 1988), pp. 215–216.

35. Cf. Larry Alexander, "All or Nothing at All? The Intentions of Authorities and the Authority of Intentions," in Andrei Marmor ed., *Law and Interpretation: Essays in Legal Philosophy* (Oxford: Clarendon Press, 1995), p. 399. Alexander accuses a number of legal theorists of conflating the questions of what the authorities' text means and what authority that text should have.

36. For a discussion of spare and rich semantic intentions in the law see Gregory Bassham, *Original Intent and the Constitution: A Philosophical Study* (Lanham, MD: Rowman and Littlefield Publishers, Inc., 1992), pp. 31–32.

37. For two very different takes on this type of example see Alexander, pp. 380–381, and Paul Brest, "The Misconceived Quest for the Original Understanding," in Sanford Levinson and Steven Mailoux eds., *Interpreting Law and Literature: A Hermeneutic Reader* (Evanston, IL: Northwestern University Press, 1988), pp. 73–76.

38. For an argument in support of the facticity of counterfactual intentions see Alexander, pp. 375–381.

39. Ibid., pp. 386–387.

40. Walter Benn Michaels, "The Fate of the Constitution," in Sanford Levinson and Steven Mailoux eds., *Interpreting Law and Literature: A Hermeneutic Reader* (Evanston, IL: Northwestern University Press, 1988), p. 391.

41. Bassham (1992), p. 74.

42. Ibid., p. 79.

43. Gregory Bassham, "Freedom's Politics: A Review Essay of Ronald Dworkin's *Freedom's Law: The Moral Reading of The American Constitution*," *Notre Dame Law Review* 72 (1997), p. 1257. Cf. Bassham (1992), p. 56.

44. Cf. Raoul Berger, *Government by Judiciary: The Transformation of the Fourteenth Amendment* (Cambridge, MA: Harvard University Press, 1977).

45. Thomas Jefferson, Letter to Wilson C. Nicholas, 7 September 1803, in William B. Parker and Jonas Viles eds., *Thomas Jefferson: Letters and Addresses* (New York: Sun Dial Classics Company, 1908), p. 154.

46. E.D. Hirsch, Jr., "Transhistorical Intentions and the Persistence of Allegory," *New Literary History* 25 (1994), p. 565.

47. Ronald Dworkin, *Law's Empire* (Cambridge, MA: Belknap Press, 1986), pp. 397–399.

48. Ronald Dworkin, *Life's Dominion: An Argument about Abortion, Euthanasia, and Individual Freedom* (New York: Vintage Books, 1994), p. 136.

49. Bassham (1997), p. 1257.

50. Bassham (1992), p. 110.

Select Bibliography

Alexander, Edwin. "Hermeneutical Violence: Heidegger's Kant-Interpretation." *Philosophy Today* 25 (1981): 286–306.

Alexander, Larry. "All or Nothing at All? The Intentions of Authorities and the Authority of Intentions." In Andrei Marmor ed., *Law and Interpretation: Essays in Legal Philosophy*, pp. 357–404. Oxford: Clarendon Press, 1995.

Apel, Karl-Otto. "Regulative Ideas or Truth Happening?: An Attempt to Answer the Question of the Conditions of the Possibility of Valid Understanding." In Lewis Edwin Hahn ed., *The Philosophy of Hans-Georg Gadamer*, pp. 67–94. La Salle, IL: Open Court, 1997.

Arthur, Christopher E. "Gadamer and Hirsch: The Canonical Work and the Interpreter's Intention." *Cultural Hermeneutics* 4 (1977): 183–197.

Austin, J.L. *How to Do Things with Words*. Second Edition. Cambridge, MA: Harvard University Press, 1962.

Barnes, Annette. *On Interpretation*. Oxford: Basil Blackwell, 1988.

Barthes, Roland. "The Death of the Author." In *Image, Music, Text*. Stephen Heath trans., pp. 142–148. New York: Hill and Wang, 1977.

———. "La Mort de l'Auteur," *Manteia* 5 (1968): 12–17.

———. "From Work to Text," Josué V. Harari trans. and ed., *Textual Strategies: Perspectives in Post-Structuralist Criticism*, pp. 73–81. Ithaca, NY: Cornell University Press, 1979.

Bassham, Gregory. "Freedom's Politics: A Review Essay of Ronald Dworkin's *Freedom's Law: The Moral Reading of the American Constitution*." *Notre Dame Law Review* 72 (1997): 1235–1276.

———. *Original Intent and the Constitution: A Philosophical Study*. Lanham, MD: Rowman and Littlefield Publishers, Inc., 1992.

Beardsley, Monroe C. *The Aesthetic Point of View*. Ithaca, NY: Cornell University Press, 1982.

———. "Aesthetic Experience Regained." *Journal of Aesthetics and Art Criticism* 28 (1969): 3–11.

———. *Aesthetics: Problems in the Philosophy of Criticism* Rev. ed. New York: Macmillan, 1980.

———. "The Authority of the Text." In *The Possibility of Criticism*, pp. 16–37. Detroit: Wayne State University Press, 1970.

Bennett, Jonathan. "The Meaning-Nominalist Strategy." *Foundations of Language* 10 (1976): 141–168.

Berger, Raoul. *Government by Judiciary: The Transformation of the Fourteenth Amendment.* Cambridge, MA: Harvard University Press, 1977.

Biriotti, Maurice and Nicola Miller. *What Is an Author?* Manchester: Manchester University Press, 1993.

Biro, John. "Intentionalism in the Theory of Meaning." *The Monist* 62 (1979): 238–258.

Blondel, Eric. "Interpreting Texts with or without Nietzsche." In G.L. Ormiston and A.D. Schrift eds., *Transforming the Hermeneutic Context: From Nietzsche to Nancy*, pp. 69–88. Albany: SUNY Press, 1990.

Booth, Wayne C. *The Rhetoric of Fiction.* Chicago: University of Chicago Press, 1961.

Brest, Paul. "The Misconceived Quest for the Original Understanding." In Sanford Levinson and Steven Mailoux eds., *Interpreting Law and Literature: A Hermeneutic Reader*, pp. 69–96. Evanston, IL: Northwestern University Press, 1988.

Burke, Seán. *The Death and Return of the Author: Criticism and Subjectivity in Barthes, Foucault and Derrida.* Edinburgh: Edinburgh University Press, 1998.

Cain, William E. "Authors and Authority in Interpretation." *Georgia Review* 34 (1980): 617–634.

———. "Authority, 'Cognitive Atheism,' and the Aims of Interpretation: The Literary Theory of E.D. Hirsch." *College English* 39 (1977): 333–345.

Carroll, Noël. "The Intentional Fallacy: Defending Myself." *The Journal of Aesthetics and Art Criticism* 53 (1997): 305–309.

———. "Anglo-American Aesthetics and Contemporary Criticism: Intention and the Hermeneutics of Suspicion." *The Journal of Aesthetics and Art Criticism* 51 (1993): 245–252.

———. "Art, Intention, and Conversation." In Gary Iseminger ed., *Intention and Interpretation*, pp. 97–131. Philadelphia: Temple University Press, 1992.

Caughie, John. *Theories of Authorship: A Reader.* London: Routledge & Kegan Paul, 1981.

Cioffi, F. "Intention and Interpretation in Criticism," *Proceedings of the Aristotelian Society* 64 (1964): 85–106.

Close, A.J. "*Don Quixote* and the 'Intentionalist Fallacy.'" *British Journal of Aesthetics* 12 (1972): 19–39.

Connolly, John M. "Gadamer and the Author's Authority: A Language Game Approach." *Journal of Aesthetics and Art Criticism* 44 (1986): 271–278.

Currie, Gregory. "What is Fiction?" *The Journal of Aesthetics and Art Criticism* 43 (1985): 385–392.

Dickie, George., and Kent Wilson. "The Intentional Fallacy: Defending Beardsley." *The Journal of Aesthetics and Art Criticism* 53 (1995): 233–250.

Dilthey, W. *Selected Writings*, H.P. Rickman trans. and ed. Cambridge: Cambridge University Press, 1976.

Donnellan, Keith. "Putting Humpty Dumpty Together Again." *Philosophical Review* 77 (1968): 203–215.

Dutton, Dennis. "Why Intentionalism Won't Go Away." In Anthony J. Cascardi ed., *Literature and the Question of Philosophy*, pp. 194–201. Baltimore: Johns Hopkins University Press, 1987.

———. "Criticism and Method." *British Journal of Aesthetics* 13 (1973): 232–242.

Dworkin, Ronald. *Law's Empire.* Cambridge, MA: Belknap Press, 1986.

———. *Freedom's Law: The Moral Reading of the American Constitution.* Cambridge, MA: Harvard University Press, 1996.

Ellis, A.J. "Intention and Interpretation in Literature." *British Journal of Aesthetics* 14 (1974): 315–325.

Ellis, J.M. *Against Deconstruction*. Princeton, NJ: Princeton University Press, 1989.

Fish, Stanley. *Is There a Text in This Class? The Authority of Interpretive Communities.* Cambridge, MA: Harvard University Press, 1980.

Foucault, Michel. "Nietzsche, Freud, Marx." In G.L. Ormiston and A.D. Schrift eds., *Transforming the Hermeneutic Context: From Nietzsche to Nancy*, pp. 59–68. Albany: SUNY Press, 1990.

———. "What Is an Author?" Josué V. Harari trans. In Paul Rainbow ed., *The Foucault Reader*, pp. 101–120. New York: Pantheon Books, 1984.

———. "Qu'est-ce Qu'un Auteur?" *Bulletin de la Société Francaise de Philosophie* 63 (1969): 75–95.

Frank, Manfred. "The Interpretation of a Text." In G.L. Ormiston and A.D. Schrift eds., *Transforming the Hermeneutic Context: From Nietzsche to Nancy*, pp. 145–176. Albany: SUNY Press, 1990.

Frege, Gottlob. "On Sense and Reference." In P. Geach and M. Black trans. and eds., *Translations from the Philosophical Writings of Gottlob Frege*, pp. 56–78. Oxford: Basil Blackwell, 1952.

Gadamer, Hans-Georg. *Truth and Method*. Second Edition. Joel Weinsheimer and Donald G. Marshall trans. New York: Continuum, 1989.

———. *Wahrheit und Methode*. Tübingen: J.C.B. Mohr, 1972.

———. "On the Circle of Understanding." John M. Connolly and Thomas Keutner trans. In John M. Connolly and Thomas Keutner eds., *Hermeneutics Versus Science? Three German Views*, pp. 68–78. Notre Dame, IN: Notre Dame University Press, 1988.

———. "Vom Zirkel des Verstehens." In *Kleine Schriften vol. IV Variationen*, pp. 54–61. Tübingen: J.C.B. Mohr, 1977.

———. "Text and Interpretation." Dennis J. Schmidt trans. In Brice R. Wachterhauser ed., *Hermeneutics and Modern Philosophy*, pp. 377–396. Albany, NY: SUNY Press, 1986.

———. *Philosophical Hermeneutics*. David Linge trans. and ed. Berkeley: University of California Press, 1976.

———. *Kleine Schriften* vols. I, II, & III. Tübingen: J.C.B. Mohr, 1967; vol. IV. Tübingen: J.C.B. Mohr, 1977.

Garrett, Jan Edward. "Hans-Georg Gadamer on 'Fusion of Horizons.'" *Man and World* 11 (1978): 392–398.

Gelven, Michael. *A Commentary on Heidegger's Being and Time*. Revised Edition. Dekalb: Northern Illinois University Press, 1989.

Gracia, Jorge J.E. "The Interpretation of Revealed Texts: Do We Know What God Means?" *American Catholic Philosophical Quarterly* 72 (1998): 1–19.

———. *Texts: Ontological Status, Identity, Author, Audience*. Albany: SUNY Press, 1996.

———. *A Theory of Textuality: The Logic and Epistemology*. Albany: SUNY Press, 1995.

———. "Can There Be Definitive Interpretations?: An Interpretation of Foucault in Response to Engel." In Barry Smith ed., *European Philosophy and the American Academy*, pp. 41–51. La Salle, IL: The Hegeler Institute, 1994.

———. "Can There Be Texts Without Historical Authors?" *American Philosophical Quarterly* 31 (1994): 248–253.

———. "Can There Be Texts Without Audiences?" *Review of Metaphysics* 47 (1994): 711–734.

————. *Philosophy and Its History: Issues in Philosophical Historiography*. Albany: SUNY Press, 1992.

————. "Texts and Their Interpretation." *Review of Metaphysics* 43 (1990): 495–542.

Grondin, Jean. *Introduction to Philosophical Hermeneutics*. Joel Weinsheimer trans. New Haven: Yale University Press, 1994.

————. *Hermeneutische Wahrheit? Zum Wahrheitsbegriff Hans-Georg Gadamers*. Königsten/Ts.: Verlag Anton Hain Meisenheim, Forum Academicum, 1982.

————. "Hermeneutics and Relativism." In Kathleen Wright ed., *Festivals of Interpretation: Essays on Hans-Georg Gadamer's Work*, pp. 42–62. Albany: SUNY Press, 1990.

Habermas, Jürgen. "The Hermeneutic Claim to Universality." In Josef Bleicher trans. and ed., *Contemporary Hermeneutics: Hermeneutics as Method, Philosophy, and Culture*, pp. 181–211. London: Routledge and Kegan Paul, 1980.

————. "Review of Gadamer's *Truth and Method*." In Fred R. Dallmayr and Thomas A. McCarthy eds., *Understanding and Social Inquiry*, pp. 335–363. Notre Dame, IN: Notre Dame University Press, 1977.

Hamlyn, D.W. "Unconscious Intentions." *Philosophy* 46 (1971): 12–22.

Heidegger, Martin. "On the Essence of Truth." In David Farrell Krell ed., *Martin Heidegger: Basic Writings*, pp. 117–141. New York: Harper and Row, 1977.

————. "Vom Wesen der Wahrheit." In *Wegmarken*, pp. 73–97. Frankfurt am Main: Vittorio Klostermann Verlag, 1967.

————. "The End of Philosophy and the Task of Thinking." In David Farrell Krell ed., *Martin Heidegger: Basic Writings*, pp. 373–392. New York: Harper and Row, 1976.

————. *Zur Sache des Denkens*. Tübingen: Max Niemeyer Verlag, 1969.

————. "Plato's Doctrine of Truth." In William Barrett and Henry D. Aikens eds., *Philosophy in the Twentieth Century* vol. 3, pp. 251–270. New York: Random House, 1962.

————. *Platons Lehre von der Wahrheit. Mit einen Brief über den Humanismus*. Bern: A. Francke, 1947.

————. *Being and Time*. John Macquarrie and Edward Robinson trans. San Francisco: HarperCollins, 1962.

————. *Sein und Zeit*. Tübingen: Max Niemeyer Verlag, 1967.

Hermerén, Göran. "Allusions and Intentions." In Gary Iseminger ed., *Intention and Interpretation*, pp. 203–220. Philadelphia: Temple University Press, 1992.

————. "Intention and Interpretation in Literary Criticism." *New Literary History* 7 (1975): 57–82.

Hirsch, E.D., Jr. "Transhistorical Intentions and the Persistence of Allegory." *New Literary History* 25 (1994): 549–567.

————. "Counterfactuals in Interpretation." In Sanford Levinson and Steven Mailoux eds., *Interpreting Law and Literature: A Hermeneutic Reader*, pp. 55–68. Evanston, IL: Northwestern University Press, 1988.

————. "Meaning and Significance Reinterpreted." *Critical Inquiry* 11 (1984): 202–225.

————. *The Aims of Interpretation*. Chicago: University of Chicago Press, 1976.

————. "Three Dimensions of Hermeneutics." *New Literary History* 3 (1972): 245–261.

————. *Validity in Interpretation*. New Haven: Yale University Press, 1967.

————. "Truth and Method in Interpretation." *Review of Metaphysics* 18 (1965): 488–507.

————. "Objective Interpretation." *PMLA* 75 (1960): 463–479.

Hoy, David C. "Must We Say What We Mean?" *University of Ottawa Review* 50 (1980): 411–426.

————. "Interpreting the Law: Hermeneutical and Poststructuralist Perspectives." In Sanford Levinson and Steven Mailoux eds., *Interpreting Law and Literature: A Hermeneutic Reader*, pp. 319–338. Evanston, IL: Northwestern University Press, 1988.

————. *The Critical Circle: Literature, History, and Philosophical Hermeneutics.* Berkeley: University of California Press, 1978.

Irwin, William. "A Critique of Hermeneutic Truth as Disclosure," *International Studies in Philosophy*, forthcoming.

————. "An Author Construct There Must Be," *Diálogos* 74 (1999): 169–177.

————. "Intention and Foresight in the British Law of Murder," *Sorites* 9 (1998): 6–15.

————. "Review of Jorge J.E. Gracia's *A Theory of Textuality: The Logic and Epistemology.*" *Sorites* 3 (1995): 64–68.

Iseminger, Gary. "An Intentional Demonstration?" In Gary Iseminger ed., *Intention and Interpretation*, pp. 76–96. Philadelphia: Temple University Press, 1992.

Iser, Wolfgang. "The Reading Process: A Phenomenological Approach." In Jane P. Tompkins ed., *Reader, Response, Criticism*, pp. 50–69. Baltimore: Johns Hopkins University Press, 1980.

Juhl, P.D. *Interpretation: An Essay in the Philosophy of Literary Criticism.* Princeton, NJ: Princeton University Press, 1980.

————. "The Appeal to the Text: What Are We Appealing To?" *Journal of Aesthetics and Art Criticism* 36 (1978): 277–287.

Knapp, Steven. *Literary Interest: The Limits of Anti-Formailism.* Cambridge, MA: Harvard University Press, 1993.

Knapp, Steven, and Walter Benn Michaels. "Against Theory 2: Hermeneutics and Deconstruction." *Critical Inquiry* 14 (1987): 49–68.

————. "Against Theory." *Critical Inquiry* 8 (1982): 723–742.

Krausz, Michael. "Intention and Interpretation: Hirsch and Margolis." In Gary Iseminger ed., *Intention and Interpretation*, pp. 152–166. Philadelphia: Temple University Press, 1992.

Lamarque, Peter. "The Death of the Author: An Analytical Autopsy." *British Journal of Aesthetics* 30 (1990): 319–331.

Lang, Berel. "The Intentional Fallacy Revisited." *British Journal of Aesthetics* 14 (1974): 306–314.

Levinson, Jerold. "Intention and Interpretation: A Last Look." In Gary Iseminger ed., *Intention and Interpretation*, pp. 221–256. Philadelphia: Temple University Press, 1992.

Lewis, David. *Convention: A Philosophical Study.* Cambridge, MA: Harvard University Press, 1969.

Lucas, George R., Jr. "Philosophy, Its History, and Hermeneutics." In Lewis Edwin Hahn ed., *The Philosophy of Hans-Georg Gadamer*, pp. 173–186. La Salle, IL: Open Court, 1997.

Lyas, Colin. "Wittgensteinian Intentions." In Gary Iseminger ed., *Intention and Interpretation*, pp. 132–151. Philadelphia: Temple University Press, 1992.

————. "Anything Goes: The Intentional Fallacy Revisited." *British Journal of Aesthetics* 23 (1983): 291–305.

Lyon, Arabella. *Intentions: Negotiated, Contested, and Ignored.* University Park, PA: The Pennsylvania State University Press, 1998.

Margolis, Joseph. "Robust Relativism." In Gary Iseminger ed., *Intention and Interpretation*, pp. 41–50. Philadelphia: Temple University Press, 1992.

Meiland, Jack W. "The Meanings of a Text." *British Journal of Aesthetics* 21 (1981): 195–203.

———. "Interpretation as a Cognitive Discipline." *Philosophy and Literature* 2 (1978): 23–45.

Michaels, Walter Benn. "The Fate of the Constitution." In Sanford Levinson and Steven Mailoux eds., *Interpreting Law and Literature: A Hermeneutic Reader*, pp. 383–391. Evanston, IL: Northwestern University Press, 1988.

———. "Against Formalism: Chickens and Rocks." In Sanford Levinson and Steven Mailoux eds., *Interpreting Law and Literature: A Hermeneutic Reader*, pp. 215–225. Evanston, IL: Northwestern University Press, 1988.

Michelfelder, D., and R.E. Palmer eds. *Dialogue and Deconstruction: The Gadamer-Derrida Encounter*. Albany: SUNY Press, 1989.

Morgan, Michael."Authorship and the History of Philosophy." *Review of Metaphysics* 42 (1988): 327–355.

Nathan, Daniel O. "Irony, Metaphor, and the Problem of Intention." In Gary Iseminger ed., *Intention and Interpretation*, pp. 183–202. Philadelphia: Temple University Press, 1992.

Nehamas, Alexander. "Writer, Text, Work, Author." In Anthony J. Cascardi ed., *Literature and the Question of Philosophy*, pp. 265–291. Baltimore: Johns Hopkins University Press, 1987.

———. "What an Author Is." *The Journal of Philosophy* 83 (1986): 685–691.

Newton-De Molina, David. *On Literary Intention*. Edinburgh: University of Edinburgh Press, 1976.

Olsen, Stein Haugom. "Interpretation and Intention." *British Journal of Aesthetics* 17 (1977): 210–218.

Page, Carl. "Historicistic Finitude and Philosophical Hermeneutics." In Lewis Edwin Hahn ed., *The Philosophy of Hans-Georg Gadamer*, pp. 369–382. La Salle, IL: Open Court, 1997.

Palmer, Richard E. *Hermeneutics: Interpretation Theory in Schleiermacher, Dilthey, Heidegger, and Gadamer*. Evanston, IL: Northwestern University Press, 1969.

Pappas, Nickolas. "Authorship and Authority." *Journal of Aesthetics and Art Criticism* 47 (1989): 325–331.

Rose, Mark. *Authors and Owners: The Invention of Copyright*. Cambridge, MA: Harvard University Press, 1993.

Rosen, Stanley. "Horizontverschmelzung." In Lewis Edwin Hahn ed., *The Philosophy of Hans-Georg Gadamer*, pp. 207–218. La Salle, IL: Open Court, 1997.

———. "The Limits of Interpretation." In Anthony J. Cascardi ed., *Literature and the Question of Philosophy*, pp. 213–241. Baltimore: Johns Hopkins University Press, 1987.

Schleiermacher, F.D.E. *Hermeneutics and Criticism: And Other Writings*. Andrew Bowie trans. and ed. Cambridge: Cambridge University Press, 1998.

———. *Hermeneutics: The Handwritten Manuscripts*. Heinz Kimmerle ed. James Duke and Jack Frostman trans. Missoula, MT: Scholars Press, 1977.

———. *Hermeneutik*. Heinz Kimmerle ed. Heidelberg: Carl Winter, 1959.

Schmidt, Lawrence K. "Recalling the Hermeneutic Circle." *Philosophy Today* 40 (1996): 263–272.

———. *The Specter of Relativism: Truth, Dialogue, and Phronesis in Philosophical Hermeneutics*. Evanston, IL: Northwestern University Press, 1995.

———. "The Enlightening Perspective: A Hermeneutic Truth Criterion." *Southwest Philosophical Studies* 10 (1988): 83–91.

———. "When the Text Speaks the Truth: The Preconception of Completion." *The Southern Journal of Philosophy* 25 (1987): 395–405.

———. *The Epistemology of Hans-Georg Gadamer: An Analysis of the Legitimization of Vorurteile*. Frankfurt: Peter D. Lang, 1985.

Shusterman, Richard. "Interpretation, Intention, and Truth." In Gary Iseminger ed., *Intention and Interpretation*, pp. 65–75. Philadelphia: Temple University Press, 1992.

———. "Interpreting with Pragmatist Intentions." In Gary Iseminger ed., *Intention and Interpretation*, pp. 167–182. Philadelphia: Temple University Press, 1992.

Sparshott, Francis. "The Case of the Unreliable Author." *Philosophy and Literature* 10 (1986): 145–167.

Stecker, Robert. *Artworks: Definition, Meaning, Value.* University Park, PA: The Pennsylvania State University Press, 1996.

———. "Art Interpretation." *The Journal of Aesthetics and Art Criticism* 52 (1994): 193–206.

———. "The Role of Intention and Convention in Interpreting Artworks." *The Southern Journal of Philosophy* 31 (1993): 471–489.

———. "Incompatible Interpretations." *The Journal of Aesthetics and Art Criticism* 50 (1992): 291–298.

———. "Fish's Argument for the Relativity of Interpretive Truth." *The Journal of Aesthetics and Art Criticism* 48 (1990): 223–230.

———. "Apparent, Implied, and Postulated Authors." *Philosophy and Literature* 11 (1987): 258–271.

Stout, Jeffrey. "The Relativity of Interpretation." *The Monist* 69 (1986): 103–118.

———. "What Is the Meaning of a Text?" *New Literary History* 14 (1982): 1–14.

Tillyard, E.M.W. and C.S. Lewis. *The Personal Heresy: A Controversy.* London: Oxford University Press, 1939.

Tolhurst, William E. "On Textual Individuation." *Philosophical Studies* 35 (1979): 187–197.

———. "On What a Text Is and How It Means." *British Journal of Aesthetics* 19 (1979): 3–14.

Wachterhauser, Brice R. *Hermeneutics and Truth.* Evanston, IL: Northwestern University Press, 1994.

———. *Hermeneutics and Modern Philosophy.* Albany: SUNY Press, 1986.

———. "Interpreting Texts: Objectivity or Participation?" *Man and World* 19 (1986): 439–457.

Walker, Cheryl. "Feminist Literary Criticism and the Author." *Critical Inquiry* 16 (1990): 551–571.

Warnke, Georgia. *Gadamer: Hermeneutics, Tradition and Reason.* Stanford, CA: Stanford University Press, 1987.

Weberman, David. "The Nonfixity of the Historical Past." *Review of Metaphysics* 50 (1997): 749–768.

———. *Historische Objektivität.* Frankfurt am Main: Peter D. Lang, 1991.

Weinsheimer, Joel C. *Gadamer's Hermeneutics: A Reading of Truth and Method.* New Haven: Yale University Press, 1985.

Westphal, Merold. "Kierkegaard and the Anxiety of Authorship." *International Philosophical Quarterly* 34 (1994): 6–22.

Wimsatt, W.K. "Genesis: A Fallacy Revisited." In David Newton-De Molina ed., *On Literary Intention*, pp. 116–138. Edinburgh: University of Edinburgh Press, 1976.

Wimsatt, W.K., and Monroe C. Beardsley, "The Intentional Fallacy." In *The Verbal Icon: Studies in the Meaning of Poetry*, pp. 3–18. Lexington: University of Kentucky Press, 1954.

Index

Aesthetics (*see also* Beautiful):
aesthetic experience, 6–7, 41, 44,
46, 51, 111, 117; aesthetic
intention, 60, 111; Gadamer and,
8, 74
Alexander, Edwin, 124
Alexander, Larry, 120, 125
Apel, Karl-Otto, 105, 109
Aristotle, 24, 45, 114–115
Arthur, Christopher E., 12
Audience: in intentionalist
interpretation, 30, 60, 61, 62, 114,
115, 117; as interpretive criterion,
5, 11
Austin, J.L., 124
Author (*see also* Intention, Ontology,
Urinterpretation): *Autor*, 15; as
owner 19; *Urheber*, 12; what is
an, 7, 12, 17
Author construct (*see also* Urauthor),
17–31, 43; Hirsch on, 28–29, 55;
historical and pseudohistorical
(Gracia), 25–27; Juhl on, 28–29;
scriptor (Barthes), 22; urauthor,
28–33; writer and author
(Nehamas), 23–25
Author function thesis (*see also*
Foucault, Michel, Lamarque,
Peter), 19, 21–22

Barthes, Roland, 17, 18, 19–23, 26, 28,
29, 101

Bassham, Gregory, 121–123, 125–126
Beardsley, Monroe C., 10, 17, 48, 58;
on authorial intention, 17–18, 40–
41; normative criterion, 6–7, 39,
40–46; principle of autonomy, 6,
40; on unconscious intention, 6
Beautiful, the, 81–83, 99
Beckett, Samuel, 19, 34
Being-in-the-world, 7, 75, 77
Bennett, Jonathan, 71
Bennett, Paula, 27
Berger, Raoul, 125
Betti, Emilio, 8, 13, 42, 68
Biography: biographicalism, 18;
relevant biographical information,
30, 49, 61–62
Blake, William ("London"), 2–3, 5, 10,
11, 41, 44
Boeckh, August, 59
Booth, Wayne C., 22, 29, 35
Borges, Jorge Luis, 36
Bradbury, Malcolm, 6
Brest, Paul, 125
Brown v. Board of Education, 121
Burke, Seán, 34

Cain, William, 68
Cardozo, Benjamin, 122–123
Carroll, Lewis, 70
Carroll, Noël, 13, 66
Certainty, 5, 49, 50, 62
Cioffi, F., 65

Close, A.J., 67, 117, 124
Cognitive discipline (interpretation as), 14, 51–54
Coleridge, Samuel Taylor, 18
Comedy, 45
Constitution, 119–123; First Amendment, 121; Fourteenth Amendment, 121
Contradiction, 9, 44; self-contradiction, 9, 83–84, 96–98, 100
Context: historical context (of a text), 26; and intentionalist interpretation, 30, 42, 44, 61
Copernican revolution, 81
Corcoran, John, 124
Criticism: 20, 48, 52, 53, 61, 64, 96, 112–114, 115, 116, 118, 122–123; authors of, 23
Cummings, E.E., 57–58
Currie, Gregory, 117, 125

Darwin, Charles, 25
Dasein, 7,8, 74–77, 85, 89, 95
Death of the author, 19–23
Death thesis (*see also* Lamarque, Peter), 19, 20–21, 22
Deconstruction, 95, 97
Derrida, Jacques, 24, 29, 97
Descriptive hermeneutics: defined, 1–3; Gadamer on, 7–9, 73–96; Grondin on, 1–2; Heidegger on, 7, 74–80; Hirsch on, 54–55; ontological basis, 3
Dialogue (*Gespräch*), 78, 81, 86, 92, 93
Dickinson, Emily, 27–28
Donnellan, Keith, 70, 71
Don Quixote, 25, 36, 67, 124
Douglas, William O., 122
Dworkin, Ronald, 121–122, 126

Écriture thesis (*see also* Lamarque, Peter), 19, 22–23; refutation of, 25, 26
Effective history (*Wirkungsgeschichte*), 8–9, 88, 89–92, 94, 95; historically effected consciousness, 89–90
Eliot, T.S., 118, 125
Enlightening (*einleuchtende*), 96–99
Enlightenment, the, 19, 86

Epistemology: Heideggerian, 8–9; normative use of, 4–6
Ethics: Aristotelian, 90–91; Kantian, 5, 51–54; and normative hermeneutics, 3, 4, 12, 50–54, 113, 116, 117
Experience: aesthetic, 6–7; *Erfahrung*, 81–82, 90, 105; and language, 93; *Songs of*, 3

Feminist interpretation, 17, 118
Feminist position on authorial repression, 27–28
Fish, Stanley, 35, 110
Foucault, Michel, 17, 18, 19–23, 24, 25, 26, 28, 29, 101
Frege, Gottlob, 42, 47, 68
Freudian interpretation, 118
Fusion of Horizons (*Horizontverschmelzung*), 8, 10, 84–89, 90, 92, 95

Gadamer, Hans-Georg: on descriptive hermeneutics, 2, 7–9, 54, 65, 73–96, 112; on effective history, 88, 89–92; on fusion of horizons, 84–89, 90, 92, 95; on language (linguisticality), 61, 92–94; on normative hermeneutics, 9, 96–102; on play, 80–83; on prejudice, 74–77, 85–88, 94, 96, 98; relativism and, 9, 90–91, 96–101; on tradition, 87–88, 91, 97–98; on truth, 78–84, 99
Garrett, Jan Edward, 106
Gelven, Michael, 103
Genre, *see* ontology, of textual genre
Gracia, Jorge, J.E., 6, 25, 27, 41, 44, 63, 103, 106, 124; on authorial intention, 25–26; on authorial repression, 26, 30–31; on authorship, 17, 25–27, 28, 29, 31; cultural function (and interpretive community), 9; interpretation (textual and nontextual), 11, 12; text, definition of, 25–26; work (as opposed to text), 65
Grice, H.P., 71
Grondin, Jean, 1–2, 100, 102, 103, 105, 109

Habermas, Jürgen, 94, 106, 108, 109
Hamill, Pete, 62
Hamlyn, D.W., 65
Heidegger, Martin, 7–8, 61, 74–80, 94;
    on the forestructure of
    understanding, 74–77, 84, 85, 86,
    95; on Kant, 116; on thrown
    projection, 75–76, 81; on truth,
    78–80, 82, 99
Hermeneutics (*see also* Descriptive
    hermeneutics, Gadamer, Hans-
    Georg, Interpretation, Normative
    hermeneutics): conflict, 1–4;
    Gadamer's definition, 73;
    universal, 3
Hermeneutic Circle, 113, Heidegger
    on, 76–77, 86; Hirsch on, 5–6, 54,
    113
Hermerén, Göran, 70, 123
Hesse Hermann (*Steppenwolf*), 117
Hirsch, E.D., 41, 42, 44, 61, 88, 90, 92,
    98, 100, 105, 106, 107, 109,
    117, 122, 124, 125; on author
    constructs, 28–29; on descriptive
    hermeneutics, 54–55;
    intentionalism, 24, 46–59;
    meaning, problems with, 56–59;
    normative hermeneutics, 1–7, 39,
    112; validation and verification, 5,
    6, 8, 48–49, 50, 54–55, 62
Historicist thesis (*see also* Lamarque,
    Peter), 19–20
Homer (and *Iliad*), 19, 63
Hoy, David C., 97, 98, 99, 106, 109
Huckleberry Finn, 40
Hume, David, 32–33
Humpty Dumpty, 56–57, 59, 60, 70
Husserl, Edmund, 42, 66, 68, 84; and
    intentionality, 4–5, 47–48

Intention (*see also* Urinterpretation):
    aesthetic intention, 60, 111;
    broad/suggestive, 117; and/as
    communication, 4–5, 12, 30, 39,
    46–47, 48, 49, 51–54, 58, 61–64,
    111, 114, 117, 119; counterfactual,
    13, 114, 119–121; future-directed,
    111, 117; Gadamer on, 85, 88; and
    law, 49; likely intentions, 30, 61;
    as normative criterion, 4–7, 11–
    12, 46–65, 91; semantic intentions

(rich and spare), 119, 120, 123;
    specific/vague, 111, 114, 115,
    117; unconscious, 4–5, 6, 41–42,
    47–48, 50, 64
"Intentional Fallacy," 6, 17–18, 40
Interpretation (*see also* Criticism,
    Hermeneutics, Urinterpretation):
    anachronistic, 24, 114; creative,
    95, definitive, 62–63; textual and
    nontextual, 11; urinterpretation
    versus non-urinterpretation, 11–12
Irony, 7, 19, 43, 60, 66, 115
Iseminger, Gary, 13, 66
Iser, Wolfgang, 110, 124

Jefferson, Thomas, 122, 126
Juhl, P.D., 13, 28–29, 41, 50, 69, 113,
    124

Kant, Immanuel (*see also* Ethics), 73,
    115–116
Kaplan, Cora, 35–36
Kierkegaard, Søren, 22, 32–33
Knapp, Steven, and Walter Benn
    Michaels, 13, 44, 50, 60, 69
Knowledge: interpretive, 5, 39, 49, 59,
    61–62, 69, 87–88; moral, 90
Kuhn, Thomas S., 49

Lamarque, Peter (*see also* Author
    function thesis, Death thesis,
    Écriture thesis, Historicist
    thesis), 19–22, 34
Language (*see also* Linguisticality), 30,
    40, 61; artificial, 43; conventional,
    31–32, 43, 44, 59, 60, 61; natural,
    43, 55, 62; unconventional, 56–58,
    59, 60
Legal texts (*see also* Constitution,
    Will), 12, 83, 111, 114, 118–123;
    failed law, 120; ordinances, 119–
    120
Lewis, C.S., 66
Lewis, David, 60, 66
Linguisticality (*Sprachlichkeit*), 9, 92–
    94, 99
Literary texts, 12, 23, 24, 40, 44, 60,
    83, 87, 111, 114, 116–118, 122;
    no definition of, 45–46;
    poems/poetry, 45, 57, 59, 60, 64,
    111

Logic: author's, 5; of common
  sense, 50
Lowes, John Livingston, 18, 34, 66

Marxist interpretation, 11, 118
Meaning (*see also* Effective history,
  Texts): an "affair of
  consciousness," 42, 47–48, 50, 55,
  56–61, 65–66; definition of, 59;
  determinate, 5, 6, 41, 51;
  indeterminate, 8; as-related-to-
  texts, 59–61; and significance, 42,
  44, 45, 46–50, 51, 61, 90, 92, 100,
  112, 114, 116, 117, 118, 122–123;
  textual, 5, 58; utterer's/utterance,
  4; verbal, 44, 58, 60
Meiland, Jack W., 14, 51–54
Metaphor, 48, 81, 94, 95
Metaphysics (*see also* Ontology), 50
Method, 3, 4, 7–8, 9, 49, 73–74, 78, 91
Michaels, Walter Benn, 121, 125
Michelfelder, Diane P., 108
Middle Ages, 19–20
Miller, Nancy, 36
Milton, John, 48–49
Montefiore, Jan, 36
Munch, Dieter, 68

Nathan, Daniel O., 66
Nazis, 114
Nehamas, Alexander, 17, 21, 23–25,
  26, 27, 29, 31, 65
New Criticism, 6, 17
Newspaper, 62
Nietzsche, Friedrich, 33, 84, 114
Normative hermeneutics: anti-
  normative, 9; authorship and, 18;
  Beardsley and, 5–6, 40–46;
  distinction from descriptive, 1–3;
  Gadamer and, 91, 92, 96–102;
  Hirsch's normativism, 4–5, 46–59;
  separating from descriptive
  (theory and practice), 10–11, 12,
  111–112, 123; terms used by
  Grondin and Hirsch, 1–2;
  urinterpretation as, 59–65

Olsen, C., 65
Olsen, Stein Haugom, 64, 72, 112, 113,
  124

Ontology: of authorship, 23, 29–31;
  and description 3, 7–8, 74; of
  textual genres, 45–46, 48, 58, 59,
  111
Ostriker, Alicia Suskin, 36

Page, Carl, 107
Paglia, Camille, 27–28
Palmer, Richard, 8, 108
Pappas, Nickolas, 23, 35
Perlocutionary act, 117
Phenomenology: and description, 2, 3,
  7; normative use of 4–5, 47–48
Philosophical texts: 12, 62, 111, 114–
  116, 117, 118; dialogues, 54, 115
Piaget, Jean, 94
Plath, Sylvia, 27
Plato, 54, 79–80, 82, 115–116
Play (*Spiel*), 80–83
Poetry, *see* Literary texts
Popper, Karl R., 49, 68
Postmodern, 21
Post-structuralist, 17, 19
Praxis, 7
Preconception of completion (*Vorgriff
  der Vollkommenheit*), 83, 96–97
Prejudice (pre-judgment, *Vorurteile*):
  condition for understanding, 74–
  77, 85–88, 94, 96, 98; New
  Criticism on, 6; as normative
  criterion, 9
Projection, *see* Heidegger, Martin

Question and answer, *see* Dialogue

Relativism, 9, 90–91, 96–101
Repression, authorial: author as
  repressive, 18, 19, 21–22; feminist
  perspective on, 27–28; Gracia on,
  26; Meiland on freedom and, 53–
  54; Nehamas on, 23–24; urauthor
  and, 30–31
Rich, Adrienne, 27
Rose, Mark, 34
Rosen, Stanley, 91, 103, 107

Sache selbst (subject matter), 9, 81, 84,
  93, 94, 96, 97, 98–99
Scientific texts, 19, 23
Schleiermacher, F.D.E., 13, 48, 61, 64,
  68, 76

Schmidt, Lawrence K. 9, 83, 93, 94, 97, 98–100
Shakespeare, William, 26, 45, 116, 117, 118
Simon, Michael A., 67
Social sciences (*Geisteswissenschaften*), 50
Socrates, 54
Sparshott, Francis, 109
Stecker, Robert, 13, 35, 69
Stout, Jeffrey, 67, 114, 124
Structuralism, 17, 19
Swift, Jonathan, 43

Teaching (pedagogy), 32, 60, 116–118
Temporal distance (*Zeitenabstand*), 88
Texts, 1, 4, 5, 27; as artifacts, 52–54, 70; bungled text, 40, 58–59; and effects, 89–92; Gadamer and, 9, 96; Gracia's definition of, 25–26; intended text, 63–64; long and complex, 52, 63, 64, 91; mental text, 63–64, 71; no meaning, 42, 60; simple and common, 27, 52, 63, 91, 95; spoken text, 63; text itself criterion, 6–7, 18, 40–46; textual identity, 91, 101
Tillyard, E.M.W., 66
Tollhurst, William E., 13
Tolstoy, Leo, 63
Tradition (*Überlieferung*), 9, 87–88, 91, 97–98
Tragedy, 45
Truth: aletheia/disclosure, 8, 78–84, 90, 95, 99; coherence, 8, 78; correspondence, 8, 78; orthotes, 80, 82; pragmatics, 78; truth claim, 8
Tugendhat, Ernst, 105

Understanding: and application, 85, 90–92, 95, 100, 116, 117; and description, 2, 3, 7–9; forestructure of, 74–77; is interpretation, 73–77; reproductive, 8; textual 8, understand in a different way, 8, 90
Urauthor: 17, 28–33, 39, 55, 57, 61, 62, 115; all texts have, 31, 42; drive to form, 32; and repression, 30–31; type of text and, 32
Urinterpretation: 11–12, 39, 55, 111, 112, 114; non-urinterpretation (significance), 12; theory of, 59–65

Virtue, 90

Wachterhauser, Brice R., 42, 91, 96, 101, 107, 109, 110
Walker, Cheryl, 18, 34, 36
Warnke, Georgia, 87, 104, 109
Weberman, David, 110
Weinsheimer, Joel, 78, 100, 102, 105, 106, 108, 109, 110
Westphal, Merold, 34
Will: last will and testament, 6, 41, 45, 119; living will, 119
Wimsatt, W.K., 6, 10, 17–18, 64, 72
Wirkungsgeschichte, see Effective history
Wittgenstein, Ludwig: family resemblance, 45–46, 67; private language, 71
Woolgar, Steve, 34
Work, 65
Writing (*see also* Écriture thesis), 101

About the Author

WILLIAM IRWIN is Assistant Professor of Philosophy at King's College in Wilkes-Barre, Pennsylvania. He is the author of scholarly articles and reviews on hermeneutics, Sartre, and philosophical pedagogy. He has edited a collection of essays entitled *Seinfeld and Philosophy*.

ISBN 0-313-31151-x

EAN

9 780313 311512

HARDCOVER BAR CODE

90000>